National Education Movement

A Saga of Quest for Alternatives to Colonial Education

Chander Pal Singh

Originals

Delhi-110052

First Published 2012

ISBN 10: 81-8454-099-X
ISBN 13: 978-81-8454-099-4

Published by
Originals
A-6, Nimri Commercial Centre,
Ashok Vihar Phase-IV, Delhi-110052
Phones: 011-27302453, Fax: 011-47061936
e-mail: info@Lppindia.com
url: www.Lppindia.com

Printed at
IIP Printers, D-17, Raja Garden, New Delhi
Phone: 25441120

PRINTED IN INDIA

Contents

Preface

Even six decades after independence, there is a general consensus that the present system of education in India has not been able to wholly rid itself of the colonial elements. In many ways it is still pro-English and pro-rich. Critics still blame Macaulay (176 years after his famous Minute of 1835) for the shortcomings of the present system, which is ironical given that in the post-independence era several Commissions have been appointed and many policy initiatives undertaken to make the education meet national requirements. In a nutshell, there is still a lack of clarity on the objectives, method and content of the education needed for the nation.

It is almost forgotten that educational reconstruction on national lines was a crucial agenda of the freedom struggle. With the growth of national consciousness, especially in the late 19th century and after, Indian nationalists were able to comprehend the mismatch between the colonial educational objectives and the national requirements. Enlightened patriotic minds, from Akshay Kumar Dutt (1820-86) to Mahatma Gandhi, participated in the educational discourse and contributed in the development of what they felt should be the ideal education for India. Under the ambit of the term national education, various models of an education on national lines and under national control were designed to meet the needs of the individual as well as the nation. Significantly, there was no single or unanimous conception of national education; multiple conceptions ranging from the ancient Indian model of Ashram style education to the modern colleges devoted solely to the study of science and technology were discussed. But there was a consensus that colonial education was not suited to the Indian national interests and hence there was need for an alternative system wholly independent of the alien Government. The ideas and experiments of national education movement in pre-independence era, coming from intellectual giants of that age, could have proved valuable not only as a source of inspiration but also to act as a guide in the post-independence educational reconstruction. But they were ignored.

One plausible cause of the ignorance of discourse on national education has been the paucity of scholarly works on the subject. The studies of individual institutions and the educational ideas of some ideologues apart, the sole full length work on the subject in English so far has been Haridas and Uma Mukherjee's *The Origins of the National Education Movement (1905-1910)*. Published in 1957, it is an excellent study of the national education movement in Bengal during the Swadeshi movement. Mukherjees' work was further supplemented by Sumit Sarkar in his monumental study *Swadeshi Movement in Bengal 1903-1908* in 1973. A quick glance at these works leads to the conclusion that so far only the national education movement in Bengal has been studied in detail and that too during the Swadeshi movement in the first decade of the twentieth century.

A valuable contribution to the subject was made in 2003 in the form of a compilation of documents: *Educating the Nation; Documents on the Discourse of National Education in India, 1880-1920*, co-edited by Sabyasachi Bhattacharya, Joseph Bara and Chinna Rao Yagati. But this unique attempt has been disappointing in the sense that instead of highlighting the achievements and constructive aspects of national education movement, the work focusses on the 'inherent antimonies' or 'differences and contestations' among the various groups, opinion leaders and spokesmen of different communities involved in the discourse of national education.

A notable exception to the general absence of good reading material on national education is a Hindi work *Rastriya Shiksha Aandolan Ka Itihas* (2007), a collection of articles edited by Devendra Swarup. Nevertheless, significant aspects of the national education movement such as the concept and the content of national education, various experiments undertaken, and the efforts of individuals involved during its different phases on an all India level up to the attainment of Independence in 1947, are still unexplored and unaddressed. Also, there is an urgent need to find answer to the question why the ideals of national education which proved their worthiness under the hostile colonial rule could not be successfully pursued in the independent India.

The present work is a modified and enlarged version of my Ph.D. dissertation on the subject. It seeks to explore in a holistic manner the ideas and experiments of national education movement during the British rule in India. The initial chapters discuss the background of the national education debate: dealing with nature and content of pre-British indigenous education in India; introduction and nature of colonial education system; and growth of nationalist consciousness. Second, fourth and fifth chapters culminate in 1905-06 as colonial education policy had fully evolved by this time and national consciousness had also reached a landmark stage in these years. The first decade of the twentieth century also marked the beginning of the institutional phase of national education. The large number of national educational institutions makes it very difficult to include all of them in this work, though an effort has been made to include all significant institutions in the fifth chapter. The concept of national education makes it clear that national education had to be completely independent and totally outside the official education system. Hence not all educational institutions working on national lines (like Banaras Hindu University) could be incorporated in this study. Similarly, out of the many workers of national education only the most prominent ideologues have been included as pioneers.

Two individuals, who hold a special place in my life, made this book possible. I am grateful to Dr R.S. Mishra, my research supervisor, for his affectionate and valuable guidance in the preparation of the dissertation. Sh. Devendra Swarup's contribution in the task of turning the thesis into a published book goes beyond prodding and support in numerous ways. My acknowledgements are also due to the staff of National Archives of India, Nehru Memorial Museum and Library and Central Secretariat Library (all in Delhi) for their kind help and co-operation. Lastly, to Sh. Pradeep Mittal of Originals, Low Price Publication, and Books For All, I owe a deep sense of gratitude for publishing this book.

Chander Pal Singh

1

Indigenous Education in India during the early 19th Century

Numerous foreign accounts of India up to the 19th century bear testimony to the fact that Indian society, since antiquity, laid great emphasis on educating its younger generation. Though, in the medieval times, several centres of higher education like universities of Vikramshila and Nalanda did perish at the hands of foreign invaders, yet the tradition of knowledge transmission continued unabated in the smaller institutions and homes. Brigadier General Alexander Walker, who served in India between 1780 and 1818, noted that "no people probably appreciate more justly the importance of instruction than the Hindus .... They sacrifice all the feelings of wealth, family pride and caste that their children may have the advantage of good education." He also observed that the love of learning was no exclusive characteristic of the Brahmins but "this desire is strongly impressed on the minds of all the Hindus. It is inculcated by their own system, which provided schools in every village."[1]

The establishment of British rule in India, proved to be catastrophic for the indigenous education system called 'the beautiful tree' by Mahatma Gandhi. Gandhiji, in 1931, squarely blamed the British rule for the decline of indigenous education which according to him contributed in the growth of illiteracy in India: "Today India is more illiterate then it was fifty or a hundred years ago. ... Because the British administrators, when they came to India, instead of taking hold of things as they were, began to root them out. They scratched the soil and began to look at the root, and left the root like that and the beautiful tree perished."[2]

Early Surveys

A glimpse of the extent, methods and nature of indigenous education of pre–British India is provided by the official and unofficial surveys conducted in the early 19th century to find out the state of native education prior to the application of the British education policies and machinery. Though these surveys of education were conducted well after the establishment of the British rule still they record the widespread extent of the native indigenous education system and its decline under the British rule.

In 1822, Sir Thomas Munro[3], the Governor of Madras, ordered the District Collectors of his Presidency to collect information about the native education system.[4] Another survey was conducted in Bombay Presidency in 1820-1823 on the orders of then Governor of Bombay, Mount Stuart Elphinston.[5] A similar statistical enquiry in Bombay was conducted by the Judicial Department in 1829. In Bengal, William Adam[6] prepared three reports on the basis of his three surveys conducted between 1835 and 1838. Adam's first report, based upon earlier survey reports, covered the whole Bengal Presidency in general. His second report was based on in-depth survey of indigenous education in Nallore *thana* of Rajshahi district. Third and final report of Adam covered four districts of Bengal - Murshidabad, Veerbhum, Burdwan and Tirhut.[7] In Punjab, G.W. Leitner[8] surveyed the state of indigenous education since the annexation (1846) up to 1882. Apart from these well known surveys many minor surveys were also conducted from time to time. For example, H.S. Reid submitted reports on indigenous education and vernacular schools in Agra, Aligarh, Barreli, Etawa, Farrukhabad, Mainpuri and Shahjahanpur in the period of 1850-54. Some of these areas were again covered by James Thomason in his survey of village schools in North-Western Provinces in 1856. R. Thornton also submitted a memoir on the statistics of indigenous education within North- Western Provinces.

Extent of Education

A bird eye view of the extent, economy and effectiveness of the indigenous education system in 1820s is provided by the following excerpt of a Minute by G.L. Prendergast (1821), a member of the Council of Bombay:

"I need hardly mention that every member of the Board knows as well as I do, that there is hardly a village, great or small, throughout our territories, in which there is not at least one school, and in larger villages more; many in every town, and in large cities in every division; where young natives are taught reading, writing, and arithmetic, upon a system so economical, from a handful or two of grain to perhaps a rupee per month to the schoolmaster, according to the ability of the parents, and at the same time so simple and effectual, that there is hardly a cultivator or petty dealer who is not competent to keep his own accounts with a degree of accuracy, in my opinion, beyond what we meet with amongst the lower orders in our own country; while the more splendid dealers and bankers keep their books with a degree of ease, conciseness and clearness I rather think fully equal to those of any British merchant."[9]

Prendergast was not the solitary observer to praise the extent of the native education system. Adam, on the basis of his survey of Bengal, also reached the conclusion that every village had at least one school.[10] Adam estimated that there was a village school for every 400 persons in Bengal and Bihar. Regarding the institutions of higher education in Bengal, Adam estimated them to be about 100 in number with about 10,800 students.[11] Survey reports of indigenous education in the Bombay Presidency reveal that almost all boys got some education in Surat district, in 1824.[12] Poona city in 1824 had 222 schools for elementary and higher instruction.[13] On the basis of reports of the Collectors of Madras Presidency, Thomas Munro observed that there was approximately one school for every 1000 of population in the presidency. Total number of those receiving education, according to Munro, was

188,000. Thus approximately one out of every 67 persons was receiving education. Munro concluded that the portion of the male population who received school education was nearer to one third than one fourth of the whole.[14]

Education at home

It would be a folly to estimate the extent of those under instruction merely on the basis of the number of schools mentioned in the reports. Survey reports indicate that more children were educated at home than at schools. Collectors of Malabar and Madras districts, in their reports also included statistical data regarding instruction at home. In Malabar, those undergoing higher learning under private tuition at home were 21 times the number of those attending the solitary college.[15] While Malabar data is solely concerned with higher learning, Madras Collectors' data also supplies information about elementary instruction at homes. In comparison to the number of school educated children, those educated at home in Madras were 4.73 times more.[16] It is no surprise that Munro refused to believe the figures about the domestic learning for it would greatly increase the figures of the educated natives. Adam's survey of Bengal brings out similar trends. In Nattore, while the total number of children in elementary or advanced schools was 659, there were 2,382 children being taught at home.[17] System of domestic instruction particularly suited the needs of girl students. Hence the absence of girl schools in the surveys did not mean the total lack of girl students as they were taught at home, though they were certainly much less in number compared to the boy students.

Education for all

Contrary to the popular notion, education in India was not monopolized by the Brahmins or the upper castes. Though the disciplines like theology, metaphysics, and ethics and to a large extent the study of law were limited to Brahmins; the disciplines of astronomy and medical science seem to have been studied by scholars from a variety of backgrounds and castes. In Malabar area out of 808 studying astronomy only 78 were Brahmins, and out of 194 studying medicine, only 31 were Brahmins. It is interesting to note that according to British medical personnel, barbers were the best in surgery.[18] Majority of the students, particularly in the Tamil speaking areas, belonged to Shudras and the castes considered below them. The percentage of upper varna pupils ranged between 13 % in South Arcot to 23 % in Madras. The Shudras and the other castes ranged from about 70 % in Salem and to over 84 % in South Arcot.[19] The fact that education was not confined to certain upper class sections of pre-British society in India is corroborated by William Adam too. His data reveals that almost every caste group was represented in the elementary school student population. In the elementary schools of Murshidabad fifty castes and sub-castes were represented. In south Bihar, 2,918 Hindu pupils belonged to 48 different castes. The largest number hailed from the Gandhabanik, Magadh and Teli castes. The native schools of Burdwan district had 61 Doms and 61 Chandal students whereas the total number of Dom and Chandal students in the 13 Missionary schools in the district, was only four. In all, these missionary schools had 86 scholars belonging to 16 lowest castes, while the native schools had 674.[20]

Native Elementary Schools

Indigenous educational institutions before the advent of British can be divided into two broad categories: elementary schools and schools of learning. Elementary schools were the main agency for spread of mass education. The average age of pupils of the elementary schools was 6 to 14 years. They spent two to four years in school. The course of instruction included elements of reading, writing and arithmetic. Throughout the country a special area of focus in the elementary education was the mastery over multiplication tables. Vernaculars were the medium of instruction in these schools. William Adam mentioned four stages of school instruction. The whole course ultimately enabled a pupil in reading epics, working accounts and writing of letters, petitions etc.[21] About the course of studies in the elementary schools, T.B. Jervis[22] has given a detailed account of the Marathi schools in South Konkan:

> "A month or even two are usually devoted to the ceremony of tracing the letters '*Shriganashayanamah*'; after this come the letters of the alphabet, and the barakuree (*Barakhadi)* or twelve combinations of consonants with vowels, and the figures which are learnt as far as 100 … They then proceed to multiplication tables called *Lekhe* as far as 10 times 20; after which they write down and commit to memory various tables …. Which are multiplication tables of fractional parts by integers; and lastly [the] tables of money, weights and measures. These rudiments, having been thoroughly acquired, the children are said to have got through the *Doolukshur* or dust writing and they proceed to writing on paper, to reading and arithmetic."[23]

Interestingly, there was no uniform curriculum at the elementary level for the schools. It varied region wise and also community wise. This shows that schools adapted their teaching to the needs of the communities for whom they catered. The Gujarati scholars being mostly Banias (traders) by caste and profession preferred to have first of all the mastery of the multiplication tables which were useful to them in business calculations of all sorts. On the other hand, the Marathi scholars, first learnt the alphabet and the letters and then proceeded to learn the multiplication tables.[24] Adam observed remarkable diversity in the curriculum of Hindu schools in Nattore where practically every school had its own curriculum.[25] The most remarkable feature of the curriculum was its utilitarian approach. Almost all the schools in the five districts Adam surveyed for his third report taught accounts and most of the schools taught both commercial and agricultural accounts.[26]

The elementary schools did not receive any endowment either from the state or from the public.[27] These schools usually possessed no building of their own and often they were conducted inside the local temple or under the shade of a tree and sometimes in a patron's house. Usually such schools had only a single teacher. Number of students generally varied between one and fifteen. There was no regular system of examination and admission. The system of regular fee was also not prevalent. But each parent paid something in cash or kind depending upon his capacity. The chief merit of these schools was their adaptability to their local environment. No wonder the system survived economic and political changes throughout the ages.[28]

Overall seen, the indigenous system of education was ideally suited to meet the requirements of the contemporary society. It was neither dependent on state nor it had any officiating agency, bureaucratic control or even a definite curriculum. The schools were maintained by the community. Apart from the transmission of knowledge, the education system was also a medium of imparting ideals, morals and values to the students. Extensive nature of this education, covering all sections of society, reflects the significance which Indian society attached to the learning of its young generations. This fact was stated in the Report of the Select Committee on the Affairs of the East India Company (1832) : "...the peasantry of few other countries would bear a comparison as to their state of education with those of many parts of British India."[29]

Schools of Higher Learning

The Hindu schools of learning in Western India were called *Pathashalas,* whereas in Bengal *Pathashala* was a school for elementary instruction and *Tol* for higher learning.[30] Schools of learning for Muslims were called *Madrassas*. Schools of learning received pecuniary assistance from rulers, chieftains, opulent and religious minded citizens. The medium of teaching in Hindu institutions was Sanskrit where as Muslim schools had Arabic or Persian as medium of teaching. Many Hindu teachers and students were associated with Persian schools, because Persian had been the court language during Saltanat and Mughal rule. Generally these institutions had special buildings of their own but sometimes they were held in temples, mosques or houses of teachers or patrons themselves. State was not associated with day-to-day activities of the schools.

Collectors of Madras Presidency reported a total of 1094 places of higher learning, termed 'colleges' in the returns. District of Rajahmundary had the largest number of colleges 279, with a total of 1,454 scholars. Coimbatore and Guntoor came next with 173 and 171 colleges respectively (with 724 and 939 scholars respectively). Several collectors reported no such institutions but they reported that in such places higher learning – the Vedas, Shastras (Law), Astronomy, Mathematics and Ethics was conducted in Agraharams (inhabited by Brahmin dwellers) or privately at home.[31] In Madras Presidency (1826) the subjects of higher learning in Hindu institutions included Vedas, various sastras, Puranas, well known books on Jyotish-shastra and epic literature.[32]

Of the subjects of higher studies in South Konkan, Jervis writes: "The Hindus have an immense variety of Sanskrit works from the Rigveda, the peculiar study of the Brahmins on the Western coast of India, and which is the most difficult of all the four grand divisions of the sacred literature, through all the range of Sciences, Philosophy, and Grammer, to the easier and most entertaining works of poetry and fiction. This country has been always famed for the eminent statesmen, expounders of law, religion and science, which it has furnished to all India."[33]

Teachers' Renumeration

Teachers were renumerated by the grants of lands by rulers, occasional voluntary presents from pupils and members of the public, allowances by wealthy citizens; payment in the form of food, clothes and other articles. Some teachers not only taught gratis but they also provided food and lodging to their students.[34] The Collector of Madura reported that "in Agraharam villages inhabited by the Brahmins, it has been usual from time immemorial to allot for the enjoyment of those who study the Vaidams and Pooranams (religious and historical traditions) an extent of maunium land yielding from 20 to 50 fanams per annum and in a few but rare instances to the extent of 100 fanams and they gratuitously and generally instruct such pupils as may voluntarily be brought to them."[35]

The tradition of teaching gratis was not limited to certain regions and seems to have been in practice throughout the land. The report of Collector of Ahmadnagar points out that the ideal of transmission of knowledge without any material return, sanctioned by the Hindu shastras, could be witnessed in practice: "The whole of the Seminaries in which the Vedas, Shastras and Astrology are studied are supposed to be taught *gratis*, in obedience to the injunction laid down in the Sacred Law Books of the Hindoos, which inculcates one of the first duties of a learned man, that he should communicate his knowledge to his fellow creatures."[36]

Relationship of the teacher and the taught at the level of higher education, unlike the present day practice, was not based on imparting education for a fee. T.B. Jervis reported that teachers at schools of learning "are forbidden to receive pay from their pupils."[37] The report of the Collector of Khandesh elaborates: "It is not usual for teachers of the Hindoo Sciences to require anything, as a matter of right, from their scholars; they consider it a charitable act to give instruction in such branches of knowledge and in return trust to the *eleemosynary* gifts of the charitable, as well as of their scholars, who, though not bound to give, always do make such offerings as they can, and at all events, in all cases, perform such menial offices, in the family of the instructor, as Brahmins may perform. The scholars also who study the highest department of Hindoo literature, are generally children of the poorer classes of Brahmins who themselves live upon charity. To such it is no disgrace to beg and sometimes therefore it is to be found that the whole of the students as well as the master live by donations which by daily circuit of the town and occasional peregrinations about the neighbouring country, they may be able to acquire."[38] Collector writes further that this custom "which is, as it were, interwoven with the feelings of the people." Such was the mighty hold of this ancient custom made sacred by passage and practice of centuries.

Teachers of the elementary schools did receive some kind of remuneration. In South Konkan the average monthly remuneration of teachers was Rs. 4. In individual cases, it was as low as Rs. 6 per year. In Gujarat no monthly fee or payment in cash was in the practice but the scholar offered gifts every day in kind. In Khandesh and Deccan the average income of school master was Rs. 3 per month.

Teachers followed the maxim of plain loving and high thinking. They commanded reverence from the people rich and poor both for their spirit of selflessness, lived a life of moderate comfort dependent on voluntary gifts.

Education as Charity

As result of the tradition of gratuitous instruction, poverty did not come in the way of a scholar going for higher studies. Giving alms to scholars was considered a charitable act. The report of Collector of Cuddapah illuminated how the poor Brahmins attain higher education: "At the age of from 10 to 16 years, if he has not the means of obtaining instruction otherwise, a young Brahmin leaves his home, and proceeds to the residence of a man of his own caste who is willing to afford instruction without recompense to all those resorting to him for the purpose."[39] The British official was bewildered to observe "how these children who are so destitute as not to be able to procure instruction in their own villages, could subsist in those to which they are strangers, and to which they travel from 10 to 100 miles, with no intention of returning for several years. They are supported entirely by charity, daily repeated ... from the inhabitants of the villages generally. They receive some portion of alms daily at the door of every Brahmin in the village, and this is conceded to them with a cheerfulness which considering the object in view must be esteemed as a most honourable trait in the native character, and its unobtrusiveness ought to enhance the value of it. We are undoubtedly indebted to this benevolent custom for the general spread amongst a class of persons whose poverty would otherwise be an insurmountable obstacle in knowledge."[40] Collector of Guntoor also observed that centers of higher education are not endowed by the state. Subjects of higher education "are privately taught to some scholars or disciples generally by the Brahmins learned in them, without payment of any fee, or reward, and that they, the Brahmins who teach are generally maintained by means of manniem lands which have been granted to their ancestors by the ancient Zamindars of the Zillah, and by the former government on different accounts, but there appears no instance in which native governments have granted allowances in money and land merely for the maintenance of the teachers for giving instruction in the above sciences."[41]

Centers of Excellence

Apart from the fact that almost every region in india had institutions of higher education and also had the facility of private tuition at home, there were some centers of excellence like Benares, Nadia and Navadweepam where the students from all over India converged for further education. Collector of Guntoor mentioned that "people desirous of studying deeper in theology & c than is taught in these parts, they travel to Benares, Navadweepum & c where they remain for years to take instruction under the learned pundits of those places."[42] Adam also mentioned that at Nadia many scholars came from "remote parts of India, especially from the South."[43] Jervis reported that in South Konkan a sizeable section of Brahmin community used to visit Benares for further studies: "it is probable that at least a tenth part of the Brahmins who attain to manhood, visit Benares, and it is there that the most learned Shastrees acquire the rudiments of Sanskrit."[44] Benares and other centers of education higher education had teachers from different parts of India. Jervis wrote that "there are about 250 houses of Concan Brahmins at Benares and there are various schools in that city for the instruction of Hindoo in Sanskrit which are under teachers of this country."[45]

Monetorial System

Besides its extent, utility and idealism, the two unique aspects of the indigenous education system in India were its low cost of operation and efficiency. A system existed, especially in the elementary schools, under which the senior pupils were appointed to teach the junior ones. The teaching scholars were called Moniters. The system attracted the attention of Dr. Bell, the Presidency Chaplain at Madras, and he introduced it in England. This system became popularly known as Monitorial system, or Madras system or Bell system, as a cheap and efficient method of education the poor. Under this system of cheap instruction, England made great advance in the instruction of her people. Bombay Education Society's report for 1817 explains the system:

"What chiefly distinguishes the Hindoo Schools and which has been so well adopted in the National System (Dr. Bell in England) is the plan of instruction by the scholars themselves. When a boy ... joins the school, he is immediately put under the tuition and care of one who is more advanced in knowledge, and whose duty it is to give lessons to his young pupil, to assist him in learning, and to report his behaviour and progress to the master. The scholars are not classed, but are generally paired off, each pair consisting of an instructor and a pupil. These pairs are so arranged that a boy less advanced may sit next to one who has made greater progress, and from whom he receives assistance and instruction. When however several of the older boys have made considerable and nearly equal progress, they are seated in one line and receive their instruction directly from master; by these means the master has sufficient leisure to exercise a vigilant superintendence on the school and of enquiring with the progress made by each pupil under his instruction."[46]

Collector of Bellary also lauded monitorial system in his report (August 1823): "the economy with which children are taught to write in the native schools, and the system by which the more advanced scholars are caused to teach the less advanced, at the same time to confirm their own knowledge, is certainly admirable, and well deserved the imitation it has received in England.[47]

A despatch dated 3rd June 1814 from the Court of Directors to the Governor General in Council of Bengal also praised the system and conceded that it has : "become the mode by which education is conducted in our national establishments, from a conviction of the facility it affords in the acquisition of language by simplifying the process of instruction."[48]

It seems that Government of Bombay initially adopted monetorial system in some form. In 1855 the number of students per teacher in Government elementary schools in Bombay Province was 68. In the same year, as a result of the Wood's Despatch, the Department of Public Instruction was established in Bombay and filteration theory or the policy of educating the native elites was put into practice. As a result of this new policy, the number of scholars per teacher was gradually reduced, so that in 1881 it stood at about 23.[49] Obviously the old mode of getting help from the scholars was discarded in the name of efficiency. Hence, a mode of instruction which India had been following for centuries was not adopted to promote the education of her people; while the same mode with some modifications but without deviating from its economic value was able to help England to make a great advance in bringing the benefits of education to her people in a short space of a few decades.

Comparison with Education in England

When compared to contemporary England, indigenous education system in India was better placed in terms of content, schools attendance and duration of study. The content of education in England was regulated by the Anglican Church while Indian system was based on the needs of the society. The school attendance in Madras Presidency was proportionally far higher than number of all types of schools in England in 1800. Besides, the conditions under which schooling took place in India schools were less dingy and more natural. In England, about half of school going pupils attended school at the most for 2-3 hours only on a Sunday. Whereas Indian students in indigenous schools attended school for most of the weekdays and for a longer duration.[50] The only aspect in which indigenous school system lagged behind the British system was the education of the girls.

Decline of Indigenous Education

A preliminary look into the available records leaves no doubt that there was a considerable decay and decline of indigenous education within a few decades of the establishment of British rule in India. The fact of decline and decay of indigenous education was openly accepted at the highest level of British bureaucracy, the Governor General of Bengal. In a Minute dated 6th March 1811, Lord Minto wrote.

"It is a common remark, that science and literature are in a progressive state of decay among the natives of India. From every enquiry which I have been enabled to make on this interesting subject, that remark appears to me but too well founded. The number of the learned is not only diminished, but the circle of learning, even among those who still devote themselves to it, appears to be considerably contracted. The abstract sciences are abandoned, polite literature neglected, and no branch of learning cultivated but what is connected with the peculiar religious doctrines of the people."[51]

By 1882, the entire Bombay Presidency had only 48 Hindu, 6 Muslim and 4 Parsi institutions of higher learning.[52] In the field of elementary education the decline was equally acute. Leitner's survey of Punjab revealed that from 1846 (British annexation of Punjab) to 1882, the number of pupils under instruction had come down from 3,30,000 to 1,90,000.[53] Adam mentioned specific villages in Nattore thana of Bengal which had only two schools but where previously there had been 10 or 11 in living memory.[54]

In Lord Minto's opinion, "the principal cause of the present neglected state of literature in India is to be traced to the want of that encouragement which was formerly afforded to it by princes, chieftains, and opulent individuals under the native governments."[55]

The onset of British rule created conditions which resulted in the destruction of indigenous education. In the pre- British socio-political setup, the system of indigenous education and other public purposes were sustained through sophisticated operative fiscal arrangements by which substantial proportions of revenue were assigned; and it was the collapse of this arrangement through a total centralization of revenue, as well as political structure that led to educational as also decay in the economy, social life etc.[56] Tax free lands which supported educational system were confiscated by the British Government in order to increase revenue. As a result, many educational institutions ceased to function and many teachers were thrown out of employment. Acknowledging this fact, Collector of Bellary wrote in his report that "it would be difficult to point out any period in the history of India when education stood more in need of the preferred aid of government to raise her from the degraded state into which she has fallen."[57] This report boldly stated that the general poverty of people increased as a result of British policy and as a result "the greater part of middling and lower classes of people are now unable to defray the expenses incident upon the education of their offspring."[58]

Besides the inbuilt revenue mechanism which supported the maintenance of schools and teachers etc in every locality, the state in the pre-British India directly promoted the learned and deserving. It is well known that Peshwas annually distributed several lakhs of rupees out of their *Dakshina* fund among learned Brahmins who assembled at Poona every year. In 1824, this *Dakshina* was much reduced, keeping it to about thirty five thousand rupees for annual distribution. In later years this practice was abondoned altogether. Shunting of the *Dakshina* immediately led to a spirit of indifference to the acquisition of higher learning among the learned. It was to this low state of higher learning throughout the province and particularly the district of South-Konkan that Jervis referred to: "It is much to be lamented, however, that in proportion as the patronage of the Peshwa and all the Hindu princes of Malewah fell of, the number of those who understand the language (Sanskrit) well, has sadly decreased."[59]

The void left by destruction of indigenous system could not be filled by the colonial education system. The old system, though it lacked the modern scientific education available in Europe, was in tune with contemporary Indian life. Moreover, it was mass based, value based and teacher based. The new system was highly bureaucratic. It focused only on a certain section of population. Foreign ideals were transmitted through it in a foreign medium. Adam had recommended that the policy of the British Government should be to extend and improve the indigenous system into a 'scheme of general or national education'. But the British Government had already decided to follow the policy of promoting European knowledge through the medium of English to a select section of the native society. In the absence of any support, or encouragement, or even utility (as the new system of laws, administration, and business demanded proficiency in English), the native schools were left to decay and die.

Notes and References

1 Cited in Ram Swarup, *On Hinduism: Reviews and Reflections*, Voice of India, New Delhi, 2000, pp. 179-180.

2 October 20, 1931, *Collected Works of Mahatma* Gandhi, Vol. 48, pp. 93-206, cited in Dharampal, *The Beautiful Tree*, 1983, New Delhi, p. vi.

3 Sir Thomas Munro (1761-1827), Governor of Madras (1820-1827), lived in India for about 47 years.

4 Reports of Collectors of Madras have been reproduced and analyzed by Dharampal in *The Beautiful Tree*, op. cit.

5 R.V. Parulekar, *A Source–Book of History of Education in Bombay Province, Part I, Survey of Indigenous Education*, 1820-1830, Bombay, 1945.

6 William Adam (1796-1881); Christian missionary; son-in-law of Charles Grant, remained in India for 20 years (1818-1838); appointed by Lord William Bentinck,Governor-General of India to survey indigenous education in Bengal.

[7] A.N. Basu, (Ed.), *Reports on the State of Education in Bengal 1835 and 1838*, by William Adam, University of Calcutta, 1941.

[8] G.W. Leitner, *History of Indigenous Education in the Punjab, Since Annexation and in 1882*, Calcutta, 1882. Leitner, member of Indian Education Service and an Orientalist, was principal of Government College, Lahore. He also worked as acting Director of Public Instruction, Punjab in 1879. He assisted in the foundation of Punjab University and later served it as Registrar.

[9] G.L. Prendergast's Minute of 1821 cited in Fisher's Memoir (7th February 1826), A.N. Basu, *Indian Education in Parliamentary Papers*, Part-I, 1832, Asia Publishing House, Bombay, 1952, p. 125.

[10] A.N. Basu, Ed., *Reports on the State of Education in Bengal 1835 and 1838*, op. cit., pp. 6-7.

[11] Ibid.

[12] R. V. Parulckar, ed., *Survey of Indigenous Education in the Province of Bombay (1820-30),* Asia Publishing House, Bombay, 1951 (First Published in 1945), p. xliv.

[13] Ibid., p. xiv.

[14] Minute of Sir Thomas Munro, March 10, 1826 cited in Dharampal, *The Beautiful Tree*, op. cit., p. 248.

[15] Dharampal, *The Beautiful Tree*, op. cit., p. 33.

[16] Ibid.

[17] Joseph Dibona, *One Teacher One School, The Adam's Reports on Indigenous Education in 19th Century India*, Biblia Impex Pvt Ltd, New Delhi, 1983, p. 20.

[18] Dharampal, op. cit., pp. 27-29.

[19] Ibid., p. 20.

[20] Ibid., p. 48.

[21] Ibid., p. 47.

[22] Thomas Best Jervis (1796-1857); British official in Bombay Presidency; 1820-36 conducted the Trigonometrical and Topographical survey of South Konkan; retired from service in 1841; 1855 founded and was first Director of Topographical and Statistical Depot, War office (later named Intelligence Division; Several publications on India.

[23] Parulekar, op. cit., p. xxxii.

[24] Parulekar, op. cit., p. xxxii.

[25] Dibona, op. cit. p. 17.

[26] Dharampal, op. cit., p. 48.

[27] Nurullah and Naik, op. cit. p. 39.

[28] Ibid., p. 40.

[29] *Report of the Select Committee on the Affairs of the East India Company*, Vol. I, p. 409, published in 1832, cited in Sunder Lal, *Bharat Mein Angreji Raj*, Vol. II, p. 683.

[30] R. V. Parulekar, op. cit., p.lvii.

[31] Dharampal, op. cit., p. 26.

[32] Ibid., p. 31.

[33] Parulekar, op. cit., p. lxi.

[34] Nurullah and Naik, op. cit., pp. 38.

[35] Dharampal, op. cit., p. 29.

[36] Parulekar, op. cit., p. lix.

[37] Ibid., p. lviii.

[38] Ibid., p. lix.

[39] Dharampal, op. cit., p. 30.

[40] Ibid.

[41] Ibid. pp. 30-31.

[42] Ibid. p. 31.

[43] W. Adam, 1941 ed., p. 78.

[44] Parulekar, op. cit., p.lxi.

[45] Ibid., p. lxi.

[46] Ibid., p. xxxvi.

[47] A.N. Basu, (Ed.), *Indian Education in Parliamentary Papers, Part I*, p. 181.

[48] H. Sharp, *Selections of Educational Records*, Part I, p. 23.

[49] Parulekar, op. cit., p. xxxvii.

[50] Dharampal, op. cit., p. 62.

[51] A.N. Basu, (Ed.), *Indian Education in Parliamentary Papers, Part I*, op. cit., p. 144.

[52] *Indian Education Commission Report, Vol I,* p. 60.

[53] G.W. Leitner, op. cit. pp. 49-50.

[54] Dibona,op. cit., p. 4.

[55] A.N. Basu, (Ed.), *Indian Education in Parliamentary Papers, Part I*, op. cit., p. 144.

[56] Dharampal, op. cit., p. 15.

[57] A.N. Basu, (Ed.), *Reports on the State of Education in Bengal 1835 and 1838*, op. cit.

[58] Ibid.

[59] Parulekar, op. cit., p. lx.

2

Introduction of Colonial Education in India

Missionaries as Pioneers of Western Education in India

The earliest schools for imparting western education in India were first established by the Christian missionaries whose educational work was designed to fulfil their main objective – to spread Christianity in India. Through education they hoped to communicate the advantages of Christianity and decry the fallacies of the native religious beliefs. Rev. Dr. D.O. Allen, an eminent missionary of the American Board in India, frankly admitted that "(the) reason for such an education, is in its procuring means and opening ways of access to the people, and opportunities of preaching to them .... School houses become chapels under the control of missionaries. Their use for this purpose is often more important than for education."[1] For the same purpose they introduced printing press for printing the Bible in Indian languages.

In 1706, two Danish missionaries – Bartholomaus Ziegenbalg and Plustschau, being the first Protestant missionaries to work in India, started their activities at Tranquebar, a Danish station in south India. As Danes failed to obtain a footing in India, most of the Danish missionaries who succeeded these pioneers worked in the territories of East India Company in south India. Ziegenbalg and his colleagues opened a printing press in Tamil in 1713. An institution for training the teachers was opened at Tranqurebar in 1716. In the following year two charity schools were opened in Madras: one for the Portugese and other for the Tamil children.

Other important contemporary missionaries in south India were Grundler, Kiernander and Schwartz. Grundler started a Portuguese school and a Malabar school a little before 1717. In 1742, Kiernander founded 'charity schools' for Europeans as well as Indians, in and near the Fort St. David (Madras). Later he shifted to Bengal and did pioneering work in the field of education in that province. Schwartz is looked upon as the pioneer of education in the province of Madras. He founded a school for European and Eurasian boys at Trichinopaly in about 1772. An English charity school at Tanjore was also founded by him with the help of the purse presently to him by Haider Ali of Mysore. In 1785 he started three schools at Tanjore, Ramnad and Shivganga with the object of teaching the English language.

In Bengal, the early missionaries based themselves in the Dutch settlements at Serampore and Chinsura. One of the first missionary to work in Bengal was Kiernander. He was followed by Carey in 1793. In 1799, two others missionaries, Ward and Marshman arrived in Calcutta. Carey, Ward, and Marshman, known as the 'Serampore trio', formed an excellent combination for mission work. Carey was a great propagandist, Ward was a printer and Marshman was a school teacher. They translated and printed the Bible in several languages. Mrs Hannah Marshman founded the first girl school in Serampore, and another in Calcutta. The Baptist Female School Society was established by the Serampore missionaries to facilitate female education. This society organized a chain of schools for girls in Calcutta, Dacca, Chittagong and other towns.[22] The other prominent missionaries who worked in Bengal during this period were Rev. N. Forsyth and Rev. R. May.

East India Company and Education

Apart from sheltering the missionaries, East India Company in its early days was also directly engaged in fostering some proselytizing and educational activities. As early as 1614, the Company was taking steps "for the recruitment of Indians for the propagation of the Gospel among their countryman and for imparting to those missionaries such education at the company expense as would enable them to carry out effectively the purpose for which they were enlisted."[3] In a despatch in 1659, the Court of Directors declared their earnest desire to propagate the Gospel by all means.[4] The Charter of 1698 also directed the Company to maintain schools in all their garrisons and bigger factories.[5]

The policy of openly encouraging the missionary enterprise continued till 1765 after which the policy of the Company towards the missionary activities underwent a turnaround in the changed circumstances. Victory in the battle of Buxor (1764) and consequently the Allahabad treaties (1765) made the Company the real master of Bengal with Diwani and Nizamat rights. Nawab of Bengal became a mere puppet in the Company's hands. East India Company thus acquired the status of a major political power of India. This fact made the Company conscious of the political importance of maintaining strict religious neutrality and it abandoned all its earlier explicit inclinations towards prosylitisation and sympathy towards the missionary enterprise. Incidents like Vellore Sepoy Mutiny (1806) further vindicated the shift in policy. Company's Directors directed their officials in India to "discourage any accession to the number of missionaries actually employed under the protection of the British Government in the work of Conversion .... Their zeal may themselves require a check, and that it may be useful and necessary to introduce the control or superintendence of Government where responsibility for the public tranquillity will force it to direct its views to those political considerations which the zeal of missionaries might overlook."[6]

But the pioneering nature of their education work apart, extent and volume of the mission work in the early years remained very small. Total number of the missionaries sent out to India up to the end of the 18th century did not cross 50, and at no time were there more than ten in the field.[7]

In 1772, the East India Company took over the administration of Bengal from the Nawab ending the confusion stemming from the duality of power and responsibility. In the beginning, education did not occupy an important place in the Company's policies because there was no precedent of public funding for education in the England. But at the same time, the new rulers found it necessary to continue the classical pattern of native education in order to get trained manpower in Persian and Sanskrit for judicial, revenue and other administrative purposes. Also, as a successor to Hindu and Muslim rulers who encouraged higher learning in classical language through grants and endowments, it was felt that the Company must continue those traditions as such measures would help in winning the confidence of the upper classes and consolidation of the British rule in India. A recent work interprets the Orientalistic education policy of East India Company in terms of the political engagement with a class of native intermediaries or informers dependence on whom encouraged the new rulers of Bengal to take up the established traditions of the public support for educational purposes.[8]

British engagement with the Indian education started with Warren Hastings, the first Governor General of British India (1773-1785). He founded the Calcutta Madrassa in 1781. Two main motives seem to have prompted this step, the first being to conciliate the Muslims, "to qualify the sons of Muhammadan gentlemen for responsible and lucrative offices in the state, even at that time largely monopolized by the Hindus."[9] Secondly, Persian being the language of the judiciary and administration, it was necessary to collect a group of Persian scholars and train some Englishmen in Persian as well at Calcutta, the seat of power. Urgency of the Madrassa project is understandable from the fact that for first two years its cost was borne privately by Hastings because a reference to the Court of Directors would have involved delay.[10] 11 years after the founding of Calcutta Madrassa, in 1792, Jonathan Duncan, the Resident at Benares, founded the Benares Sanskrit College. Two principal advantages, which Duncan hoped to derive out of this College, were 'endearing our Government to the native Hindoos' and 'preserving and disseminating a knowledge of the Hindoo Law and providing a nursery of future doctors and expounders thereof, to assist the European Judges' in the administration of justice.[11] Working on similar lines, Lord Minto, the Governor General of India from 1807 to 1813, laid a plan for remodelling of a Hindu college at Benares and for the establishment of similar colleges at Nuddea and Tirhoot, two prominent traditional centres of the Hindu learning. Lord Minto also favoured the setting up of colleges of Muslim learning at Bhaugulpore, Jaunpore and some other places along with the reform of Calcutta Madrassa.[12] Continuing the same spirit, Commissioner of Deccan, Mountsuart Elphinstone, established a college for Hindu learning at Poona in 1821.[13] Schools were also opened in Delhi for instruction in Persian and Hindi.

So we find that the first generation of British statesmen in India like Warren Hastings adopted a sympathetic approach towards the Indian knowledge system, literature and civilization in general. Proponents of this policy, known as 'orientalists', believed that their respect for Indian laws, institutions and religions would reconcile the natives to the nascent British rule. They embarked on an ambitious project of studying the Indian antiquity and native languages and also translated Indian classics into English. With the foundation of Asiatic Society in 1784 to systematize the Indic studies and establishment of Fort William College in 1800 to train the British civil servants coming to the India, the group of oriental scholars like William Jones, H.T. Colebrooke, Nathanial Halhead, Charles Wilkins, H.H. Wilson and H.T. Princep made remarkable contribution in the 'discovery of India's past'. But along with being serious students of indology, the orientalists were also consciously performing the imperial function of deepening the roots of British rule in India. It was in this context that Warren Hastings wrote, "Every accumulation of knowledge, and especially such as is obtained by social communication with people over whom we exercise a dominion founded on the right of conquest, is useful to the state."[14]

Pressure from Groups in Britain for Change in Education Policy in India

The policy of encouraging the oriental education was soon questioned by some influential groups in England like the Evangelicals, the Liberals, the Utilitarians and the Free Traders. All of them demanded changes in the prevalent education policy in India for different reasons. Evangelicals viewed India as a place of moral degeneration and ignorance. Hence, according to them, introduction of western sciences through English education and conversion of the natives to the Christianity should be the policy of East India Company in India. The Liberals were convinced of the superiority of western education over the indigenous education. The Utilitarians also pleaded for the promotion of useful learning rather than what they considered 'obscure and worthless knowledge.' The Free Traders had commercial interests in their mind; they hoped that anglicized Indians would be the potential customers of British goods. Impact of these groups in England began to be felt in India in the early nineteenth century as military and political supremacy of British in India became obvious. Establishment of British paramountcy in India was seen by the majority of Englishmen as the confirmation of racial, cultural and religious superiorly of England over India. Consequently, educational worth of the indigenous knowledge began to be considered of little value. At the same time a perception developed in England that Englishmen's duty was to civilize the backward civilization of India. Overall seen, the general attitude in England with respect to India underwent a transformation. From being admirers of India and its civilization, the new perception was to see it as an inferior civilization in need of massive reform. Proponents of this new imperial attitude challenged the educational policies initiated by Warren Hastings.

Charles Grant and his *Observations*

The new imperial cultural onslaught on India seems to have begun with Charles Grant (1746-1823), an influential Evangelist, who has been called as the 'father of modern education in India.' He first came to India in 1767 and worked at various positions as a servant of East India Company. After 1775 he associated himself with the missionaries and became committed to the evangelization of India. He returned to England in 1790 and became a prominent member of the famous 'Clapham sect', a powerful group of evangelicals led by William Wilberforce, committed to evangelization and reform. Grant was also elected as the Chairman of Board of Directors of East India Company in 1805, 1809 and 1815. He was also a Member of Parliament from 1802 to 1818. It was mainly his work and influence that led to the educational clause of the Charter Act of 1813.

In 1792, Grant wrote his famous pamphlet: "*Observations on the State of Society among the Asiatic Subjects of Great Britain, particularly with respect to Morals and Means of Improving it.*"[15] This pamphlet, being a strong appeal to the Christian sentiments of Britons to introduce English as medium of education in India, became central to the evangelical propaganda campaign. The pamphlet described the Indian society, particularly the Hindus as 'utterly immoral and wretched' due to their 'ignorance' and 'want of a proper religion'. The remedy which Grant suggested was Christianization of India. According to Grant, Britain had a mission of regenerating the Hindu society. Which was only possible through introduction of western knowledge and Christianity and the best medium through which these could be communicated to the people was English education. "The most important communication which the Hindoos could receive, through the medium of our language, would be the knowledge of our religion".[16] He was convinced that western knowledge will free Indians from 'ancient laws of customs that made them victims of the corrupt of the corrupt Brahminical priest craft.' 'Idolatry with all its rabble of impure rights, would fall' and the people having arisen 'in the scale of human beings, would live in peace, comfort and justice under British rule. Regarding the introduction of English language, he remarked that British would only be following the example of other ruling groups in India and elsewhere. He forcefully advocated that English be made the language of administration. If Indians, under the Mughals could master the Persian language, a foreign language, so would be the case with English, language of the new rulers. Grant also noted that "introduction of the language of the conquerors...seems to be an obvious means of assimilating a conquered... people to them."[17] English, he noted, would not only improve the Company's administrative efficiency but through its use the natives would inevitably learn the arts, the religion and the philosophy of the governing race. All this, he said, would ultimately lead to extension of British commerce in India. Grant advocated the establishment of free schools for teaching English.

The Evangelical propaganda in the form of Grant's '*Observations*' was timed to change the policy of East India Company in 1793, at the time of renewal of Company's Charter. The move failed in 1793, but the propaganda continued. The '*Observations*' was published for public circulation in 1797. This pamphlet played a crucial role in influencing the contemporary public opinion in England. Many members of British parliament also began to realise the urgent necessity of imparting English education to the people of India. Significantly, most of Charles Grant's recommendations and prophesies mentioned in the pamphlet, with the mojor exception of his hopes of Missionaries' success in conversion, came true in 1830s: Indians evinced great interest in learning English; English became the medium of education in 1835 and finally replaced Persian as the language of the Government in 1837.

The Evangelical enterprise gathered strength in 1790s. New missionary societies like London Missionary Society (1795) and Church Missionary Society (1799) were established in England. Sir John Shore, the Governor General of Bengal from 1793 to 1798, being a member of the Clapham sect, personally sympathised with the missionary efforts. In 1799, two important missionaries, Joshua Marshman and William Ward reached India without a license. In 1801, William Carry, another prominent missionary was appointed as a teacher in Fort William College. In England, both groups of missionaries- Baptists and Anglicans, under the leadership of Wilberforce, launched a vigorous campaign to legalise Missionary activities in India and no less than 850 petitions were laid down on the table of the House of Commons on behalf of the missionaries. Their efforts ultimately yielded result in 1813 when the British parliament, while renewing East India Company's charter, removed restriction on the missionaries to preach and settle in India.

Charter Act of 1813

The Charter Act of 1813 contained in itself two issues related with education. Firstly, it gave permission to the missionaries to go to India for proselytisation and education. Secondly, the Company accepted the responsibility for education of the people of India. The Act provided that 'a sum of not less than one lac of rupees in each year shall be set apart and applied to the revival and improvement of literature and encouragement of the learned natives of India and for the introduction and promotion of a knowledge of the sciences among the inhabitants of the British territories in India.'[18] It is worth noting that if 'the revival and improvement of literature and encouragement of the learned natives of India' signified the continuation of Orientalist line, the 'introduction and promotion of a knowledge of the sciences' depicted the concession granted to the Utilitarians. Thus the Charter Act of 1813 was more of a compromise which accommodated the diverse stands of Evangelicals, Orientalists and the Utilitarians regarding the education policy to be followed in India.

But this momentous step failed to produce any immediate impact for the first ten years. During this period the education policy could not be given a definite shape due to the conflicting interests and ideologies involved in the educational question. Moreover, during this period, the British rulers were preoccupied with conquests and consolidation of their empire in India. In such circumstances education became a neglected issue. Hence the money allotted by the act of 1813 could not be put to use for next ten years.

Despite the ambivalent nature of the Charter Act of 1813, the policy of supporting the classical learning of India continued on the ground. In their first despatch on the subject of education after the 1813 Act, dated 3rd June 1814, the Court of Directors made it clear that the provisions of the Act must not be implemented through the medium of colleges or universities as in England but by "our leaving them (Hindoos) to the practice of an usage, long established amongst them, of giving instruction at their own houses, and by our encouraging them in the exercise and cultivation of their talents, by stimulus of honorary marks of distinction, and in some instances by grants of pecuniary assistance."[19] The despatch stressed that for political advantages, it was necessary to conduct the educational policies and practices "with due attention to the usages and habits of the natives."[20] Directors noted the native veneration for Benares as a religious centre and as a great repository of learning and suggested a survey of the sacred city with regard to its educational establishments, branches of studies conducted and means of support of the teachers involved in teaching. The purpose of the survey was to introduce and establish among the learned of Benares a gradation of honorary distinction. The despatch of 3rd June 1814 is also remarkable for its praise of various aspects of the native education system like inbuilt financial arrangements for teachers of village schools, cheap and effective instruction, ability to withstand shock of revolutions, and richness and utility of ingenious knowledge system contained in the Sanskrit texts.

General Committee of Public Instruction

The Government appointed a General Committee of Public Instruction (GCPI) in 1823 with the objective of:-- "ascertaining the state of public education … and of public institutions … and of considering and from time to time submitting to the Government the suggestion of such measures as it may appear expedient to adopt with a view to the better instruction of the people."[21] The grant of one lakh of rupees was placed at the disposal of the Committee.

GCPI continued the policy of supporting and promoting traditional education in India. Most of its members had sympathetic views towards the classical learning of India. Moreover, key officials like Thomas Munro, John Malcolm and Mount Stuart Elphinstone had faith in a policy of conciliation towards their Indian subjects. They believed that the native public opinion had a direct bearing on the stability of British Empire in India. The native public opinion in a conservative society like India, as they understood, would not tolerate any interference in the domain of culture and education. Western sciences was considered desirable but they wanted it to be introduced slowly and cautiously. Initial work of the Committee reflected these views: reorganization of Calcutta Madrassa and the Benares Sanskrit College; establishment of a Sanskrit College at Calcutta in 1824; printing and publication of Sanskrit and Arabic books on a large scale; and employment of oriental scholars to translate English books containing useful knowledge into oriental classical languages.[22]

Native Demand for English Education

Meanwhile the native demand for English education was growing up. Some sections of Indian society had come to recognize the utility of English language. Raja Ram Mohan Roy, Ram Camul Sen and Tagores can be cited as examples of those who rose to prominence through their command over English. Knowledge of English could easily fetch employment with Company or private agency houses. As Adam also found in his survey of indigenous education in 1830s, the knowledge of English was for the "native aspirant the grand road to distinction", and opened to him 'the prospect of office, wealth and influence'.[23] Consequently, English education was becoming immensely popular. While Government had to pay Arabic and Sanskrit Scholars, those who learnt English were willing to pay themselves.[24] Thousands of Arabic and Sanskrit books printed by the GCPI lay unsold, but the Calcutta School Book Society was selling seven to eight thousand English books every year.[25] The desire to obtain a knowledge of the English language was so great, Adam wrote, that a school was 'sure to dwindle away' unless it taught English.[26] Thus, English, the language of rulers, was gaining practical importance.

Enlightened Indians of that time saw the usefulness of English education for different reasons. Raja Ram Mohan Roy wrote a letter to Lord Amherst (dated 11th December, 1823), the acting Governor General, vigorously protesting the establishment of Sanskrit College in Calcutta. "This" he said "would only load the minds of youth with grammatical niceties and metaphysical distinctions of little or no practical use to the possessors or to society."[27] The students of Sanskrit College drew up a petition pathetically representing the uselessness of their education.[28] In the press and elsewhere, educated Bengalis were demanding more facilities for English education. *Sudhakar,* a Bengali journal, wrote on 7th September, 1833, "Government ... no doubt spends a lakh rupees on education ... But we are at a loss to understand the benefits accruing from it ... The Government should sow the seeds all over the country, of that type of learning which can remove the darkness of ignorance and makes a man fit for administration and other public activities. It is necessary to establish an English school for this purpose in every village."[29]

As a result of the popular demand, schools imparting English began to be set up through local initiatives. As far back as 1800, a school was established at Bhawanipore, a suburb of Calcutta. Another school was opened in 1814 at Chinsura. Rich citizens of Calcutta and Bombay organised Native School Societies and Native School Books Societies. Bombay Native Education Society, established in 1823, had the objective of spreading modern education among the Indian people. On the recommendation of Elphinstone, the Court of Directors sanctioned grants–in–aid to the Bombay Native Education Society and accepted it as the principal agency for the spread of education among the people. By 1840 the society was conducting four district English schools and 115 district primary schools.[30] Similar cooperation between wealthy natives and official as well as non- official Englishmen resulted in the foundation of Hindu College in 1817 and Elphinstone College in 1834. The Hooghly College, opened in 1836, witnessed a surge of enrolment. Within the first three days, 1200 hundred joined the English department alone.[31] In 1855, a report of the Council of Education said, "a demand for English education has arisen in every district ... Schooling fees are willingly paid and increasing number of teachers are supported in private schools ... Gradually but surely, the vernacular schools established by Lord Hardinge have disappeared."[32]

Imperial Objectives Begin to Shape the Education Policy

By early 1820s, the exercise to replace the oriantalist education policy had already begun. A brief survey of this exercise leads us to the conclusion that much before the Macaulay's famous Minute or the Lord Bentinck's resolution on education (both in 1835), the British authorities in India had finalized the objectives and the main contents of the education policy.

Holt Mackenzie, Secretary to the Bengal Government and also a member of the G.C.P.I., in a Note[33] dated 17th July 1823, underlined the need to follow a systematic and long term approach while dealing with the education policy. "The first step is to settle the ultimate object to be aimed at: for otherwise we may debate about the means without end .... Nothing therefore can be more comprehensive than the design. Its different parts must indeed be filled gradually and with well measured steps. Its completion we must leave to our children's children." Mackenzie called for an end to Government's hesitation regarding the introduction of European sciences in India: "If there be truth and excellence in European Science, that the introduction of it among the Natives of India, must necessarily be one, and an early part of the general scheme, and should authoritatively be indicated by Government as such."

It was Mackenzie who for the first time argued that the object of the education policy must be the education of a select, influential class and Government must leave to this class education of the masses. "Government should apply itself chiefly to the instruction of those who will themselves be teachers....To provide for the education of the great body of the people seems to be impossible, at least, in the present scheme of things....Natural course of things in all countries seems to be that knowledge introduced from abroad should descend from the higher or educated classes and gradually spread through their example."

Mackenzie repeated Charles Grant's argument that it was necessary to introduce the language of the rulers just as Mughals had done by making Persian the language of the administration. Mackenzie also emphasized that education policy should be so formulated so as to be fully subservient to the various requirements of the apparatus of the British Government in India:

"In framing any rational scheme of public instruction, we must necessarily consider in a general way, at least, how far our other institutions are suited to the state of things, which the diffusion of knowledge may be expected ultimately to produce, and more immediately, how the acquirements of the students at the public seminaries can best be rendered subservient to the public service, and how the constitution of public offices and the distribution of employments can be made the means of exciting to study and rewarding merit."

A despatch from Court of Directors, dated 18th February 1824, openly admitted that the policy of supporting and promoting only oriental education was erroneous. According to the despatch, the objective of education should be to promote useful learning not the denominational learning.[34]

In September 1827, Court of Directors directed the Governor-general in Council of Bengal to concentrate educational endeavours only at the places of greater importance and that too to a select class of natives only. Directors stressed that "the first object of improved education should be to prepare a body of individuals for discharging public duties".[35]

A Minute dated 24 March, 1828, by Francis Warden endorsed the downward filtration theory of educating a select few. Warden emphasized on "making the study of the English language the primary, and not the merely secondary object of attention in the education of the natives". Among the various advantages of introducing English, according to Warden, a significant advantage will be that English "might become the most durable tie between Britain and India" and rightly predicted that "the English tongue would in India, as in America, be the lasting monument of our dominion."[36]

William Bentinck, the Governor General of India, in a letter to the GCPI dated 26 June 1929, declared that its policy was to eventually make English the language of public business in India. "It is the wish and the admitted policy of the British Government to render its own language gradually and eventually the language of public business throughout the country, and that it will omit no opportunity of giving every reasonable and practical degree of encouragement to the execution of this project."[37]

In 1830, while expressing a strong desire to employ natives in civil administration, the Court of Directors emphasised on their being proficient in western education.[38] Keeping this in view, changes in the curriculum of three now oriental colleges were made. Study of modern (European) science was introduced into the Calcutta Madrassa and Benares Sanskrit College.[39] Districts English Schools were established in Delhi and Benares.[40]

Anglicist-Orientalist Controversy

While the Government had made up its mind to introduce the western pattern of education through the medium of English language, the majority opinion of General Committee of Public Instruction (GCPI) was against the introduction of English education. A long and bitter struggle took place in GCPI between the supporters of classical literature and supporters of western education. This is known as 'Anglicist-Orientalist controversy'. In the end, Anglicist viewpoint prevailed due to the crucial role played by some prominent individuals on their side–James Mill, Alexander Duff, Charles Travelyan and William Bentinck.

One of the first to support the Anglicist cause was James Mill. The above mentioned despatch of 18th February 1824 was apparently written by him.[41] James Mill worked in the London Office of East India Company, overseeing the correspondence with India. From this position he was able to influence the policy in India through despatch writing and influencing the opinion in London. He adhered to utilitarian philosophy. James Mill was of the opinion that as a superior civilization it was the duty of the British to use their power for good by directly introducing their superior system and ideas wherever possible. Indian society, in his opinion, was a barbarous one and hence it needed the superior ideas and institutions from the West. James Mill gained fame through his book- *The History of British India*. Published in 1817, this book was a direct attack on orientalistic view point. Mill found little of value in either ancient or modern Indian civilization. He argued that 'useful learning' did not mean 'Hindu or Mahomedan learning'. Through his personal influence and the ideas contained in his book, James Mill was able to prepare a favourable background for radical changes in the education system.

Besides Utilitarians, the Anglicist endeavour also had the solid backing of Evangelicals, spearheaded by Alexander Duff. Alexander Duff, one of the greatest Christian missionary in India, came to India in 1830. He at once realized that the growing demand for English education was not being met by the official efforts. In the popular demand for English education he saw a great opportunity for Christian proselytisation of Indian middle classes. Duff was convinced that the English language alone could be the suitable means for conveying the Christian culture to the Indians, as the native languages were underdeveloped[42]: "The English language I repeat it, is the lever which, as the instrument of conveying the entire range of knowledge, is destined to move all Hinduism."[43] Duff organized a network of schools where western education was imparted along with teaching of Christianity. He developed a new English language curriculum which was able to attract native students despite its Christian message.[44] Duff received the cooperation of Raja Ram Mohan Roy in his efforts of establishing schools and popularizing western education. Raja Ram Mohan Roy helped in mitigating the native fears that by reading Bible one becomes a Christian. Duff- Ram Mohan cooperation went a long way in preparing the foundation of western education in India.

Among the pioneers of English education, Charles E. Trevelyan occupies a very high place for his seminal contribution. He was appointed to G.C.P.I. in 1833 to replace the retiring H.H. Wilson. Like Alexander Duff Trevelyan shared Charles Grant's convection that 'English language would morally and intellectually transform the subcontinent.'[45] Soon after his appointment he orchestrated a campaign to overturn the orientalistic policies. He praised Duff for his efforts and criticized the working of orientalistic policies. He campaigned for introduction of western sciences directly through English language and not through Indian languages. In 1834, he campaigned to replace the various scripts of South Asia with the Roman script.[46] Trevelyan also maintained a private correspondence with Governor General Bentinck, seeking to persuade him that the conditions were just right for a radical change in the education policy.[47]

The confrontation between the Anglisits and Orintalists was brewing up for a long time. Anglicist opinion was getting stronger day by day because it was supported by the natives' increasing demand for English. The attitude of the Government, except the orientalist group, was overwhelmingly in the favour of the Western education. But G.C.P.I., dominated by Orientalists somehow continued to resist the pressure. Appointment of William Bentinck, a reformist Governor-General turned the tide in favour of the Anglicist position. William Bentinck was a liberal influenced by the utilitarian ideas. As we have seen, Bentinck had made up his mind regarding the changes in education policy well before the Macaulay's Minute. In a private interview given to Alexander Duff in February 1833, Bentinck "heartily approved of the design of giving a higher education to a select few, in preference to the plan of giving a common education to the many." He told Duff that "if there was one opinion on which he was more decided than another, it was the expediency of teaching English in all our Higher Seminaries gradually substituting it throughout every department of Government business, instead of the Persian which ought as soon as possible to be abolished."[48] Bentinck appointed known Anglicists in GCPI as a result of which the overwhelming majority of Orientlists was lost. It was he who appointed Trevelyan to replace Wilson in GCPI. Bentinck was also influenced by the successful efforts of Alexander Duff. Macaulay, the recently appointed law member of the Governor– General's Council, was also in close contact with Bentinck. Macaulay's ideas on education bore a marked similarity to Trevelyan, his future brother-in-law. Macaulay used his proximity with Bentinck to convince him to take the side of Trevelyan.

So by 1835 major forces in the British administration had already aligned to replace classical learing by English education. Governor General, his Law Member and Court of Directors, all had made up their minds by this time. Anglicists in the GCPI led by Trevelyan called for some radical changes in the education policy: reforming the curriculum at Sanskrit College; introduction of English at the Calcutta *Madrassa*; and halting the publication of Hindu texts authored by Orientalists.

Orientalists held their ground in the beginning. They defended their policy in terms of interpretation of 1813 Act, continuity of the policy of conciliation and continuity of historical traditions. They said that they were not against disseminating western education but against English as the medium of education. GCPI at this stage was evenly divided between the Anglicists and Orintatists. Orientalist group was constituted of W.H. Macnaughten, H.T. Princep, James Princep, H.D. Shakespeare and J.C.H. Sutherland. On the other hand Anglicist group had W.W. Bird, G.A. Bushby, J.R. Calvin, G.W. Saunders and C.A. Trevelyan.[49] In such circumstances the issue was submitted to the arbitration of the Governor General. Governor General Bentinck asked Macaulay, then President of GCPI, for a ruling. The result was his famous Minute of 2nd February 1835.[50]

Macaulay's Minute

Macaulay's minute was a severe critique of the orientalistic education policy. He advocated total shift to western education through the medium of English language. He also explained the reasons behind such a radical change. In his opinion, Indian classical literature did not contain useful knowledge. Vernacular languages of India were poor mediums for communication of real knowledge. On the basis of these assumptions, Macaulay emphasized that funds allocated for education would be better utilized by supporting a system of western education. He recommended the stopping of stipends and publication of books for oriental education. Macaulay agreed with Orientalists on only one point, that Government should focus on educating a select class, not the general masses.

Anglicist Education Policy Comes into Practice

Macaulay's Minute became the basis of Lord William Bentinck's resolution on education. It put an end to a phase which had its beginning in the times of Warren Hastings. The policy of conciliation and sympathy towards oriental learning was abandoned. But it is important to note that Macaulay's Minute and Lord Bentinck's resolution merely marked a formality. The policy, as the preceding pages show, was long in making. By the time of the arrival of Bentinck (in 1929), the fundamentals of the coming policy had already been decided. The credit usually given to Bentinck and Macaulay for propounding a new education policy is overstated.

In a way the developments in the education policy were in tune with other historical development of the time. British in India had emerged as the paramount power. With British hold over India and its people more secure than ever, the old fears of an Indian reaction against the cultural interference had diminished substantially. Oriental studies were losing their administrative utility after the new legal codes had come into effect. New revenue settlements and other administrative apparatus were already in place. Moreover the new generation of British administrators had confidence in the supremacy of European culture, knowledge and morals. Influenced by the Utilitarian and the Evangelical ideologies, they believed that England represented a higher civilization and had a mission to reform.

The supporters of the English education also had other motives in their minds. As Macaulay said in his Minute, an anglicised class of natives was needed to act as a class of interpreters or a buffer between the English rulers and Indian masses. English education was also expected to provide a positive bond between the rulers and the ruled. "The spirit of English literature cannot be but favourable to the English connecting", wrote Trevelyan. In his opinion, English education would stop the Indian from regarding their rulers as foreigners. It would make them "intelligent and jealous co-operators."[51] Thus English education was perceived as a factor contributing to the permanence and stability of the British Empire.

Besides the imperial motives, practical and administrative considerations also guided Bentinck. In the midst of the financial crisis in 1830's Bentinck's principal task was to economise. One of the major items of expenditure was the high salary of British officers. He therefore considered employing Indian subordinates in various branches of administration.[52] In 1831-32, Halt Mackenzie, in his evidence before the Parliament Committee, adduced facts and figures to prove that the finances of India would be improved by the employment of natives.[53] Charter Act of 1833 opened the doors for employments of Indians. Knowledge of English language was considered a prime qualification for employment with the company

Government. Hence a prominent aim of British education policy was to turn out lowly paid subordinates.

Along with the economizing potential of English language and learning some other factors also worked in its favour. Trading interests in England hoped that once Indians were educated in English, they would develop taste for products of England. For the missionaries, as shown before, new education was the first step towards the conversion of Indian to Christianity. Liberals considered western education as a vehicle for 'civilizing and humanizing' the society of the East. As also discussed earlier, the natives demand for English was another crucial factor for its introduction in India. Thus the decision to introduce English education was the result of a combination of different factors: economic, administrative, political, religious and moral.

Bentinck's resolution had left Oreintalists completely discontented. Lord Auckland's minute of 24th November 1839 was meant to assuage the feelings of Orentalists. It guaranteed the continuation of existing institutions of oriental learning, payment of adequate grants and scholarships, and printing of oriental books.[54] At the same time Lord Auckland's minute restated the new policy in clear terms- " I would make it my principal aim to communicate through the means of the English language, a complete education in European literature, philosophy and science"[55] The Minute also gave official approved to the 'downward filtration theory'. The Minute declared that "the great primary object is the extension (of education) among those who have leisure for advanced study."[56]

Wood's Despatch

The new educational policy was firmly entrenched and elaborated in 1854 by the 'Wood's Despatch.'[57] The despatch was the result of a committee set up to survey the educational scene in India in connection with the renewal of Company's Charter in 1853.[58] Its main recommendations are as under:-

1. It declared that the aim of British Government's educational policy was 'the diffusion of the improved arts, science, philosophy and literature of Europe'.

2. English language was declared as the most suitable medium for higher education. Vernacular languages were regarded as the suitable mediums through which European knowledge could percolate to the masses.
3. A Department of Public Instruction was to be created in each of the five provinces.
4. Universities in Calcutta, Bombay and Madras were to be established on the model of London University. Their functions were to hold examinations and confer degrees.
5. It recommended a system of grants- in- aid to encourage and foster private enterprise in the field of education.
6. The despatch emphasised the importance of technical education, training of teachers and women education.

Thus the educational policy, which was evolving since the beginning of missionary enterprise, was given finishing touches by Wood's Despatch.[59] The policy followed up till now was not steady as the work of education was dealt by officials who were generally unacquainted with it.[60] Wood's Despatch, for the first time, laid clearly the policy regarding the dissimination of education as well as the necessary administrative channels.

Within two years of the Despatch, Departments of Public Instruction were created in all existing provinces. These bodies advised the provincial Governments in all educational matters, administered the funds allocated to education, managed those institutions which were directly under the Government, supervised private institutions which received Government grants-in-aid, prepared reports on the progress of education and worked for the improvement and expansion of education.[61]

The system of grants-in-aid spread the Government control on education far and wide through numerous private schools and colleges. In lieu of the Government aid, Government imposed conditions and inspections on private schools and colleges. The

Government kept only a few institutions under its direct control. Thus in substance, education was left mostly to the private enterprise. Hence the supervision of institutions, but not their establishment, became the primary function of the Government. But, inadequate financial assistance, which usually was the case, made the supervision ineffective. The Government schools and schools covered by grants-in-aid system could never compensate the vast network of indigenous schools which were allowed to disappear. Few surviving indigenous schools were prevented from receiving the Government aid due to the complex nature of the Government rules and conditions. Thus ultimately, the system of grant-in-aid did not help the cause of mass education.

Wood's despatch laid the foundation of Universities in India. Universities of Calcutta, Bombay and Madras were established in 1857. Following the model of the London University, the universities in India were affiliating and examining bodies but not teaching bodies. Higher education was imparted in the colleges affiliated to universities.

Table depicting progress of education in India from 1855 to 1882[62]

S. N.	Type of Institutions	1855 Institutions	1855 Pupils	1882 Institutions	1882 Pupils
1.	Arts Colleges: English & Oriental	15	3,246	38	4,252
2.	Professional colleges & schools	13	912	96	3,670
3.	Secondary Schools	169	18,335	1,363	44,605
4.	Primary Schools	1,202	40,841	13,882	681835
5.	Normal Schools and Claris	7	197	83	2,814
	Total	**1,406**	**62,731**	**15,462**	**737176**

When seen from the Indian standpoint, several drawbacks can be pointed out in the Wood's Despatch. It does not refer to the ideal of universal literacy, or the state's obligations for educating the poorer classes. Its authors did not aim at education for leadership, education for the industrial regeneration or education for the defence of motherland.[63] The Despatch is credited with establishing universities and thus introducing higher education in a systematic manner. But its author, Charles Woods, did not have any benign intentions towards the higher educated Indians. He wrote that "I do not see the advantages of rearing up a number of highly educated gentlemen at the expense of state, whom you cannot employ, who will naturally become depositories of discontent ... I am against providing our own future detractors and opponents and grumblers."[64] It was not the intention of British Government to make universities the vehicles of modernization in India. Modernizing tendencies of universities were checked by the policy of Government to provide selective educational content to select, elite class students.[65]

The Government control over the universities was very rigid. The strict control over the universities is well illustrated by the example of the Calcutta University. Here, the Governor General serving as the Chancellor nominated the Vice Chancellor and appointed and could dismiss all the fellows of senate except the ex-official fellows. The Governor General in Council approved the making of bylaws and regulations, controlled the fee fund and raised annual statement of accounts. These universities made little contribution to learning and knowledge as 19th century Indian universities were merely examining and affiliating bodies, not associated with in-house teaching and research. The Act of 1904 empowered the universities to set up post graduate teaching departments but these powers were not used until 1916.

Despatch of 1854 contained clauses which reveal some of the imperial objectives behind the education. Need for an educated and cheap work force was one of them.[66] Similarly, commercial interests of England were sought to be promoted through the educational policy. "This knowledge," the Despatch said, "will secure to us a large and more certain supply of many articles necessary for our manufactures .... as well as, an almost, inexhaustible demand for the produce of British labour."[67]

The chief beneficiaries of Wood's Despatch were the missionary institutions. The grant-in-aid system provided indirect subsidies to the missionary work, in a way encouraging proselytisation through education. Apart from grants-in-aid system, missionaries benefited from the Despatch in other ways too. Some of these advantages are brought out by John Wilson (one of the most prominent missionaries of 19th century in India), in a letter dated 16 May 1855. The Despatch, Wilson was happy to note, recognised the principal concerns of missionaries; made Bible accessible within Government seminaries; encouraged missionary press and Bible and Tract Societies; and called "for an increase of missionary agency with a view to the hollowing of the secular instruction which it directly encourages.'[68]

Hunter Commission

Nearly three decades after the Wood's Despatch, the need to review the entire educational system was acutely felt. The extension of education achieved till now was utterly insufficient for India. In 1881, 95.20% of Indian population was enumerated as illiterates. The condition of female literacy was particularly pathetic. Only 0.39 % of females could read and write.[69] Primary education was being neglected. Educational policy was being criticised from all quarters. In such conditions, Lord Ripon appointed the first Indian Education Commission under the chairmanship of W.W. Hunter in February 1882. The Commission had 20 other members including Syyed Ahmad Khan and Anand Mohan Bose. The objective of the Commission was "enquiring into the working of the existing system of public instruction and to the further extension of the system on popular basis."[70]

The Hunter Commission focused its work on primary education. It suggested improvements and aid to the indigenous schools for the extension of primary education. It declared that primary education "possesses an almost exclusive claim on provincial revenue."[71] Primary education was to be provided even in the absence of adequate local funds and cooperation. The Commission admitted that "for many years the cause of primary education had to struggle against the theory described as that of "downward filtration theory."[72] In this perspective the commission recommended that it is desirable "in the present circumstances of the country, to declare the elementary education of the masses, its provision, extension, and improvement, to be that part of the educational system in which the strenuous efforts of the state's hand now be directed in a still larger measure than hereafter."[73] The Commission also stressed on making the contents of primary education more useful than merely "a portion of instruction leading up to the University."[74]

Regarding the secondary education, the Commission recommended the bifurcation of subjects. One group of subjects should qualify the pupils for higher general education, and the other group for commercial and technical purpose. The further extension of the secondary education was also desired through more liberal grants-in-aid. The Commission also recommended uniting high schools and middle schools under the single term 'secondary schools.'

The Commission also sought improvement of collegiate education through new grants-in-aid rules and diversification of studies. It felt the necessity of a university in the United Provinces. As a result Allahabad University was established in 1887. Punjab University had already come into existence in the very first years of the Commission's work in1882.

The Government of India accepted most of the recommendations of the Hunter Commission. The management of the primary education was transferred to the newly created municipalities and local boards. But the recommendations of the Commission failed to initiate any rigorous change. College education continued to avoid the practical needs of the Indian society. There was no concrete proposal for the spread of scientific and technical education. Recommendations for making secondary schools more useful by bringing in practical subjects did not prove practical. Similarly, the changes conceived in the primary education system did not show the necessary extension."[75]

Lord Curzon's Education Policy

Most visible effect of the Indian Education Commission was the great increase in the number of educational institutions and students. Most of the newly opened institutions were privately managed schools and colleges. Most of them were inefficient, badly housed, poorly staffed, ill-equipped and overcrowded. They had become in fact coaching institutions with too many students and too little learning.[76] Lord Curzon upon his arrival in 1898 felt that Indian education was in a mess and 'must be lifted from this furrow' before it was finally 'dragged down and choked in the mire'[77] Curzon's object in attacking the education system was not merely to make it more efficient but also politically safe for the Raj.

From the time of Lord Dufferin, higher education had come to be regarded as the root cause of the political unrest in the country. British Government realized that political associations formed in the later half of the 19th century and the rising political consciousness were the work of English educated Indians. As educated class became more vocal in the criticism of the Raj, wisdom of a liberal education policy was soon questioned. Later, the advent of extremist ideas, with the murder of Mr Rand, the Collector of Poona, and his associate Lt. Ayerst in June 1897, by Chapekar brothers, was also attributed to anarchical ideas transmitted by English education. George Hamilton, the Secretary of State, while dealing with the Poona murders, found it "impossible to dissociate their ideas and their hatred of England from the course of education and training through which they passed."

Curzon felt that by decentralizing the education, the Government (during Lord Ripon's tenure) had surrendered its control to a dangerous degree, According to Curzon the Indian majority in education management showed "a mischievous independence of Government."[78] In his opinion "there were ill educated *'vakils'* in the senates and too many *'babus'* in text book committee."[79] Curzon's intention was to reassert Government's "responsibility which there had been a tendency to abdicate."[80] Curzon was convinced that if left unreformed, the Indian Universities would develop into "nurseries of discontented characters and stunted brains."[81] Hamilton commended Curzon for his initiative in the field of educational reforms: "You never, I am sure, undertook a task which was more necessary than that of looking into the control of education in India. It is almost, if not quite, the first duty of an autocratic Government, and in this, as in many other things, we have been terribly misled by false analogies derived from the English practice."[82]

Indian Universities Act 1904

In order to frame a new education policy, Curzon called for an educational conference at Simla in September 1901. Directors of Public Instruction from the provinces attended the conference. The conference was followed by the appointment in 1902 of the Indian University Commission with Sir Thomas Relaigh as its chairman. The report of the Commission became the basis of the Indian Universities Act 1904. The main provisions of the Act are summarized as under :

1. Functions of the University were enlarged. From now the Universities were involved in teaching, appointment of professors and lecturers, managing endowments, establishing libraries, laboratories, museums and others areas of studies and research besides affiliating colleges and conducting the examinations.

2. Stricter conditions for affiliations and periodic inspections were provided in the Act.

3. The Act sought to increase official control over university by limiting the number of fellows and increasing the nominated element over elected fellows. The Government was vested with the authority to veto the regulations period by the Senate.
4. Entrance for university was made tougher and Government tried to fix the minimum college fees.

The Act drew angry protests from Indian leaders who regarded it as a political move designed to throttle the aspirations of the educated classes. Even moderate leaders like Gopal Krishna Gokhle and Pheroj Shah Mehta called this step as retrograde. Gokhle, during the debate on University Bill in the legislative Assembly observed that "for the present the hands of the clock have been put back ... there can be no doubt that the work done today in this council chamber will be remembered with sorrow all over the country for a long time to come."[83] Sole Indian member of the Commission, Gooroo Dass Bannerjee strongly disagreed with the recommendations of the Commission. In his 'note of dissent', he boldly mentionable that "it (effects to raise the standard of education) is only a partial solution of the problem, and that we should not only aim at raising the height, but also at broadening the base of our educational fabric."[84] The University Act failed to achieve anything substantial and system of higher education remained as it had been before. In 1917-19, Calcutta University Commission noticed that university system "was fundamentally defective in almost every respect."[85]

The University Act of 1904 gave significant impetus to national education movement. The Act was regarded as an official mischief to counter the Indian aspirations in higher education and thus caused deep anguish. It led to final termination of hopes of many Indians about the intentions of the Government with respect to education. From now onwards it began to be felt very strongly that Indians must control their own education. In the words of Annie Besant, "the educated Indians ought to take up the question of education into their own hands, this has been essentially necessary in consequence of the late University Act."[86] In the following year the boycott of Government schools and establishment of national schools became an important aspect of the Swadeshi Movement. The concept of national education had been developing much earlier. But during the Swadeshi Movement it was formalised as a radical programme of establishing an alternative system of education under national control and on national lines.

Notes and References

1 R.G. Wilder, *Mission Schools in India*, pp. 36-37, cited in Nurullah and Naik, *The History of Education in* India, 1951, p. 60.

2 Tarachand, *History of the Freedom Movement in India,* vol. II, Delhi, 1961, p. 178.

3 N.N. Law, *Promotion of Learning in India by Early European Settlers*, London, 1915, pp. 7-8.

4 H. Sharp, (Ed.), *Selections from Educational Records, Pt. I*, (1789-1839), Calcutta, 1920, p. 3.

5 Nurullah and Naik, *History of Education in India during the British Period*, Bombay, 1955, p. 53.

6 Despatch of Court of Directors dated 7th September 1808 cited in H. Sharp, op. cit., pp. 5-6.

7 Cited in Nurullah and Naik, op. cit., p. 66.

8 C.A. Bayly has highlighted the role of intermediaries or informers in establishment of British Empire. Crucial intermediaries in this process were the Munshis. They were skilled in Persian language and literature. They are denoted as keepers of diplomatic, court and elite culture. Munshis were desperately needed by the British as they maneuvered their way through the diplomatic changes and political intrigues in their rise to power. For their part, the Munshis saw themselves as educating their British employees and thus keeping alive the political culture of which they were the guardians. (Bayly, *Empire and Information*, p. 15, pp. 69-88, 196-7, 284-7, cited in Lynn Zastoupil and Martin Moir, eds., *The Great Indian Education Debate: Documents Relating to the Oriantlist – Anglicist Controversy, 1781-1843,* 1999, pp. 1-2.).

9 H. Sharp, op. cit., p. 7.

10 Nurullah and Naik, op. cit., p. 57.

11 Letter from J. Duncan to Earl of Cornwallis, Governor-General in Council, dated 1st January 1792, cited in H. Sharp, op. cit., pp. 10-11.

12 Minto's Minute dated 6th March 1811, *Indian Education in Parliamentary Papers*, part I, op. cit., pp. 144-148.

13 Ibid., p. 11.

14 David Kopf, *British Orientalism and the Bengal Renaissance*, Firma K.L. Mukhopdhyay, Calcutta, 1969, p. 18.

15 A.T. Embree, *Charles Grant and British Rule in India*, p. 155.

16 Ibid, p. 142-151.

17 Ibid.

18 H. Sharp, op. cit., p. 22.

19 A.N. Basu, *Indian Education in Parliamentary Papers*, part I, p. 149.

20 Ibid.

21 Ibid., p. 10.

22 Nurullah and Naik, op. cit., p. 10.

23 Cited in Aparna Basu, *The Growth of Education and Political Development in India, 1898-1920,* Delhi, 1974, p. 73.

24 Aparna Basu, *Essays in the History of Indian Education.* pp. 4-5.

25 H.Sharp, op. cit., p. 114.

26 Aparna Basu, *The Growth of Education and Political Development in India, 1898-1920*, op. cit., p. 73.

27 *The Great Indian Education Debate*, op. cit., p. 111.

28 H. Sharp, op. cit., p. 113.

29 R.C Majumdar, *History and Culture of People of India*, Vol. X, pp. 35-36.

30 Nurullah and Naik, op. cit., pp. 97-98.

31 Aparna Basu, *The Growth of Education and Political Development in India,* op. cit., p. 73.

32 Ibid.

33 *The Great Indian Education Debate*, op. cit., pp. 99-103.

34 H. Sharp, op. cit., pp. 91-92.

35 *Indian Education in Parliamentary Papers, Part 1,* op. cit., p. 160.

36 Minute of Francis Warden, March 24, 1828, cited in ibid., p. 221.

37 Suresh Chandra Ghosh, *Birth of a New India*, Originals, Delhi, 2001, p. 26.

38 Chopra, Puri, Das, *A Social, Cultural and Economic History of India, Vol. III*, p. 236.

39 *The Great Indian Education Debate*, op.cit., p. 20.

40 Nurullah and Naik, op.cit.,p. 94.

41 Eric Stokes, *English Utilitarians and India*, p. 324.

42 Tarachand, *History of Freedom Movement in India, Vol. I*, p. 180.

43 Speech of Alexander Duff in the General Assemble 25th May 1835, cited in ibid, p. 75.

44 *The Great Indian Educational Debate*, op.cit., p. 25.

45 M.A..Laird, *Missionaries and Education in Bengal, 1793-1837*, pp. 233-34.

46 The *Great Indian Education Debate*, op.cit., p. 27.

47 Ibid.

48 Bentinck to Alexander Duff, February 1833, *Duff Papers* cited in Suresh Chandra Ghosh, *op. cit.*, p. 26.

49 Hazel Marie Griffin, *Thomas Babington Macaulay and the Anglicist-Orientalist Controversy in Indian Education, 1833-37*, (Unpublished Ph.D.thesis), p. 120.

50 H. Sharp, Part I, op.cit., pp. 97-107.

51 C.E.Trevelyan, *On the Education of the People of India*, pp. 189-90.

52 Aparna Basu, *Essays in the History of Indian Education*, op. cit., p. 7.

53 Parliamentry Papers (House of Lords) No. 445 (iii) 1833 p.142, quoted in ibid., p. 7.

54 H. Sharp, op.cit., pp. 149-150.

55 Ibid, p. 157.

56 Ibid, p. 155.

57 J.A. Richie, *Selection from the Educational records, Pt. II, (ed.)*, pp. 364-393.

58 Aparna Basu, *Essays in the History of Indian Education*, op. cit., p. 8.

59 D.P.Sinha, *The Educational Policy of the East-India Company in India in Bengal upto 1854*, p. 307.

60 Ibid., p. 304.

61 Chopra, Puri and Das, op. cit., p. 230.

62 *Report of the Indian Education Commission*, 1882, Table No.I.a, p. V.

63 M.R. Paranjape, *Progress of Education*, pp. 51-52.

64 Wood to Halliday, 24-07-1854, *Wood Papers*, cited by S.R. Mehrotra, op.cit., p. 244.

65 Susane, H. Rudolph and Lyod I.Rudoplh, *Education and Politics in India*, pp. 14-15.

66 J.A. Richie, (Ed.), op. cit., p. 365.

67 Ibid.

68 George Smith, *The Life of John Wilson*, London, 1878, pp. 531-533.

69 *Report of the Census of India*, 1891, p. 214. The figures for literacy include those who were already literate and those under instruction.

70 *Report of the Indian Education Commission*, op. cit., p.1.

71 Puri, Das, Chopra, op.cit., p. 267.

72 *Report of the Indian Education Commission*, op. cit., p. 112.

73 Ibid.

74 Ibid, p. 81.

75 Puri, Das,Chopra, op. cit., p. 268.

76 Aparna Basu, *Essays in the History of Indian Education*, op. cit., p. 10.

77 T. Raleigh (ed.), *Lord Curzon in India (Speeches)*, P. 318. quoted in ibid., p. 11.

78 Curzon to Godley, 18-10-1899, Curzon Papers (158), cited in ibid.

79 Curzon to Godley, 31-1-1901, Curzon Papers (161), cited in ibid.

80 T. Raleigh, op. cit., p. 325.

81 Curzon to Hamition , 22.8.1907, Curzon Papers (161) cited in ibid.

82 Hamilton to Curzon, 10th November 1899, cited in Aparna Basu, *The Growth of Education and Political Development in India*, op. cit., p. 10.

[83] Bhola Chatterjee, *Indo-British Cultural Confrontation*,Calcutta,1979, p. 136.

[84] Ibid., p. 133.

[85] Calcutta University Commission Report, 1904, Vol II, p. 302.

[86] Haridas Mukherjee and Uma Mukherjee, *Origins of National Education Movement*, p. 15.

3

Nature of Colonial Education

It is an undisputed fact that in countries under the colonial rule the educational policy promoted the needs of the colonizer, ignoring the aspirations of the colonized. The educational policy of British Government in India is a good illustration of this practice. The British replaced indigenous education in India with an education which promoted the colonial interests. Although the education policy had different priorities at different times and under different situations, the needs of the empire remained its guiding principle.

Travelyan's Vision

On the role of a new system of education in protecting the British imperial interests in India, perhaps the most explicit and impressive argument was provided by Charles Travelyan in 1838 in his book *On the Education of the People of India.*[1] As a first step, Trevelyan and others who shared his opinion considered it necessary to strangle the indigenous system of education to its death because continuance of the native system of education was inconsistent with the maintenance of the British rule in India for long. Trevelyan warned the British policy makers that revival and popularization of the Hindu and Muslim systems of education "would be perpetually reminding the Mahommedan that we are infidel usurpers of some of the fairest realms of the Faithful, and the Hindus, that we are unclean beasts, with whom it is a sin and a shame to have any friendly intercourse. Our bitterest enemies could not desire more than that we should propagate systems of learning which excite the strongest feelings of human nature against ourselves." English education on the other hand, Trevelyan noted, would further the cause of the British rule in India: "The spirit of English education ... cannot but be favorable to the English connection. Familiarly acquainted with us by means of our literature, the Indian youth almost ceases to regard us as foreigners. They speak of our great men with the same enthusiasm as we do. Educated in the same way, interested in the same objects, engaged in the same persuits with ourselves, they become more English than Hindu, just as the Roman provincials became more Romans than Gauts or Italians." About the English educated Indians he wrote, "From violent opponents, or sullen conformists, they converted into zealous and intelligent co-operators with us."

Trevelyan rightly concluded that all conquered communities try to regain their independence and India was no exception. "As long as the native are left to brood over their former independence, their sole specific for improving their conditions is, the independence and total expulsion of the English ... It is only by the infusion of European ideas, that a new direction can be given to their national views. The young men, brought up at our seminaries, turn with contempt from the barbarous despotism under which their ancestors groaned, to the prospect of improving their national institutions on the English model."

It goes to the credit of Trevelyan that he was able to visualize the entire spectrum of India's struggle for freedom in future led by the educated class against the British rule. After reading the next two paragraphs, one cannot but marvel at the astonishing clarity of vision behind the introduction of new education policy.

"No effort of policy can prevent the natives from ultimately regaining their independence. But there are two ways of arriving at this point. One of these is, through the medium of revolution; on the other, through that of reform. In one, the forward movement is sudden and violent; in the other, it is gradual and peaceful. One must end in a complete alienation of mind and separation of interests between ourselves and the natives; the other in a permanent alliance, founded on mutual benefit and goodwill."

"The only means at our disposal for preventing the one and securing the other class of results is, to set the natives on a process of European improvement to which they are already sufficiently inclined. They will then cease to desire and aim at independence on the old Indian footing. A sudden change will then be impossible; and a long continuance of our present connection with India will even be assured to us. A Mahratta or Mahommedan despotism might be re-established in a month; but a century would scarcely suffice to prepare the people for self-government on the European model. The political education of a nation must be a work of time; while it is in progress, we shall be as safe as it will be possible for us to be. The natives will not rise against us, because we shall stoop to raise them: there will be no reaction, because there will be no pressure: the national activity will be fully and harmlessly employed in acquiring and diffusing European knowledge, and in naturalizing European institutions. The educated classes, knowing that the elevation of their country on these principles can only be worked out under our protection, will naturally cling to us. They even now do so. There is no class of our subjects to whom we are so thoroughly necessary as those whose opinions have been cast in the English model; they are spoiled for a purely native regime; they have everything to fear from the premature establishment of a native government."

As Trevelyan had professed, the English educated classes never supported any violent upheavel to overthrow the British rule. They remained aloof from the great revolt of 1857. Some sections of educated Indians even prayed for the British victory in the revolt. Later, nationalist educated class adopted western mode of organisation and method of protest. Their objective was to create western political institutions in India. After India won her independence, the Constituent Assembly chose to adopt a constitution based on the Westminster model of democracy.

Missionary Designs

Missionary interests had been influencing the British education policy much before 1854 and they continued to do so well after 1854. In 1871, Madras census report expressed the hope that rationalizing effects of modern education might iead the Hindu masses to adopt Christianity.[2] To support the missionary cause tacitly, prominent missionaries were appointed at influential positions in the education systems. In this context, case of Dr. John Wilson can be cited as a suitable example. Besides being one of the founders of Bombay University, John Wilson was a member of syndicate, dean of faculty of arts, and examiner in Sanskrit, Persian, Hebrew, Marathi, Gujarati, and Hindustani. Later he became the Vice Chancellor of the university. In his correspondence with Alaxander Duff, Wilson gave a detailed account of how he was able to promote Christianity through his position in University. He was able to induct the study of new subjects in undergraduate courses like 'Evidence of Christianity', which promoted his cause. Some of the books chosen for university studies had the material to lay 'good foundation for Christian tuition.' He gives examples of text-books for Sanskrit course which were selected because they promoted certain principles of Christianity. At the same time some texts which put the Hindu learning on rational grounds were eliminated from the course. In the last part of the letter Wilson points out the consequences for missionary cause if they (missionaries) withdrew from the arena of education.[3]

Wilson's latter reveals how the unsuspecting mind of Indian students was being subtly imbued with fundamental features of Christian teachings. By designing curriculum, missionaries were able to elude the violent reaction which the open preaching of religion would have led to. Selection of the suitable texts to suit the missionary or imperial purposes was going on from the time of Macaulay. For instance, Macaulay and Travelyan had selected certain texts to be taught under literary curriculum including Shakespeare for his 'sound protestant Bible principle'; Addison's Spectator Papers for their 'strains of serious piety' and Bacon for his 'scriptural morality'.[4] By the middle of 19th century, missionaries were able to play a leading role in text book writing and thus shaped the school pedagogy to a great extent. At the same time, under the pretext of teaching secular education, the teaching of Indian religions or morals was carefully avoided.

Text-books as Carriers of Colonial Ideology

Indirect propagation of the Christian teachings through the curriculum was but only one aspect of the school pedagogy. During the British rule the job of selecting and shaping the school knowledge was performed primarily with colonial motives. Indigenous knowledge was considered to be deficient for educational use. In its place, the curriculum and the textbooks prescribed to operationalize it represented the values and vision of the colonial bureaucracy. The recipients of the new education were required to disown their own images of the world and to internalize the world view of the colonial rulers. The purpose was to train a small minority (educated class) in attitudes and skills of the rulers. This class was needed to supply the subordinates. Such a class of persons saw themselves as sharing power and privileges with the rulers. They also intended to place themselves above the masses, intellectually and morally. Moreover, as consumers of knowledge supplied by the rulers, the educated class considered themselves as people incapable of producing the new knowledge.[5]

Selective study of the English literature played a crucial role in the transmission of colonial ideals. Interestingly, British emphasized on literary study in India while in England classical study was considered more respected. The reason was that the literary study was more suitable for transmitting colonial cultural ideals and values. As pointed out by Gauri Viswanathan, greater the support literature gave the state in its tasks of ensuring form of behaviour and taught conducive to its well being, the more strengthened was its status as a cultural ideal and the more insistently was its nature constructed as morality, true belief and knowledge.[6] Achieving a distinction in the literary study was made compulsory for Indian aspirants for higher positions in administration. The purpose was to imbue native public servants with colonial cultural norms so that they would perceive or react in a way similar to a British public servant. Hence literary study was a potent tool designed to regulate public behaviour of native elites. Colonial rulers were following Edmund Burke who had said "give me the making of the ballads of a nation and I will give you the making of its laws."[7] Thus, literary traditions were used as a medium to transmit the cultural norms which in turn were expected to regulate the society. James Mill had also advocated a similar theme. Mill equated education to 'trains of thought passing in an individual mind by means of words, images or other signs through repetition and reinforcement'. These 'trains' form the habits and impressions of individuals. Thus the entire set of beliefs, thoughts and values (which to Mill was equivalent to culture) was embedded in the structure of education and could be used to control the individuals' mind.[8]

The theory that those who control the trains of thought passing through the mind also control the society found concrete evidence in 'downward filtration theory' or 'trickle down theory'. This theory had originated out of the necessity of creating a small elite group as well as the availability of limited funds for the education. A letter from the Court of Directors to the Bombay Government in 1830 explained the objective behind the filtration theory. The letter emphasised the argument that the elevation of the moral and intellectual condition of a people depended upon the education of higher classes. Natives educated directly by British would make the best teachers and translators of useful books. They will become the medium of communication of 'improved spirit' or the influence of European ideas and sentiments on the native mind and native literature.[9]

The European ideas and sentiments which served the colonial purpose were conveyed through the textbooks designed for the purpose. The textbook came to acquire a permanent role in the prevalent school system so much so that it became the central character of the school pedagogy. The dominance of text books in the school pedagogy, termed as 'textbook culture' by Krishna Kumar, portrays the following:

1. Teaching in all subjects is based on textbooks prescribed by the state authorities.
2. The teacher has no freedom to choose what to teach.
3. Teaching resources other than text book are not available generally.
4. Assessment and examinations are based on the text book.

The textbook culture was a manifestation of highly bureaucratised system of education. Even the indigenous schools desirous of getting the government aid were brought under its ambit. The supply of textbooks was big business and interests of big publishing concerns were involved. Business interests and bureaucracy often mingled together to allow inferior books to be recognized as textbooks. The *Hindustan Review* of 16th October 1903 reported that United Province had became "the dumping ground for all sorts and conditions of books published by an influential Landon firm of publishers whose books were 'rushed through.'[10] Biggest loser in the whole scenario was the native student.

Another casualty of textbook culture was the native teacher. Teacher now had no power to select the teaching material. Moreover, the performance of the students was not decided by the teacher but by the examination results. In the pre-British education system, the teacher was supported by the society and was highly respected for his services. But under the colonial system, the teacher became a junior functionary of the state. His professional training was brief and insufficient. Substantial part of the school teacher's daily routine consisted of clerical activities. Besides, he lived in constant dread of school inspector as school inspector's report decided his performance and a chance of promotion. Teacher was paid very less in comparison to inspectors and other officials of the Education Department. The average salary of a primary school teacher varied between Rs. 5 and Rs. 15 whereas Inspector of Schools drew between Rs. 100 and Rs. 500. Salary of Directors of Public Instruction in the Provenances was more than Rs. 2000.[11] Low salary, hard working conditions and low status made teaching profession acquire a low status when compared to other professions like legal and medical practice. Inferior position of teacher symbolized the degradation of creativity of the teachers. By subjugating the position of teachers, the colonial state made them intellectually passive. In this situation, knowledge created especially for the colonial purpose could be transferred to students without any distortion. This would not have been possible had the teaching class been intellectually alive.

Foreign Nature of Education

The knowledge passed through a passive teacher was foreign in nature and unsuitable to meet the Indian requirements. On the foreign nature of education system in British India, Max Muller had stated in 1871 that "the education system now in force in India, with certain indispensable modifications, has been framed after the model of the schools and universities of England."[12] Higher education was imparted in English, a foreign medium. The mind of native student was taxed not only with learning a foreign language but also by the content which was not always relevant to Indian conditions. An article in *Hindu Patriot* of 19 May 1873 noted that "a beginner's mind is distracted at the outset with the difficulties of a foreign language and names of things which are not within everyday experience ... The books, which are now in fashion have been designed especially for English youths.... and for more reasons than one they are utterly unsuited to Bengali lads."[13] The main defect of such an education imposed on India, in K.M. Panikkar's opinion, was that "its social ideas were entirely different from and to a great extent hostile to Indian conditions....The social philosophy that is current in the colleges is not applied critically and nationally in our institutional life and it gives to our education an air of unreality."[14]

The foreignness of the education during the British times was nowhere as explicit as in the promotion of English at the cost of vernacular languages. Medium of English became the greatest obstacle in the spread of education. Even some British officials recognised the need of instruction through the mother tongue. In this context Col. Jervis, a member of the Board of Education in Bombay, made the following observations in a minute in 1847 - "it must be admitted that instruction cannot be afforded, except through the medium of language with which the mind is familiar. In our endeavour to make the knowledge of English among the native so prominent and so essential a qualification, we are neglecting the benefits of three hundred years' experience in Europe, and we are retrograding to the days in which Latin was the sole language of literature."[15] The implication of such a policy, Jervis rued, was that knowledge became confined to a 'few Men of Letters' and it was only after the exclusive use of Latin language was abrogated and modern tongues of Europe emancipated that the learning became widespread. "Should we then", asked Jervis, "forget this lesson, and insist so much on imposing the burden of the foreign language of handful of Rulers on the Millions of our Native population?" About a century later Mahatma Gandhi lamented the ill effects of the foreign medium upon the country: "Among the many evils of foreign rule this blighting imposition of a foreign medium upon the youth of this country will be counted by history as one of the greatest. It has sapped the energy of the nation ... It has estranged them from the masses ... The sooner therefore educated India shakes itself free from the hypnotic spell of the foreign medium, the better it would be for them and the people."[16]

Denial of Technical Education

Another great defect of the British education system was the overwhelming literary bias and neglect of technical education. Madras census report for the year 1871 stated in unambiguous words that "the present system of general education is wholly literary and its chief result hitherto has been to provide an excessive number of clamorous candidates for the civil services."[17] Official education policy, right from the time of Macaulay's Minute, had focussed on the European literature in place of the European science. Enlightened Indians including Raja Ram Mohan Roy were demanding facilities for the teaching of sciences. But the teaching of sciences and technical and vocational subjects was by and large neglected. In place of these subjects the emphasis was on the study of literature, logic, politics and philosophy. Macaulay's Minute ignored the scientific education of the Indian people. As Pramath Nath Bose, pioneering Indian geologist and palaentologist noted- "at the time he (Macaulay) wrote, Europe had begun to make amazing progress in natural sciences and its application to industry. If useful knowledge of the West had been imparted to the Indian alumni from the very beginning the annihilation of Indian industry might possible have been averted."[18] Initially the science was excluded from the course of studies completely. It was largely due to the effort of Father Lafont of St Xavier's College, Alexander Padler (Director of Public Instruction in Bengal), and Mahendralal Sircar that an alternative B.A. course in science was adopted by the senate of Calcutta University. In 1891, out of the 1000 pupils who received education, only one belonged to technical institutions.[19] In 1899-1900, only 10 students obtained the degree of B.Sc. in India. Opportunities for Indians to advance in the colonial educational and scientific services were limited. That the university studies had an 'art bias' is also evident from the fact in 1901-02, while there were 1,476 pupils enrolled for the B.A. degree, there were only 14 for B.Sc. and 16 for B.E. In the matter of employment in the scientific institutions, qualified Indians were usually ignored. The first appointment of an Indian to a graded post (that of Pramath Nath Bose) in Geological Survey took place only in 1880, though the Geological Survey was established in 1851.[20]

One of the major reasons for the slow growth of engineering education was the lack of employment opportunities for highly trained Indians. The main employers for engineering jobs were government and private industry. The former reserved the Imperial Service of Engineers and other superior services for Europeans. Only 9 to 10 appointments to the provincial services were made each year from the five engineering colleges.[21] Railways could have provided a vast ground for training of Indian engineers but Government discouraged the indigenous growth of Railways and ancillary industries, along with the discrimination against the Indians in the appointments to these avenues. In 1913, European and Anglo-Indians formed 0.08 % of the population but held 90 % of the posts in railways carrying the salary of Rs. 500 and above.[22] Irrigation Department ranked text to the railways in European and Anglo-Indian predominance.[23] Government ordinance factories rarely trained Indians for supervisory jobs. In the Posts and Telegraph Department also, natives held a disproportionately small number of posts in the higher paid jobs.[24] In the private sector too, except the cotton textile industry in Bombay Presidency and the Tata Iron and Steel Works, there were few industries before 1920 which were financed and controlled by Indians. European managers doubted the ability of Indians to handle technical jobs efficiently. The Director General of Education regarded this lack of confidence in the natives' ability as one of the serious obstacles to the growth of higher technical education in India.[25]

The Atkins-Dawson Committee, appointed in 1912 to enquire into bringing technological institutes into closer touch with employers in India, reached the conclusion that there were no openings for those who possessed higher theoretical training.[26] Thus due to lack of openings for technically and theoretically trained Indians, growth of higher science and technology education suffered. As late as 1919, senior Government officers were arguing that one single engineering college would be sufficient for the whole of India.[27]

'The plant of technical and industrial education', Lord Curzon admitted, subsisted mainly on 'platitudes in viceregal and gubernatorial speeches'.[28] Curzon's admission sums up the official response to consistent public demand from Congress platform and elsewhere since 1880s for more government expenditure and facilities for technical education. Extreme apathy to the subject of higher technical education apart, British officials were not even convinced about the genuineness of the native intelligentsia's demand. Some went as far as to call the native fascination for the subject as merely 'an extraordinary fascination for the tongue in India'.[29] "Rage for so-called technical education in India", wrote Curzon to Lord Ampthill (Governor of Madras), "is merely one more aspect of the craze for posts, for the finding of billets, for young men of educated classes, who, if they fail, as nine out of ten will fail, will only add to the discontented hordes."[30]

Socio- economic Disparities

Apart from the denial of technical education, the new education created steep social, economic and regional disparities. English education was expensive in nature. Poor had no place in the new system. In 1883-84, only 9% of the college students in Bengal came from families with annual income less than Rs. 200.[31] Non-access to the higher education further broadened the gap between the rich and poor. Moreover, the education was concentrated around port cities of Calcutta, Madras and Bombay. Rest of India had little access to higher education. In terms of number of educated natives, various provinces showed large variations. The Public Service Commission Report of 1886-87 found 18,390 educated natives in Madras; 16,639 in Bengal, 7196 in Bombay,3200 in United Province, 1944 in Punjab, 608 in Central Provinces and only 274 in Assam. The data presented in the Government reports depicts rapid growth in the number of institutions and the pupils studying in them. But when compared with the total population of the country, these figures represent a miniscule proportion of the population. The census figures for literacy presented below demonstrate a pathetic picture of the state of literacy in the country.[32]

Census Literacy Figures per 1000

Year	Male literacy per 1000	Female literacy per 1000
1881	67	3
1891	87	4
1901	98	7
1911	106	10
1921	139	21
1931	156	29

Thus, the literates (male & females) in 1901 were 53 per thousands.[33] It means that about 95% of the population was illiterate. Dadabhai Naoroji in his note to the Education Commission of 1882, pointed out the gross inadequacy of the state effort in education. Comparing the school attendance figures from different countries Naoroji said that while in United Kingdom about 1 child in 7 attends the elementary school, the corresponding figure for India is only 1 in 114.[34] In 1903, Gopal Krishna Gokhle in his budget speech presented comparative data relating to the ratio of enrolment to the total population of various countries including India. In India this ratio was 1.4 while in United States it was 20.9, 18 in Australia, 17.7 in England, 17.6 in Ireland and 14.4 in France.[35] In 1919, Prof. P.C. Roy, the celebrated chemical scientist, wrote that illiterate population of India is highest in the civilized world.[36] In 1931, 90.5 % of population was illiterate.[37] Literacy rate at the time of independence was about 15%. Independent India had to carry the great burden of 85 % of population being illiterate.

Very low literacy rate and poor quality of education were obviously due to the colonial policy of resource allocation for the education. In 1855 (one year after Wood's Despatch) the expenditure on education was less than one percent of the total revenue.[38] Budget speech of Gokhle (1903) gives a comparative account of the expenditure on primary education per head of population.[39] If Indian expenditure is taken as one unit Australia was spending 14 units of money per head, United States 11 units, and England 6 units. The relative difference in expenditure per head on higher educating was steeper. Ireland spent 44 times, Australia 32 times, USA 25 times and France spent about 24 times the per head expenditure of India on higher education.[40]

Apart from poor resource allocation for education and neglect of mass education, gender bias or preference to education of males over females is clearly evident in British education policy in India. According to the census figures for 1881, ratio of males under instruction was 1in 42 while the ratio of females under instructions was 1 in 858. Similarly the literate males not under instruction was 1 in 16 whereas in case of females this figure was1 in 434 .[41] While every report emphasised on the need of special efforts in female education, very little was actually done. The following table highlights the statistics of special institutions for girls in 1881.[42]

Institutions	**Number of special institutions for girls**	**Number of pupils enrolled**
Colleges	1	6
Secondary schools	81	2054
Primary schools for girls	2600	82420
Mixed primary schools	—	42071
Training Institutions for primary school teachers	15	515
Total	**2697**	**127066**

The gender bias in education continued to exist till the very end of British rule in India. The following table depicts the member of girls for every 100 boys at school in 1946-1947.[43]

Institutions	Number of girls for every 100 boys at school
Universities and colleges of general education	12
College of professional and special education	7
High schools	14
Middle schools	22
Primary schools	36
Other special schools	12
Total	30

Notes and References

1 Charles Travelyan, *On the Education of the People of India,* London, 1838, pp. 189-193.

2 Madras Census Report, Part I, 1871, p. 107.

3 Wilson to Duff, cited in George Smith, *The Life of John Wilson,* London, 1878, *The Life of John Wilson*, op. cit., p. 535.

4 Krishna Kumar, *Political Agenda of Education*, Delhi, 1991, p. 62.

5 Krishna Kumar, *Origins of India's Textbook Culture*, Occasional Papers, Nehru Memorial Museum and library, New Delhi, 1987, p. 7.

6 Gauri Vishwanathan, *The Ideology of Literary Education in British India*, Unpublished Ph. D. thesis, p. 179.

7 Ibid.

8 Ibid., p. 180.

9 *Great Britain Parliamentary Papers 1831-32*, Vol. 9, p. 383, cited in ibid., pp. 184-185.

10 Krishna Kumar, *Origins of India's Textbook Culture*, op. cit., p. 13.

11 Krishna Kumar, *Political Agenda of Education*, op. cit., p. 75.

12 John Murdock, *Education in India*, Madras, 1881, p. 44.

13 Ibid., p. 38.

14 K.M. Pannikkar, *Essays an Educational Reconstruction in India*, Madras, 1920, pp. 6-7.

15 J. Richie, *Selections from Educational Records, Vol.II*, op. cit., pp. 111-112.

[16] Aparna Basu, *The Growth of Education and Political Development in India, 1898-1920*, Delhi, 1974, pp. 78-79.

[17] *Madras Census Report*, Part I, 1871, p. 366.

[18] J.C. Bagal, *Pramatha Nath Bose*, Calcutta, 1955, p. 3.

[19] *Census Report for India*, 1891, Vol. I, part I, p. 224.

[20] Deepak Kumar, (ed.), *Science and Empire*, Delhi, 1991, pp. 128- 129.

[21] *Progress of Education in India*, 1897-1902, Vol I, p. 249.

[22] *Report of the Royal Commission on Public Services in India*, 1917, Vol. I, p. 24, cited in Aparna Basu,, *'Essays in the History of Indian Education*, op. cit., p. 50.

[23] Ibid., p. 289.

[24] Ibid., pp. 290-291.

[25] *Progress of Education in India*, 1902-07, Vol. I, pp. 590-91.

[26] Deepak Kumar, *Science and Empire*, op. cit., p. 131.

[27] Home Education A, July 1919, No. 36.

[28] Aparna Basu, *The Growth of Education and Political Development in India*, op.cit., p. 93.

[29] Ibid. p. 86.

[30] Ibid, p. 82.

[31] Sumit Sarkar, *Modern India*, p. 6.

[32] The figures for 1891 and 1891 include those literate and those under learning. The figures and taken from the Report of 1901 (p. 158), 1911 Report (p. 295), 1921 Report (p. 177) and 1931 Report (p. 339).

[33] Census Report, India, 1901, p. 158.

[34] *Educating the Nation*, 2003, p. 56.

[35] *Modern Review*, March 1911, p.p. 261-263.

[36] *Census Report of India*, 1931, p. 339.

[37] Aparna Basu, *Essays in the History of Indian Education*, op. cit., p. 65.

[38] Nurullah and Naik, op.cit., p. 162.

[39] *Modern Review*, March 1911, p. 262.

[40] Derived from ibid.

41 Cited in the *Report of the National Committee an Women's Education*, May 1858 to January 1859, Ministry of Education, Government of India, 1959, pp. 18-19.

42 Ibid. p. 20.

43 Ibid. p. 28.

4

Growth of National Consciousness in India

Along with the introduction and spread of the English education by the colonial regime, 19th century India also witnessed the expression of a sense of nationality in an idiom hitherto unknown in India. National consciousness expressed itself in multiple forms – political, economic, social, art, literature and also educational. The underlying spirit of this consciousness lay in looking at the issues from a national perspective and national requirements and how British interest were antagonistic to national interests. The awareness about the national requirements in education vis-à-vis the prevalent education policy later led to the concept of national education. A brief discussion of the origins, dimensions, growth and impact of the national consciousness will not be out of context here before discussing the educational consciousness and the early efforts in that direction.

The rise of national consciousness in India has been explained by some scholars as purely a product of the western impact.[1] Their argument is that "national feeling did not germinate of its own accord in the soil of India, rather it was an exotic growth imparted by foreign hands and influences ... Foreign rule produced an atmosphere favourable to the growth of national sentiment, and foreign education in time created a native intelligentsia in whose rank such ideas found a ready welcome".[2] But views of such kind do not stand the test of a careful study of history. Without belittling the role of the West it can be established that development of nationalism in India was a process quite unique to India. Moreover, a sense of national consciousness can be traced since the ancient times.

Nationalism as viewed by the Western scholars and British administrators was 'European' in nature. It envisaged five unities essential to make a nation: territory, state, language, race and religion or culture. India with its great cultural and geographical diversity and lack of political unity did not fit in this definition of nationalism. A careful study of the subject leads us to the conclusion that European and Indian nationalism are essentially different in many respects. European nationalism was mainly political in nature, Indian nationalism was largely cultural. Nationalism in Europe emerged after the French Resolution, whereas the roots of Indian nationalism can be traced to the ancient times. As Bipin Chandra Pal wrote in 1913, European nationalism, being isolationalist and materialist in nature was anti-humanity, while the Indian nationalism represented a higher stage of group consciousness and was a positive step towards human brotherhood and spirituality.[3]

Antiquity of National Consciousness in India

Explorations into Indian history have revealed with conclusive evidence not only the nature but also the antiquity of the idea of Indian nationalism. In this context, Radha Kumud Mookerjee's work[4] deserves a special mention. Mookerjee concluded, "A close examination of Sanskrit literature will easily reveal the truth that it contains within itself all the elements that are needed to develop the different interests of national life, mental or moral, spiritual and political".[5] Mookerjee said that India was preaching the gospel of nationalism when Europe was passing through what has been aptly called the Dark Age of her history, and was labouring under the travails of a new birth.[6]

With its varied physical features and climatic diversity India enjoys a clear divide from its surrounding areas so much so that it is known as a subcontinent, a separate geographical unit; a fact accepted universally. Since Kautilya, people inhabiting this land were keenly conscious of the geographical boundaries of their homeland, a fact celebrated in the Puranas:

"Uttaram yat samudrasya
Himadreschaiva dakshinam,
Varsham tad Bharatam nama
Bharati yatra santatih."

(*Vishnu Purana,* II, 3.1; *Vayu Purana*, 45)

"The country that lies north of the ocean and south of the snowy mountains is called Bharata; there dwell the descendents of Bharata".

Puranas and several other ancient texts such as Pali texts, Panini's *Astadhayai, Artashastra, Ramayana,* and *Mahabharata* contain lists of sacred places, sacred mountains, and sacred rivers so as to provide education about the country and instil a spirit of cultural consciousness and patriotism among the educated classes. But nowhere is the geo-cultural consciousness of the Indian civilization so visibly portrayed as in the *Samkalp Mantra*[7], a part of the daily prayers of every Hindu and also recited before the start of every sacred ritual, describes every individual of this land in terms of time and space down to every possible detail.

The country has had a common name since the time immemorial: Bharatavarsha or Jambudvipa or Prithvi[8]. Notwithstanding its division into numerous political divisions during different periods of time, inhabitants of this land have proudly referred themselves as the descendants of Bharata. Through the ages, this geographical unity has also preserved a cultural unity on a macro level. Chief carriers of the cultural unity have been a common sacred language[9] i.e. Sanskrit and common sacred body of literature of the Vedas. Sects like Jainism and Buddhism, though not believing in the infallibility of the Vedas, also contributed to the unity of this land, their idols and places of worship interspersed all over the country. Pilgrim places and shrines are also dispersed all over the territory including the remote corners of India. Indian tradition of visiting the major pilgrim centers at least once in the lifetime provided a unique way of familiarizing with the far off corners of the country. It is in this light that the establishment of the four revered mathas (Shringeri in far south, Dwarika in far west, Puri in the east, and Joshi Math in higher Himalayas in the north) in the four corners of India by Shankaracharya must be seen. Reverence for the holy places and the religious merit associated with pilgrimage preserved the idea of India in the minds of the common folk for thousands of years.

Apart from the continuity of the cultural unity of the country what strikes one's mind is the fascinating sense of lofty patriotism and deep admiration for the land and its people since the ancient times. Wide spread consciousness of a keen sense of patriotism - pride, love and gratitude for the motherland, is expressed by aphorisms like "*Janani Janmabhumischa svargadapi gariyasi*" (The mother and Motherland are greater than Heaven itself) Sanskrit literature contains hymns which could be called national songs in modern terminology. Perhaps the best representative of such poetry is *Prithvisukta,* a string of 63 hymns full of reverence to the motherland. *Prithvisukta* expresses a most beautiful description of the motherland, its riches, values and ideals. The last passage of *Pritvisukta* is truly remarkable as it recognizes the national unity despite the inherent diversity of Indian life - the land "bearing in many places people of different speech, of diverse customs,"[10] yet the motherland feeds them without distinction, like a cow will do.

The fact of fundamental unity of India is not only conveyed in the sacred idiom, but also as in the terminology of the political concepts like *Chakravartin*. Elucidated in Chanakya's *Arthashastra* of 4th century B.C., *Chakravartin* literally meant a King who has conquered the four directions, meaning thereby a single power dominating the whole country or the attainment of the highest form of sovereignty. Radhakumud Mookerjee also compiled a crop of terms denoting political sovereignty in both pre-Kautilya and post- Kautilya periods in the Ancient India.[11]

Thus the religious scriptures and spiritual milieu functioned as vehicles for development and continuance of national consciousness, a process which helped maintain a sort of cultural unity in India for thousands of years. India and the essence of Hinduism are organically related as body and soul. The entire ancient literature from *Rigveda* to *Puranas* covers a vivid description of the expanding geographical basis of a national culture.[12] Common sacred literature, cultural traditions and festivals point out a deep cultural unity in spite of an outward diversity. Over the centuries, this unity was preserved and strengthened by pilgrims, merchants and scholars who frequently toured the entire country. The sense of belonging to an all-India community cut across regional and linguistic affiliations.

It is the peculiar feature of the national consciousness in India that since antiquity it has expressed itself in the religio-cultural domain and not in the political domain. A plausible cause of this apparent shortcoming was the immense difficulty in establishing and then maintaining an all-India state in the face of vastness of distance and physiographical diversity. At the same time it must be said that Hindu mind was little bothered about the political convulsions. During the Great Revolt of 1857 Indian sepoys revolted only when they felt that their religion was in danger.

Role of the British Rule in Making India a Nation

Establishment of the British rule in India created suitable conditions for the emergence of national consciousness in the domain of politics. For the first time after Mauryas and Mughals, under the British rule, Indian subcontinent witnessed a political unity. Regarding the impact of political unity provided by British rule, it has been said that "the British Raj was like a steel frame which held the injured body of India together till the gradual process of internal growth had joined the dislocated bones, knit up the torn fibers, and enabled the patient to regain inner coherence and unity".[13] A single administration, a common official language (English) and a newly developed accessibility to the whole of India with the help of modern means of communication and transport combined with the ancient ethos of spiritual and cultural unity to give birth to a new type of national consciousness.

People living under a common rule were brought closer by modern means of communications and transport: the post, the telegraph, postal system, railways and press. Press has been hailed as the chief instrument used by Indians to spread modern social, economic and political ideas and thus creating an all-India consciousness on modern lines. Native press fearlessly criticized the official policies and gave expression to the wants and views of the people. Some native newspapers made it their conscious policy to inculcate an all-India outlook. Press broke the regional barriers. It enabled the people in one part of the country to become aware of the existences of those in the other parts of the country, their feelings, their grievances and their aspirations. It is hardly surprising that almost all the nationalist leaders were intimately associated with one journal or the other.

The growth of vernacular and Anglo-vernacular press deserves a brief description as it provided expression to different sections of population. At the same time it assisted powerfully in overcoming the barriers which the foreign learning had erected between the educated community and the rest of the population. The first vernacular paper appeared in Calcutta in 1819 and was followed by vernacular newspapers in Bombay and Madras. In 1877, William Digby estimated that the total number of Anglo-vernacular and vernacular papers in circulation amounted to 382.[14] Of these 102 were published in Bengal where two newspapers, *Amrit Bazar Patrika* and *Salobha Samachar* had circulation of 2217 and 3000 approximately. In 1878, among the 86 papers published in Bombay Presidency the largest were the Gujrati *Rast Goftar* and the Marathi *Subodka Patrika* with a circulation of 1800 apiece. In the NWP where every principal town had its local paper, there were 65 papers in1878 which increased to 90 in 1884. Madras in 1877 had 55 vernacular papers. In 1877, total number of papers in C.P., Oudh, Sindh and Rajputana amounted to 63. Among the native newspapers in English Bengal had *Indian Mirror*(founded in 60s, daily circulation of 1500), *Hindu Patriot* (organ of British India Association), *Bengalee, Reis and Rayyet, Indian Nation;* Bombay had *Indian Spectator* and *Sind Times;* Madras had *Hindu* and *Tribune* belonged to the Punjab.

The combined circulation of Anglo-vernacular newspapers was estimated at about 150,000 in 1877.[15] But this number gives little indication of the total readership. In 1880, Roper Lethbridge, Press Commissioner under Lytton wrote: "The date of a paper goes for nothing among Hindus and it continues to be read as long as it hangs together. It may safely be said that if a single copy reaches a village, or even a larger collection of villages, its contents will sooner become known to nearly every man residing in the neighborhood."[16] The growth of vernacular press along with its impact assumed so alarming a proposition that Government felt compelled to gag it by passing the Vernacular Press Act in 1878.

Steady improvements in the postal system under the British rule and finally the introduction of a cheap and uniform rate of postage in 1854, also served to unify the country. Now people could communicate with all parts of India at a cheap rate. It helped in enlarging the circulation of newspaper and thus promoting the social, economic and intellectual advancement of the people in various ways.

Introduction of the railways also had a profound impact on the contemporary India. Railways not only brought people physically nearer but also socially closer. It can be said that the railway compartment in which people of all castes, creeds, and provinces were huddled together, became the symbol of a new and united India in the making. "Railways may do for India", Edvin Arnold wrote in 1865, "what dynasties have never done… they may make India a nation."[17] Travelling across the country increased familiarity with the native land and led to growth of understanding and attachment among the people.

Seen in its entirety, the growth of Indian national consciousness during the British rule was the result of processes both negative and positive. In the positive sense, the imposition of political unity, peace and security, and introduction of modern means of transport and communication unified Indian people. On the other hand, the negative reaction to the foreign nature of British rule, colonial policies, racial bias and a common threat to indigenous religions united India as a nation against a foreign government.

Unlike the other foreign invaders, British could not become a part of the Indian society. Differences in political situation, colour, languages, religions and social habits shut the British out of acquaintance with Indians and Indian society. Their sense of superiority went further than their being the ruling class. It led to racial arrogance resulting in racial discrimination of the native people. This made Indians conscious of 'national' humiliation, and led to think of themselves as one people, irrespective of differences in caste, creed or religion, when facing Englishmen. Again unlike the rulers of the past, the British excluded Indians from all the higher offices of state, civil and military. This was one of the common grievances which united Indians of all creeds and provinces against their alien rulers. *Indian Statesmen* of Bombay (16 May 1872) expressed the mood of educated Indians in the following words: "From Peshwar to Cape Camorin, throughout an empire of 150 millions of people, there is hardly a native of the country, we say in any position of real dignity or large emolument ... the position is so unprecedented and so false, that it cannot last ... The exclusion of the people from the higher ranks of the service is a real scandal and in our own eyes the most potent blot in our administration of the country."[18]

Apart from the racial bias what hurt the natives most was the abusive onslaught of Christian Missionaries on their belief systems. Native religions were projected by missionaries as primitive, based on myths and superstitions. Missionaries kept on insisting that great end of British dominion in India was to Christianize India. Despite the official denials, missionaries continued to receive some official help and backing as many British officials were sympathetic to their cause. Hence Indian people perceived the administration and missionaries as two faces of a single coin.

Missionary propaganda was supplemented with the justification of English rule over India. Charles Grant, Macaulay, Trevelyan, James Mill and many others launched a campaign to destroy the native faith in their culture, their social traditions and knowledge system. Indian response to this propaganda has been called as 'reawakening and reformation'. One of the facets of reawakening was to rediscover India's heritage and cultural achievements particularly in the field of polity, literature, science and technology, philosophy, art and architecture. The rediscovery went a long way in arousing the self confidence and self respect of Indians. In R.C. Majumdar's words, "sense of rich heritage from the past generated in their mind a spirit of self confidence and held out before them a bright vision of their future destiny ... the revelation of India past was one of the strongest foundations, on which India's nationalism was built."[19]

Role of Western Education and English Language

In such a fertile background for the growth of nationalism, western education played the role of a catalyst. Surendranath Banerjea, speaking in the Imperial Assembly in 1915, while supporting the teaching and development of Indian languages, could not ignore the contribution of English education to the Indian national life in the recent decades:

"... it may be a silent and bloodless revolution but one of the greatest resolutions ever witnessed in any age or country. If, today, India is instinct with a new spirit and a new life, if new ideas have broadened the horizon of our vision, it is all due to English education."[20]

Though designed to produce cheap clerks and enslave the native mind, English education, by default, also acted as a medium for access to progressive movements and thoughts of the West. As R.C. Majumdar said, "It is a happy coincidence that India's first contact with the West dated precisely from the period when the ideas of nationalism, freedom, and democracy exercised greatest influences in that part and permeated the English literature through which that contact was mainly estabilished."[21] The ideas and events culminating in the American independence, French revolution, European revolutions of 1830 and 1648, Irish struggle for home rule, and liberation of Greece and Italy made profound impact on the English educated class in India. Rousseau, Paine, J.S. Mill and other western thinkers became their political guides. Mazzine, Garibaldi and Irish nationalist leaders became their political heroes. Enlightened among the English educated Indians inculcated the European ideas of patriotism and public service, rationalism, duties of state and the rights of subjects.

Apart from enabling the Indians to absorb the European ideas, English language also provided a common medium of expression to the scattered Indian intelligentsia. As a result, the English educated people, regardless of the fact that they were Bengalis, Madrasis, Sindhis, Maharastrians or north Indians, for the first time, could communicate in a common medium, exchange views and take a united position vis-a- vis the British administration. Writing in 1878, S.N Banarjea noted that "English education has uplifted all those who have come under its influence to a common platform of thoughts, feelings and aspirations. Educated Indians, whether of Bengal, Madras, Bombay or the N.W.P. are brought under the same intellectual, moral and political influences; kindred hopes, feelings, and ideas thus generated. The educated classes of India are thus brought nearer together."[22]

Thus the role of English education lay in the elevation of a dormant sense of belonging to a common cultural and emotional entity, to a modern kind of nationalism based on a commonality of problems, aspirations and future. Political and administrative unification, availability of new technology to develop the means to travel and communicate with the fellow countrymen, common subject status and a common master, all provided the necessary bond missing up till now. Western ideas and idiom made concrete what was up till now abstract.

It must be kept in mind that only a very small section of society was in direct contact with western studies. Census figures for 1891 show that, of the total literates only 4.4 % knew English. If the Europeans and Eurasians and subtracted from this account, the ratio of those knowing English came out to be 1.4 in every 1000 of the community.[23] A section of this small minority of English knowing persons was inspired by western liberal and nationalist ideas. It were they who started political activity in India, although following the British model of liberal democracy. This group led what became later the national movement.

Another important factor which contributed to the growth of nationalistic sentiments was the growing knowledge of India's glorious past. The rediscovery of India's past had started in the fourth quarter of 18th Century by William Jones and other early Indologists but it was only after the archeological excavations started (In 1861 under Alexander Cunningham), Indological studies taken up on larger scale in Europe particularly Germany, and the results of such research started appearing in journals and books that the Indians in general became aware of their glorious past. These findings put Indian civilization on the same pedestal with ancient Greece and Rome and provided much needed self-confidence during the freedom struggle. Past greatness of Hindu civilization countered on one hand the colonial propaganda about the 'white men's burden' and on the other it held a vision to attain that glorious status again.

It must be reemphasized that even before the British rule India had the necessary elements of national life- an intrinsic underlying unity among all the apparent external diversities. The sense of belonging to an all-India community cut across regional and linguistic loyalties. The conditions created by the British rule provided the necessary stimuli to transform a dormant cultural and spiritual unity into an anti-colonial nationalist movement. Growth of modern nationalism in India thus rested on the twin rocks of ancient tradition and modern influences. The plant of Indian nationalism had ancient roots but above the surface it needed a graft of new ideas under new circumstances to restore its vitality. Some of the new ideas came from the West but the roots remained Indian. How could an imported sapling survive without indigenous roots?

Nationalism: A Unique Phenomenon

It is also necessary to underline the fact that origins and growth of nationalism is a complex phenomenon depending upon the culture, history and geography of a nation. Since these three factors are unique to every nation, every nationality is unique and so is the case of Indian nationalism. There cannot be a fixed criteria for nationalism. Not all the communities become nationalities. Scholars like Ramsay Muir, G.P. Gooch, and MacDougall rejected the old definition based on five unities. G.P Gooch explicitly stated, "The core of nationalism is group consciousness.... neither the occupation of a well defined area, nor community of race, language, religion, government or economic interests are indispensable to national self-consciousness"[24]

Carlton J.H. Hayes, a distinguished authority on nationalism, arrived at a similar conclusion in his work *Nationalism: A Religion*: "In simplest terms nationalism may be defined as a fusion of patriotism with a consciousness of nationality" and that "a nationality receives its impress, its character, its individuality from cultural and historical forces". He wrote further, "historical tradition mean an accumulation of remembered or imagined experiences of the past". Hayes defined patriotism "as a people's territorial past, its ancestral soil, involving a popular, sentimental regard for a homeland where one's forefathers lived and are buried or cremated".[25] Rejecting the nineteenth century belief that nationalism was a political phenomenon and the existence of state was a prerequisite in nation-formation, Hayes said, "If we are to grasp what a nationality is, we must avoid confusing it with state or nation". Accepting the idea of cultural nationalism, Hayes wrote, "Cultural nationalism may exist with or without political nationalism. For, nationalities can do and exist for fairly long periods without political unity and independence."[26]

Hans Kohn, another authority on the history of Nationalism, discovered that in Europe the 'state' was mainly instrumental in nation formation, while in Asia nationalism had cultural origins. Even in Europe, political unity of Germany and Italy was preceded by vigorous intellectual and cultural movements led by Herder, Goethe and Kant etc. in Germany and by Mazzini in Italy. As Sukumar Dutt pointed out, Indian nationality has to be studied and understood in the psychological perspective and not viewed through the colored glasses of such western conceptions such as 'unity of race', 'unity of language', 'unity of religion', etc. The simple fact should be constantly born in mind that the connotations of all such facile terms, as race, language and religion, differ in India vastly from their connotations in the west.[27]

Socio-religious Reform Movements

Initially the Indian nationalists were not averse to British rule. Instead of political opposition to the British rule, early nationalist activity focused on consolidating nationalism along social, cultural and economic lines. Their emphasis was on obtaining social unity, and social equality of different sections of Indian society. It involved active opposition to various forms of social discrimination, social obscurantism, religious superstition, bigotry and other social evils. All the reformers agreed that ignorance was the root cause of all social evils prevalent in Indian society. They laid high emphasis on use of education as a tool for social progress and ultimately the national regeneration. So the reformers were the first to demand and strive for a system of education, suited to the needs of Indians.

The efforts of reform movements towards development of national consciousness were further corroborated by the native reaction to the proselytising activities of missionaries. Missionary activities gave rise to three-fold reaction from Indian society. Firstly, the social reformers countered the missionary propaganda that Hinduism was superstitious in nature by projecting its rational elements. Reform movements such as Brahmo Samaj and Arya Samaj were the manifestation of this realization. Tattwabodhini Sabha, an offshoot of Brahmo Samaj admitted openly that "it was to counteract influences like those, and inculcate on the Hindu religious mind doctrines at once consonant to reason and human nature, for which he has to explore his own sacred resources the Vaidik, that the society was originally established."[28] Second form of Indian reaction was to attack Christianity and its doctrines through press and speeches etc. Thirdly, reaction was against the missionary inroads in the domain of education including boycott of certain institutions, setting up of alternate institutions, and petitions to the Government in protest of missionary influence on education. For instance, baptism of two Parsi boys in Bombay in a mission School in 1839 led to withdrawal of hundreds of boys. A petition was also sent to the Governor accusing the missionaries of insidiously carrying on the work of conversion 'under the cloak of education and the Government of giving countenance and encouragement to the efforts of missionaries.'[29] In the same year a petition signed by over 70,000 inhabitants of Madras prayed for an education which did not interfere with their religion.[30] In 1842, a school (Pacheappa's School) was established in Madras to accommodate students withdrawn from missionary institutions as a results of conversion of three Hindu students.[31]

The growing awareness to defend the native culture against the combined efforts of Government and missionaries can also be seen in the Indian protests against Lex Loci proposals. These proposals were introduced in October 1840. Most controversial provision of the proposals was to remove disabilities imposed by native communities against converts to Christianity. Proposals became a law called Act XXI of 1850. Passing of the Act led natives to believe that Government was actively helping the missionaries in their endeavour of Evangelization of Indian society. The period from 1840 to 1852 saw vigorous protests organized by Indian intelligentsia against the Act. Many memorials were served to the Government against the Act from a cross section of Indian society. One of them was signed by 14,000 Hindus. The issue also led to an active and prolonged debate in the press involving *Bengal Hurkaru*, *Sambad Bhaskar*, *Sambad Prabhakar*, *Sambad Purnachandrodaya*, *Englishman*, *Hindu Intelligencer* and *Friend of India*. Native reaction over this issue may be called as the beginning of organized public opinion against a common grievance. Moreover, protesters were joined by orthodox section and also some Muslims in opposing the Government move.[32] Thus Christian proselytisation drew a combined response from Indians, irrespective of different regions and religions. Later on, in 1857, religious cause became the immediate cause for what some scholars have referred as the first war of Indian independence. During this great event, Indians forgot their own religious differences and fought against a common enemy. Religious activities of Christian missionaries continued to incite Indian people and became one of the causes for many of tribal uprisings.

Economic Nationalism

Side by side with the rise of national consciousness along social and religious lines, economic aspect of national consciousness acquired an important dimension. Enlightened Indians of 19th century, from Ram Mohan to Vivekananda, were concerned about the poverty, under development and colonial exploitation. As in the case of social reform, they tried to evolve a vision for India's prosperous future. Domain of economic nationalism centred around 'drain of wealth'. It included demands for protection of Indian capital and handicrafts, industrialization, tariff protection and relief to peasantry.

Among the leaders who analyzed the causes of poverty and economic backwardness of India, one of the earliest was Gopal Hari Deshmukh(1823-1892). On this subject he wrote two books-

'*Laxmi-Jnan*' and '*Hindustanas Daridrata Yenyachi Karane*' He said that India was economically backward because there was no enthusiasm about economic progress, industrial development was neglected, technical and professional education were non existent, and in place of these realism and rationalism Indian society was engaged in ritualism.[33]

Early nationalists began to realize that the chief cause of economic backwardness of India was its colonial status. They began to grasp the reality that for Britain utility of India lay in becoming a supplier of raw material, being a market for manufactured goods and being a field for the investment of British capital. Economic development of India using western knowledge and resources was not on the agenda of British Government. Early nationalists started educating the public about colonial exploitation and galvanising the public opinion against colonial policies. In 1849, Gopal Hari Deshmukh (Lokhitwadi) was exhorting the Indians that they "should buy Indian goods only. They should avoid purchasing foreign goods-especially goods made in England; Indian merchants should sell clothes made in India, but they should not sell cotton produced in India to the English traders The Indian farmer toils...becomes poorer and poorer while the stream of the wealth goods to the West."[34] On similar lines, Bholanath Chandra, a great publicist and literary figure of his age, urged the people to boycott the foreign goods so as to rejuvenate native Industry according to Bholanath Chandra, the 'most effective weapon' against the drain of wealth was active 'moral hostility of the people'.[35] Thus Lokhitwadi and Bhola Nath Chandra were among the pioneers of economic nationalism in India.

Economic analysis of colonialism became more mature with time and soon a nationalist critique of colonial rule was developed. In this context, contribution of three leaders deserve special mention- Dadabhai Naoroji, M. G. Ranade and Ramesh Chandra Dutt. Dadabhai Naoroji through his numerous writings and speeches popularised the 'drain of wealth' concept. Justice M.G

Ranade taught an entire generation of Indians the value of industrial development. Ramesh Chandra Dutt authored the *The Economic History of India* in which he examined in minute detail the economic policies of the British Government since 1757. Other prominent leaders who made valuable contribution in this direction were G.V. Joshi, G. Subramania and Gopal Krishna Gokhle.

Nationalist economic critique of the colonial rule that finally emerged can be summed up into the following major themes:

1. Foreign capital investment, instead of developing India served the colonial interests, economically and politically. Industrialization of India must be done through the Indian capital.
2. Foreign trade and railways facilitated the decline of indigenous industries. India became an exporter of the raw goods and importer of the manufactured goods. Tariff policy overwhelmingly favoured the British industries.
3. Land revenue and taxes raised by the British Government overburdened the poor and favoured the rich.
4. A large part of India's wealth was being drained to England without an economic return. According to calculations made by nationalists, this drain amounted to one-half of government revenues, more than the entire land revenue collection and over one third of India's total savings.[36] It look the form of salaries and pension of British officials working in India, interest on loan taken by Indian Government, profits of British capitalists in India and various expenses of the Indian Government in Britain.

According to the nationalist opinion the economic transformation of the country must be achieved by industrialisation through modern technology and capitalistic enterprise. Industrialisation of the country was also seen as an effective response to aggressive western imperialism. In the opinion of Pramatha Nath Bose, western imperialism is a manifestation of search for the markets. If the Indians are able to develop their own industries with the help of their own resources and by applying western methods, western manufactures would not be able to exploit Indian markets. In his view "western imperialism would then die a natural and peaceful death, at least in its present highly militant form."[37] Western countries have shown that the real strength of a nation lies in her economic strength. If India was to become a strong nations if was imperative that Industrialization of the country must be given top-most priority. Views of Pramatha Nath Bose on industrialization were shared by most of his contemporaries.

The issue of industrialization was directly associated with the growth of national consciousness. As Ranade said, factories could "far more effectively than schools and colleges give a new birth to the activities of the nation."[38]

Modern industry was seen as a major force which could unite the diverse people of India into a single national entity having common interests. *Bengali* of 18 January1902, elaborated this point: "The agitation for political rights may bind the various nationalities for a time. The community of interest may cease when these rights are achieved. But the commercial union of the various Indian nationalities, once established, will never cease to exist. Commercial and industrial activity is, therefore, a bond of very strong union and is, therefore, a mighty factor in the formation of a great Indian nation."[39]

In 1870s, G.V. Joshi led a popular movement for the revival and encouragement of native arts and industries in Gujarat and Maharashtra.[40] For this purpose societies or associations were established in many cities and large towns. Members of these societies took an oath not to use European articles where the corresponding indigenous articles could be procured at around the same price. Some enthusiastic members including G.V. Joshi vowed not to use any foreign manufactured articles under any conditions. Cooperative shops were opened in many towns to sell indigenous goods. Indigenous manufacture of simple articles like ink, candles, soaps etc was encouraged. Exhibitions of indigenous arts and manufactures were organized. Joshi and his co-workers made use of popular lecturers and songs to spread the message of swadashi among people.

As a result of nationalist emphasis on industrialization and its positive implications, an industrial conference was organized for the first time in Calcutta in 1891. In his presidential address, Pramatha Nath Bose said that industries alone can relieve the distress of the masses by lightening the pressure over land and offering openings to middle classes other than clerkship.[41] Most important outcome of this conference was the establishment of the Indian Industrial Association. Main objectives of the Association included adopting measures for the spread of technical education, collecting information about Indian products and manufacturers, and pointing out new openings for industrial entrepreneurs and to facilitate their establishment.[42] The Association also organized lectures on industrial subjects for some years. It also organized industrial exhibitions, the first of which was held in 1893.

Popularising Science for National Development

Indian intelligentsia of 19th century was unanimous in their belief that scientific knowledge, imperative for industrial development, is vital for national development. They were also influenced by the 19th century European view that wealth of a nation was closely related to the development of scientific institutions and the capacity for technological innovation.[43] Science and technology had facilitated industrial revolution in Europe. Moreover, the great powers of that time were those nations which had taken up rapid industrialization.

But science and technology in India under the British rule were a colonial monopoly. Very little official effort was made to popularise science. Even after the advent of railways and other modern means of transport and communication, no significant effort was made to train the Indians in the modern technology. Nearly all the technical manpower continued to be sourced from England. As a result, industries, medicine and other scientific avenues in

India remained totally dependent on the England-the mother country.

The task before the Indian pioneers involved in the popularization of science was two fold. First, they had to redefine the new knowledge keeping in mind the Indian social and cultural context.[44] Second, they had to convince the native population that modern science could be a useful instrument in social transformation. They attempted to achieve these objectives through newspapers, journals and by forming various associations and societies.

Sambad Koumudi (founded by Raja Ram Mohan Roy) often published scientific articles in the second decade of 19th the century.[45] Around the same time, other journals catering to the scientific education began to come up. Journals especially dedicated to popularization of science included *Paswabali* (est. 1822), *Bijnan Sewadhi* (est. 1832) and *Bignam Sar Sangraha*[46] (est. 1833). *Bignan Sar Sangraha* was a bilingual journal (Bengali and English). Its objectives stated in its first issue may represent the general objectives of all who were associated with popularization of science at that time. Its aim was "to communicate ... such selections from the works of European literature and science as may ... infuse a spirit of activity and enterprise in all pursuits which conduce to the happiness or glory of men. Our object is not so much to amuse as to instruct, not so much to lull them into self complacency as to stimulate them to greater exertions and noble purposes."[47] Another notable development in the field of propagation of science was establishment of 'Society for Translating Sciences' in Calcutta in 1825. The society published 15 volumes of '*Vigyan Sebadi*', a periodical devoted to the propagation of scientific knowledge.[48] Soon after, the society established a 'Mechanical Institute' with Tarachand Chakrabarty, one of the important leaders of Young Bengal, as its president.[49]

In Calcutta, students of Hindu College formed several forums where scientific matters were discussed. Students of Medical College also participated in them.[50] One such prominent forum was, the 'Society for the Acquisition of General knowledge' founded in Calcutta in 1838. The Society was committed to application of 'useful studies' and acquiring 'respectable Knowledge'.[51] Another association, Academic Association was formed at about the same time in Calcutta with similar objectives. *Tattvabodhini Patrika* often published scientific debates in form of articles. Students of Elephinstion College started a 'Students Scientific and Literary Society' in Bombay in 1848. This society also discussed questions related to science and its popularization.

Among those who were involved in popularization and dissemination of science in 19th century, some individuals stand apart for their exceptional contribution: Master Ramchandra, Akshoy Kumar Dutt, Mahandra Lal Sircar, Syyed Ahmed Khan and P.C. Roy. Out of these, Akshoy Kumar Dutt and his work have been discussed else where.

Master Ramchandra[52] (born in 1821 at Panipat), taught at Delhi College and later at Thomson Civil Engineering College, Roorkee. He started translating English scientific works into Urdu so that common people had access to the western scientific knowledge. He was instrumental in the formation of Vernacular Translation Society in 1843. In 1846, he started a weekly called *Qiran-Us-Sadain.* This paper carried articles on new inventions, discoveries and research in modern science and technology. Ramchandra was also associated with the activities of Delhi Society, founded in 1865. Many prominent personalities of that time including Mirza Ghalib and Syyed Ahmad Khan were members of this society. The Society was instrumental in translations of European scientific works into local languages. Ramchandra later joined the services of the Maharaja of Patiala, as the Director of Education. There he was able to introduce the teaching of science in the local Punjabi language. Ramchandra wrote profusely against all prevalent beliefs which he considered to be irrational and unscientific. To reach out to the people he chose the popular medium of Urdu. Ramchandra belonged to a group of educators who brought modern science to the people in their own idiom and familiarised them with the new knowledge. The process of translation also led to the growth of indigenous scientific terminology. Vernacular school books in science which they produced, laid the foundation of the science studies in the schools.

Among those who considered science as a medium of national regeneration, the brightest luminary was Mahendra Lal Sircar (1833-1904).[53] Mahendra Lal Sircar studied at the Here School and later at Hindu college. He excelled in mathematics. To study systematic experimental science he joined Medical College in 1855 and was awarded M.D. in 1863. Later he became Vice-President of British Medical Association. Sircar was much conscious of the exclusion of natives from effective participation in the governmental scientific undertakings. Not hopeful of any Government cooperation, he relied on self-help to use science as a means of national regeneration.[54] He presented his views on the subject in an article named "On the Desirability of a National Institution for the Cultivation of Science by the Natives of India" in August 1869 issue of *Calcutta Journal of Medicine*. Sircar wrote in this article that although under foreign yoke, Indians have inherited a mind that is inferior to none. The Government offering no help to pursuit of science by natives, the regeneration of India is in our own hands. He wanted this institution to combine the character, the scope and the object of the Royal Institute of London and of the British Association for the Advancement of Science. He wished that 'the institution be entirely under native management and control."[55] After persistent efforts he was ultimately successful in establishing the Indian Association for the Cultivation of Science in 1876.

Syyed Ahmad Khan (1817-1898) was another crusader for the cause of science in 19th century India. He was convinced that only modern scientific knowledge can ameliorate India's condition. The best method according to him was to translate all relevant works into vernacular languages.[56] In order to give shape to his ideas, Syyed Ahmed Khan founded the Aligarh Scientific Society in 1864. Objectives of the Society included: translation of western works into local languages of the country; publication of the translations and other material considered useful to the native mind; and organization of demonstrative lectures on scientific subjects. Inspired by Syyed Ahmad Khan's efforts, Maulana Imdad Ali founded Bihar Scientific Society in 1868 with similar objectives.[57]

Prafulla Chandra Roy (1861-1944), a distinguished chemical scientist, was a firm believer in the inter-relation between science and national prosperity. After the partition of Bengal, he promoted the spirit of swadeshi through his researches and entrepreneurship. P.C. Roy represented the Indian men of science who endeavoured to use science to make India self-reliant in industrial products and food production. His work in this direction can be summarized under three dimensions. Firstly, P.C. Roy was closely associated with National Council of Education. The Council attempted to impart higher technical education on national lines and under national control. Secondly, Roy considered chemistry as a tool to develop the resources of the country and increase its wealth. He chose his research problems with the objective of developing self-reliance in preparation or extraction of chemical products that were hitherto being imported from England.[58] And thirdly, he set up Bengal Chemical and Pharmaceutical Works for the local preparation of various chemical and pharmaceutical products. Roy's contributions were not limited to science and industry. He also wrote a treatise on the history of chemical sciences in ancient India called *A History of Hindu Chemistry*.

Using Vernaculars to Disseminate Knowledge

Early nationalist workers recognized the importance of vernacular languages as a medium for dissemination of knowledge. Being intimately associated with regional cultures of India, vernacular languages act as the vehicles of regional history, traditions, folklore and literature. Hence the strengthening and development of vernaculars was needed to counter or resist the imperial cultural attack. The task of popularising, enriching and development of vernaculars involved starting vernacular newspapers and journals, producing and compiling vernacular literature and establishing associations and societies.

19th century saw many new vernacular newspapers and journals coming up. Following can be cited as examples: Ram Mohan Roy's *Sambad Kaumudi*, Young Bengal's '*Gyananveshan*', Devendra Nath and Akshoy Kumar's *Tatwa Bodhini Patrika* and Keshab Chandra Sen's *Sulabh Samachar* in Bengal; Balshastri Jambhekar's *Dig Darshan* and *Bombay Darpan*, Bhau Mahajan's *Prabhakar* and Dadabhai Naoroji's *Rast Goftar* in Bombay; Veerasalingam's *Viveka Vardhini* and B. Pantalu's *Jana Sanskarini* in Andhra.

A Native Literary Society was formed on September 9, 1830 by the followers of Ram Mohan Roy.[59] Sarbatatva Deepika Sabha, formed in 1835, was also dedicated to the vernacular literature. Members of this Sabha, pledged to speak to each other only in Bengali during the proceedings of Sabha.[60]

Sensitive issue of the vernacular languages was taken up very passionately in the proceedings of various Associations and Societies. For example, Uday Chandra Addhya, a member of Society for Acquisition of General Knowledge, presented his views on the subject in following words: " My heart bleeds and tears stream down my face when I think about the lack of knowledge in my mother tongue among the natives of this country ... Only when the people of this country learn properly the languages of this country - then and only then alone will they acquire that efficiency which can enable them to shake off the present slavery and become masters of their own land."[61] At the same time the tendency to use the English by educated class was attacked. They were asked to follow the example of Englishmen who use only their own languages and not any other European language. In this context *Tattvabodhini Patrika,* in one of its editorials, asked - "by using English words in every respect why do we insult our own mother tongue?" ....."a true patriot will never do this."[62] In the same journal Rajnarain Bose later wrote that "the development of a nation depends much an the development of its national language and culture."[63]

Cultural Nationalism

Various aspects of the expression of national consciousness discussed above had a common thread i.e.the reassertion of Indian culture. Without the reassertion of native cultural identity and heritage it was not possible to arouse the national consciousness. Moreover the battle against colonialism was to be first fought and won on the cultural turf as Bernard S. Cohn has rightly observed, "colonialism was made possible, and then sustained and strengthened, as much by cultural technologies of rule as it was by the more obvious and brutal modes of conquest that first established power on foreign shores."[64] British propaganda about India as a country with an inferior culture and denationalized past formed an important part of this 'cultural technology of rule'. Several British officials and writers of the time propogated the thesis that Indians had never been able to rule themselves in the part, that Indians were destined to be ruled by foreigners, that their religious and social life was degraded and uncivilized, and hence making them unfit for democracy or even self government.[65] Early nationalists tried to arouse the self-confidence and self-respect of the people by countering this propaganda. They pointed to the cultural heritage of India with pride. Political achievements of great Indians rulers like Ashoka and Akbar were also brought out. They were helped in this task by the work of contemporary Indian and European scholars in rediscovering the India's national heritage in art, architecture, literature, philosophy, science and politics. The inter-relationship between nationality, self respect and past glory was elaborated by Brahma Bandhab Upadhyaya, a contemporary nationalist, "The nationality of a people was based upon self-respect. We should learn how to respect ourselves before we can rise in the scale of nations. Self respect can be effectively engendered by dwelling upon the glories of the past."[66]

The issue of growth of national consciousness in India will remain incomplete without mentioning the contribution of Rajnarain Bose, Nabgopal Mitra, Bhudev Mukhnopadhyaya, and Bankim Chandra Chatterjee. All of them were products of the western education but at the same time they were also ardent admirers of the ancient Indian spiritual thought. Rajnarain Bose (1826-1899) was perhaps the earliest to predict the dawn fall of British power in 1845.[67] His 'Prospectus for the Society for Promotion of Nationalist Feelings among the Educated Natives' (1866) included physical training, patriotic music, rejuvenation of Ayurveda, and glorification of ancient heritage.[68] He talked of social unity and revival of great past. He also gave a call for the boycott of foreign products, dress and food. In collaboration with Devendra Nath Tagore and Nabgopal Mitra, he started a Hindu Mela (1867-1880). Highlights of this annual gathering were rendering of patriotic songs and lectures; detailed review of overall conditions of the nation, exhibitions of indigenous crafts and arts and performance related to physical strength. After the fourth session of 'Mela', a 'National Society' was founded by Nabagopal Mitra (1840-1894). Its object was to promote unity and national feelings.[69] Nabagopal Mitra was also called as 'National Mitra' because of the many societies and institutions he founded with the prefix 'national' such as 'Natonal Press', 'National Paper' and 'National Society'.

Bhudev Mukhopadhyaya (1827-1894) was a political thinker deeply attached to orthodox tradiation, yet liberal in outlook. His line of action was to promote national culture through a system of national education.[70] He emphasised that objectives of the prevalent system of education must be redefined to meet the needs of the Indian society.[71] He strongly favoured the vernacular medium for education. He wrote many vernacular school textbooks besides a teaching manual. He advocated Hindi as the link language of India in place of English.

Bankim Chandra Chatterjee (1838-1894) is known as 'the high priest of nationalism in India'.[72] Bankim was of the view that national consciousness will not be 'national' in essence unless it moves the masses of India. He noted with contempt that political agitation was being carried on by a few western educated elite, and the rural masses were untouched by it. He analysed in detail why the feeling of nationalism was alien to the majority of Indians. He was convinced that western methods of promotion of nationalism could not appeal to the Indian mind. To promote national consciousness it was necessary to raise nationalism to the dignity of a religion as nothing can move the hearts of Indians as much as religion. So he preached patriotism as the highest religion.[73] Bankim was a precursor of Aurobindo Ghosh in imparting a divine status to the motherland. His immortal song '*Bande Matram*' stirred the imagination of millions and made them staunch nationalists, perhaps more effectively than thousands of platform speeches and news paper articles could have done.[74]

His famous novel *Anandmatha* has been called as the Bible of modern Bengali patriotism. National consciousness, according to Bankim, was possible only through vernacular languages, because masses could not understand English. He himself devoted his life to the cause of Bangla literature. He was also fully aware of the value of the history for rousing national consciousness. He wrote several articles in his journal *Bangadarshan* to emphasise the importance of making diligent researches in the history of the Bengali people.[75]

The process of national consciousness also involved dissuading the Indians who had already come under the influence of alien ideology and culture. Such individuals had begun to adopt everything English- language, dress, thoughts and some times even religion. Great Bengali writer Michael Madhusudan Dutt (1824-1873) in his early life can be cited as a prime example representing such misguided youth. Launching a vigorous attack an anglicized Bengalis, Dwijandra Nath Tagore (1840-1926) wrote in *National Paper* of 5th May, 1869 :"With all our present inferiority and infirmities we are little better respected by the world than the

Christian Negro of North America who speaks English, drones himself with the jacket and pantaloon, and whose habits of life and fact are mostly borrowed from the European settlers there. And why so? Simply because his civilization is nothing more than an image of European manners and habits, and he is no more like the true European than the monkey in the red-coat riding on the she goat is like a human being. By means of mere imitation we can be just so much like the Europeans as slaves are like their masters."[76]

Such attacks on blind imitation of West by the likes of Dwijendranath Tagore definitely had some effect. Because the same paper after three years (7th August 1872) claimed that "the tide of denationalization has sustained ebb, a happy reaction has taken place in native feelings. People have begun to disbelieve in the theory that for a nation's progress they have simply to learn the art of borrowing."[77]

The maturity of the nationalist sentiment in India is evident in the fact that it was not chauvinistic in native. Perhaps this was the result of age-old universalistic cultural traditions of India such as '*Vasudhev Kutumbakam*' and '*Sarve Bhaventu Sukhina*'. Indian Nationalists did not reject every thing European or accept everything indigenous. This unique aspect of Indian nationalism was appropriately articulated by Rajendra Lal Mitra (1823-1891) in a speech in 1870. He said that patriotism does not mean unjustified love for everything indigenous. True patriotism is "an intelligent love for the welfare and advancement of our race." Moreover, patriots do not "hesitate a moment to spurn everything that stands in the way of progress, and import from foreign lands whatever is calculated to raise her in the scale of nations."[78]

Nationalist Political Consciousness

Western influence on the growth of national consciousness is clearly evident in the realm of political consciousness. Gradually the ambit of both political methods and objectives widened. Better understanding of the Indian problems and the nature of British rule resulted in better comprehension of the colonial reality. Gradually it became apparent that interests of Indian people and the British rulers were mutually antagonistic. This realization marked the final evolution of national political consciousness. Thus the process of evolution of nationalist political consciousness passed through the stages of individual politics, organised politics and finally mass movements leading to complete independence from foreign rule.

The pioneer of political consciousness in India was Raja Ram Mohan Roy (1772-1833). Through his speeches, petitions and writings, Ram Mohan Roy demanded individual rights for Indians and reforms in the administration. He boldly asserted that "enemies to liberty and friends of despotism have never been and will never be ultimately successful."[79]

Ram Mohan Roy's passion for liberty was common to Henry Vivian Derazio (1809-1831), a teacher at Hindu College, Calcutta. Derozio is known for installing ardent patriotic feelings and liberal yearnings among a whole generation of English educated young men in Bengal.

Derozio's legacy was carried forward by his students. A series of public meetings were held during 1830-1835, on such issues as trial by jury, Indianization of services, freedom of press, amendment of Charter Act of 1833 and protest against exploitation of coolies.[80] The spread of political consciousness is evident from the numerous newspaper articles and latter to editors. Question of racial discrimination was also taken up. "Why India should groan for ages under foreign yoke," asked a latter to *Reformer* of February 1831.[81] Similar sentiments were being conveyed through the pages of periodicals such as *Enquirer*, *Kaleidoscope*, *Indian Gazette*, *Calcutta Monthly Journal*, *Bengal Chronicle* etc.

Educated Indians started forming various associations to share their views and put forward combined demands. One of the first societies thus formed was 'The Society for Acquisition of General Knowledge' in 1838. Another society, 'Deshahitaishunee Sabha' was formed in 1841. This was frankly a patriotic organization and its proceedings mainly dwelled upon political issues. A speech on the occasion of establishment of the Society openly stated that "our deprivation of the enjoyment of the political liberty is the cause of our misery." The remedy suggested by the speaker included unity, love for country and patriotism so as to be "freed from the tyranny and oppression of local Government."[82]

The growth of national consciousness was being witnessed in Maharastra too. Bhaskar Pandurang Tarkadkar (1816-1847) and Gopal Hari Deshmukh (1823-1892) were the pioneers of national consciousness in Maharastra. Bhaskar Pandurang Tarkadkar, in a series of letters to *Bombay Gazette* in 1841, touched upon the racial and exploitive nature of British rule in India.[83] He came to the conclusion that the British rule in India was the "most bitter curse India was ever been visited with."[84]

Gopal Hari Deshmukh wrote prolifically on the social and political conditions in Western India. In letters to a Marathi weekly, *Prabhakar* during 1848-1850, he visualized the entire course of national movement. He made the prophecy that, "It may take 200 years but the Indians would definitely make a demand for their independence."[85]

The beginning of organised political activity in India is marked by the establishment of Landholders Society on 19th March 1838. It gave the people the first lesson in the art of fighting constitutionally for their rights and taught them how to give expression to their opinion.[86] The society was in communication with British India Society of England (est.: July 1839), which represented the first attempt of organized agitation on behalf of India in England. At around the same time, three other associations were formed - Patriotic Association (9 February, 1839); Deshitashooni Sabha (3 October, 1841) and Bengal British India Society (20 April, 1843). Another important association formed during this time was British East India Association (October 1851). The primary goal of British East India Association was to represent Indian interests in connection with the approaching Charter Act of 1853. Radha

Kant Deb (1784-1867) was its President and Debendra Nath Tagore (1817-1905) the Secretary of this Association. *Hindu Patriot* was the organ of this Association.

Growth of political consciousness through organized political activity in the Western India is witnessed by establishment of Deccan Association on 1st February 1852. In Madras the first such association was Madras Accociation, estabilished on 13th July 1852. In the same year Bombay Association was established in Bombay on 26th August 1852.

Apart from British India Society, three other societies or associations were formed in England for the Indian cause. One of them, India Reform Society (12 March 1853) was formed by some Englishmen, sympathetic to India. In 1865, Indian students, merchants and other members of Indian community formed an association called London Indian Soceity. Dada Bhai Naoroji was elected its president and W.C. Bannerji was its secretary. The society was later amalgamated with East India Association when the latter was formed in December 1866. East India Association launched a campaign for inclusion of Indians in the civil services. They were successful in getting an Act passed in 1870 by which one fifth of appointments were to be made from India. East India Association also tried to establish its branches in different parts of India. Dadabhai Nairoji (1825-1917) in a pamphlet exhorted various associations in India to adopt such methods of organising public opinion such as public meetings, drafting petitions, signature campaigns, educating the public opinion through use of vernacular medium and coordinating political activity in different parts of the country.[87] In this pamphlet, the grand old man of Indian politics charted out the whole course of constitutional agitation that was to follow shortly.

Back in India, some intellectuals of western India like M.G. Ranade, G.V. Joshi, and S.H. Chiplunkar established Poona Sarvajanik Sabha on 2nd April 1870. The work of Poona Sarvajanik Sabha was not limited to submitting petitions and organizing meetings. The sabha organized a 'swadeshi' movement in Deccan; contributed to famine relief work in 1872 and 1876-78; raised funds for famine relief in Bengal; campaigned for an enquiry into conditions of agricultural class; and setup arbitrations courts for settlement of civil disputes without taking recourse to the ordinary courts of justice.[88]

By the 1870s, political consciousness, especially among the educated classes in the major urban centres of the country, had become well established. At this time a major fillip was provided by Surendra Nath Bannerjea to political activity in the country. He attempted to elevate the political associations from their regional and elitist nature by establising Indian Association (26 July 1876). Association was to be the centre an all India movement and hence the name, India, in place of 'Bengal' was adopted.[89] In order to expand the social base of those participating in political activities, Bennerjea kept the membership fee low.

The range of issues covered by the petitions and memorandums of the various associations in the last quarter of 19th century reflects the level of political consciousness. For instance, major issues covered by a petition of British Indian Association were as follows: reconstitution of Legislative Councils; employment of Indians in civil services and simultaneous conduction of exam in England and India; reduction of government expenditure and home charges; separation of judiciary from the executive; education grant; Indian parliamentary affairs; racial discrimination; famine policy; epidemics; administrations of police, justice; and municipality affairs.[90]

Along with the submission of petitions and memorandums, some issues were taken up in the form of nationwide campaigns. A country wide agitation took place during1859-71 against the bill for imposition of a license tax on traders and professions which proposed to exempt officials, land holders and fund holders. The agitation later turned against income tax too. A no tax return campaign was also organised and Government was forced to give concessions.

The political consciousness at this stage was further intensified and consolidated by the reactionary policies of Lord Lytton (1876-80). His policies in the office not only went against the Indian interests in general but also hurt the dignity of Indian people . They included: abolition of import duties on sugar and cotton; wastage of Indian men and money at Afghan front; unnecessary pomp and show of Delhi Durbar in times of famine; his efforts to deny employment in civil service to Indians; Vernacular Press Act (1878) and Arms Act (1878). Lytton's policies drew strong response from various sections of Indian society which proved that informed public opinion had come to identify and defend the collective interest of the people. The collective interest above the personal interest, group interest or class interest can be called as national interest. Concern of educated urban class for the hardships of peasants in famine affected areas or indebtedness of the weavers in remote villages and a common indignation against racial bias or denial of democratic rights produced strong sense of brotherhood among the fellow Indians. These conditions afforded excellent conditions for various associations to organize all-India agitations on the issue of Indianisation of civil services. *Madras Standard* of 31 December 1877 declared that civil services movement was "becoming a national movement".[91]

Reactionary policies of Lytton were repealed by Lord Ripon (1880-84). Ripon initiated constructive steps in education and local self government. But his policy could not proceed beyond certain limits. His policy of bringing Europeans under the jurisdiction of Indian judges was bitterly opposed by the Anglo-Indian community. Ultimately he had to bow before their pressure. This controversy known as Ilbert Bill controversy was seen as a national humiliation by Indians. Native press began to talk of an urgent need for national unity, greater organization and self reliance. It was felt that a national organization was needed to achieve these objectives.

The idea of a national organization was in the air for quite some time. The roots of this idea lay in the nationwide campaigns which had begun earlier. 1870s witnessed campaigns over the issues of opposition to Afghan policy, Vernacular Press Act, Arms Act, plantation labour and India Emigrations Act etc. All India efforts were also made to raise a National Fund (1883), right to join the Volunteer Corps (1885) and to support the India-friendly candidates in the British elections (1885). Indian Association in December 1883 organised an All- India National Conference. At the same time new political associations dominated by younger and more radical nationalists also started forming. Madras Mahajan Sabha (1884) was founded by M. Viraghawachari, G. Subramaniya, P. Ananda Charlu and others. In Bombay, K.T. Tailang, Pheroj Shah Mehta and others formed Bombay Presidency Association in 1885. Poona Sarwajanik Sabha was already staunch nationalist in is approach. A section of press had also become staunch nationalist. The newspapers and journals which came under this category were: *The Amrit Bajar Patrika*, *The Indian Mirror*, *Sanjivani*, and the *Bengalee* in Bengal; *The Hindu*, *Swadesh Mitran*, *Andhra Prakasika*, *Kerela Patrika* in Madras; the *Mahratta*, the *Kesari*, the *Indu Prakash* and the *Sudharak* in Bombay; *The Advocate*, the *Hindustan* and the *Azad* in U.P. *Akhbar-I-aam* and the *Koh-i-noor* in the Punjab were some of the prominent nationalist newspapers of the period.[92]

So, by 1885, stage was set for the birth of Indian National Congress, as a national organization. The first session of Indian National Congress was held in Bombay on 25th December 1885. Indian National Congress became the mainstream organization of the many faceted national movement. The aims of Indian National Congress in its early phase represented the objectives of national political consciousness in general. They were: promotion of friendly relations between nationalist political workers from diffrent parts of the country; development and consolidation of the feeling of national unity irrespective of caste, religion or province; formulation of popular demands and their representations before the Government; and the training and organization of public opinion in the country.[93]

The period of first twenty years of Congress has been called as 'moderate phase' because during this phase Congress leaders adopted moderate methods of political activity. Though their method was mild they never failed to lodge protest against those measures of British Government which might affect Indian people adversely. Moderates attempted to educate Indian people politically. At the same time they made efforts to influence the British Government and the public option in Britain to introduce the desired changes. A direct confrontation with the Government as well as a clear vision for political independence was not on their agenda. Moderates succeeded in creating political awakening among the educated class. They trained a large number of political workers in the art of modern politics.

By the end of 19th century, new trends started emerging. In the new circumstances, moderates started losing their relevance. British policies were becoming more reactionary and repressive. Moreover, moderates could not keep pace with the growing national consciousness. Their methods of work as well as their philosophy began to be criticized. The policies of Lord Curzon as Viceroy in India (January 1899-November 1905), left no stone unturned to reduce Congress to 'impotence' and 'assist in its peaceful demise.'[94] These circumstances gave the message that moderate methods were no longer relevant. The need of the hour was to adopt new methods of political activity and hence achieve new levels of national political consciousness. Administrative initiatives of Lord Curzon such as Calcutta Corporation Act (1899), University Act (1904) and finally division of Bengal (1905) proved to be very unpopular. These repressive policies in an environment of growing unemployment, repeated famines, epidemics and increasing tax burden produced discontent among Indians. The potential base for political activity was also expanding fast. This is also depicted by huge increase in circulation of vernacular newspapers: from 29900 in 1885 to 81700 in 1905.[95]

The situation threw up a number of new leaders who believed in a more militant form of nationalism. They were called 'extremists' by their critics. According to Amles Tripathi, extremism was a response to the challenge of haphazard and superficial westernization of Indian life. "Spiritually it countered the threat to traditional Hindu religion, ethics and social values posed by Christianity and Utilitarianism ... Culturally, it resisted a mechanistic and individualistic civilization, which seemed to be destroying the indigenous tissues of growth. Politically, it withstood a slow merger of Indian national identity in the vast and inchoate British empire."[96] Thus extremism signified a new and higher stage in the growth of national consciousness in India.

The new and higher stage in the growth of national consciousness in the form of extremism was an evolution of the Indian spirit which had lain dormant for many centuries. It symbolized a new belief in the capacity of Indians to create indigenous institutions. Politically, extremists visualized a sovereign self-dependent nation. Socially and economically, the focus of extremists was on self reliance and constructive work. Culturally, indigenous arts, crafts, industries, literature and vernaculars were to be revived and promoted.

National education was a vital component of three-dimensional programme of extremists, other two being *swadeshi* and boycott. In a way it embodied the entire ideology of extremist philosophy: the regeneration of India along cultural, economical, political and of course educational lines. Broad programme of national education which included promotion of Indian national culture, vernacular languages, national heritage and the necessity of the imparting technical education, attempted at reasserting national identity of India as different from a subject colony of Britain. Thus the growth of national consciousness was in fact the evolution of Indian nation and the evolution of a nation could not be complete without a national system of education.

Notes and References

1 For example see B.T. McCully, *English Education and the Origins of Indian Nationalism*, New York, 1940; L.S.S.O' Mally, *India and the West*, London, 1941; Anil Seal, *The Emergence of Indian Nationalism Cambridge,* 1968; Percieval Spears, *Oxford History of India*, Cambridge, 1974.

2 B.T. McCully, op.cit., p. 388.

3 Devendra Swaroop in preface to Poornima Singh, *Indian Cultural Nationalism*, New Delhi, 2004, p. 14.

4 Radha Kumud Mookerji, *The Fundamental Unity of India*, Bombay, 1954; *Nationalism in Hindu Culture* (First appeared as an article in *Dawn and Dawn Society's Magazine* in January, 1909, appeared in the present form in *The Modern* Review of March 1913, First published in book form in 1914 in London.

5 *Nationalism in Hindu Culture,* London, 1914, p. 9.

6 Ibid. p. 47.

7 अद्य ब्रहमणो द्वितीय परार्धे श्रीश्वेतवराह कल्पे वैवस्वत मन्वन्तरे अष्टाविंशतितमे कलियुगे कलिप्रथम चरणे बौद्धावतारे जम्बुदीपे भरतखण्डे आर्यावर्तेक देशान्तर गते....अमुकक्षेत्रे ....अमुकस्थले ....संवत्सरे ....ऋतौ ....मासे ....तिथौ ....समय ....गोत्रः अहं ....करिष्ये।

8 Using the evidence from *Kautilya Arthashastra*, *Mahagovinda Sutta*, *Aitreya Brahmana* and *Atharvaveda*, Devendra Swarup suggests that the earliest name of this land was Prithvi.

9 p. 29-30. ff. Monier Williams (*Hinduism,* p. 13): "India, though it has, as we have seen, more than 500 spoken dialects, has only one sacred language and one sacred literature, accepted and revered by all adherents of Hinduism alike, however diverse in race, dialect, rank, and creed. The language is Sanskrit, and that literature is Sanskrit literature- the only repository of the Veda or knowledge in its widest sense; the only vehicle of Hindu theology, philosophy, law or mythology; the only mirror in which all the creeds, opinions, customs, and usages of the Hindus are faithfully reflected."

10 *Fundamental Unity of India*, op. cit., p. 13.

11 Ibid., pp. 80-84.

12 Devendra Swarup, op.cit.

13 E. Bevan, *Indian Nationalism*, London, 1913, pp. 45-46.

14 B.T. Mccully, op. cit., p. 234.

[15] Ibid. p. 235.

[16] Ibid.

[17] Edvin Arnold, *The Marquais of Dalhousie's Administration, vol. II*, London, 1865, pp. 341-42, cited in S.R. Mehrotra, Delhi, 1971, p. 112.

[18] S.R. Mehrotra, op. cit., pp. 136-37.

[19] R.C. Majumdar, *History of the Freedom Movement in India, Vol-I*, Calcutta, 1962, p. 327.

[20] Aparna Basu, *The Growth of Education and Political Development, 1898-1920*, op. cit., p. 76.

[21] R.C. Majumdar, *History and Culture of the Indian People, Vol. X*, Mumbai, 2007, p. 434.

[22] *S.R. Mehrotra*, op. cit., p. 141.

[23] *Report of the Census of India*, 1891, Vol. I, p. 224.

[24] G.P. Gooch, *Nationalism*, London, 1920, pp. 5-6.

[25] J.H. Hayes, '*Nationalism: A religion*', New York, 1960, pp. 2-4.

[26] Ibid. p. 6.

[27] Sukumar Dutt, *Problem of Indian Nationality*, Calcutta, 1926, p. 9.

[28] Annual Report of Tattawabodhini Sabha for 1843-44 cited in Mohammad Mohar Ali, *The Bengali Reaction to Christian Missionary Activities, 1833-57*, Chittagong, 1965, p.17.

[29] *Bombay Courier*, 28 January 1840, cited by S.R. Mehrotra, op. cit., p. 34.

[30] *Bombay Courier*, 4 February 1840, cited in ibid.

[31] *Madras Native Herald*, 18 March 1843, cited in ibid.

[32] Mohammad Mohar Ali, op.cit., pp. 117-136.

[33] S.G. Malik, ed., *Indian Movements: Some Aspects of Dissent, Protest and Reform*, Delhi, 1970, p. 224.

[34] N.R. Inamdar, *Lokhitwadinchi Shatpatre*, p. 339 cited in S.G. Malik, op. cit., p. 226.

[35] *Mookerjee's Magazine*, January-June 1876, p. 12 cited in J.C. Bagal, *Pramatha Nath Bose*, p. 87.

[36] Bipan Chandra, *India's Struggle for Independence*, New Delhi, 1989, p. 97.

37 J.C. Bagal, *Pramatha Nath Bose*, Calcutta, 1955, pp 94-95.

38 M.G. Ranade, *Essays an Indian Economics*, p. 616, cited in Bipan Chandra, op.cit., p. 93.

39 B.N Ganguli, *Indian Economic Thought: 19th Century Perspectives*, cited in ibid. pp. 93-94.

40 S.R. Mehrotra, op.cit., p. 134.

41 J.C. Bagal, o.p. cit., p. 69.

42 Ibid. p. 70.

43 *Studies in the History of Science*, Santimoy Chatterjee, ed., Calcutta, 1992, p. 26.

44 Santimoy Chatterjee, ed., op. cit, p. 2.

45 J.C. Begal, *Pranatha Nath Bose*, op. cit, p. 4-5.

46 Ibid., p. 3.

47 Gautam Chattopadhyay, Awakening in Bengal in the Early 19th century Bengal, Calcutta, 1965, op. cit., pp. XXV-XXVI.

48 Bela Dutt Gupta, *Sociology in India*, 1972, p. XV, cited in K.N. Pannikkar, Presidential speech , 1HC Proceedings, Aligarh, 1975, p. 372.

49 Ibid.

50 J.C. Bagal, op. cit., p. 5.

51 Gautam Chattopadhye, op.cit, p. XXVII.

52 Irfan S. Habib in *Studies in the History of Science*, ed.by Santimoy Chatterjee,op.cit., pp. 10-18.

53 Deepak Kumar, *Science and Empire*, Delhi, 1991, pp. 152-153.

54 Ibid., p.132.

55 Ibid, pp. 154-155.

56 *Writings and Speeches of Syyed Ahmed Khan*, ed., Shan Mohammad, Bombay, 1972, pp. 231-32.

57 *Studies in the History of Science*, op.cit., p. 14.

58 Ibid., p. 29.

59 K.C. Vyas, *The Development of National Education in India*, Bombay, 1954, p. 19.

60 Gautam Chattopadhyay, op.cit., pp. XXV.

61 Ibid., p. XXXIV.

62 Cited by Arundhati Mukhopadhyaya in an article in '*Studies in History*, January- June 1987, p. 22.

63 David Kopf, op. cit., p. 168.

64 B.S. Cohn, *Colonialism and its Forms of Knowledge*, Delhi, 1997, p. ix.

65 Bipan Chandra, *Modern India*, p. 199.

66 David Kopf, op. cit., p. 210.

67 Ibid., p. 168.

68 Ibid., pp. 179-180.

69 R.C. Majumdar, *History and Culture of Indian people*, Vol. X. op. cit., p. 473.

70 *Concept of National Education*, Calcutta, 1967, p. 9.

71 Ibid., p. 10.

72 B.B. Majumdar, *History of Indian social and Political ideas from Ram Mohan to Dayananda,* Calcutta, 1967, p. 171.

73 Ibid., pp. 172-173.

74 Ibid., p. 173.

75 Ibid., p. 179.

76 David Kopf, op. cit., p. 183.

77 S.R. Mehrotra, op. cit., p. 129.

78 A full Report of the Public Meeting of the Native Inhabitants of Bengal on the Education Question Held at the Town Hall of Calcutta on 02 July 1870, pp. 13-14.

79 R.C. Majumdar, *History of Freedom Movement in India*, Vol.I, op. cit., p. 323.

80 Gautam Chattopadhyay, op.cit., p. XVII.

81 Ibid., p. XIV.

82 Ibid., pp. XII-XIII.

83 K.N. Pannikkar, "The Intellectual History of Colon[illegible]" in *Situating Indian History*, pp. 423-424.

84 B.B. Majumdar, op. cit., p. 199.

85 N.R. Inamdar, *Lokhitwadi Shatpatre*, Poona, 1960, p. 258 cited in *Indian Movements : Some Aspects of Dissent, Protest, and Reform*, op.cit., p. 226.

86 S.R. Mehrotra , op. cit., p.14.

87 Dadabhai Naoroji, *'The Duties of the Local Indian Associations in Connection with the London Association*, cited in S.R. Mehrotra, op. cit., pp. 99-100.

88 S.R. Mehrotra, op.cit., p. 192.

89 S.N. Bannerji, *A Nation in the Making*, Calcutta, 1925, p. 37.

90 S.R. Mohrotra, op. cit. 192.

91 Ibid., p. 275.

92 Bipan Chandra, Amlaes Tripathi and Barun De, (eds.), *Freedom Struggle*, pp. 55-56.

93 Bipan Chandra, *Modern India*, New Delhi, 1971, op. cit., p. 159.

94 Bipan Chandra & others, *India's struggle for Independence*, op. cit. p. 137.

95 Sumit Sarkar, *Modern India*, New Delhi, 1983, op. cit., p. 96.

96 Amles Tripathi, *The Extremist Challenge*, Calcutta, 1964, p. 1.

5

Growth of Nationalist Educational Consciousness

Education could not remain indifferent to the rising tide of nationalism in the late 19th century India. As education was considered a vital tool for nation building, nationally conscious Indians critically analyzed the official education policy vis-à-vis Indian interests and requirements. At the same time, indigenous efforts also began to emerge in order to fill the gap between national requirements and the official efforts. This concept of nationalism in education later came to be known as national education.

Natives Welcome English Education

As mentioned earlier, English recieved enthusiastic welcome from educated Indians when it first appeared on the Indian horizons. Indians saw English as a gateway to western knowlege. They also realized the other advantages of learning English like getting jobs and business opportunities. But as the Government at that time was following the policy of promoting the classical learning only, the initial efforts towards dissemination of English language and western knowledge were made by the Indians themselves. Raja Ram Mohan Roy was among the pioneers who wanted the fellow countrymen to have access to western knowledge. At that time Europe was churning out revolutionary ideas. Moreover, it was the application of modern science which had led to the industrial revolution in the Europe. Raja did not want the isolation of India from the progress made in Europe. In his opinion, English education would create new opportunities for the Indians and also make them acquainted with politico-administrative system of the European countries.[1] His efforts in this direction led to the establishment of Hindu College in Calcutta in 1817. Other contemporary Bengali intellectuals including Radha Kant Deb were also associated with Hindu College. In the same year Ram Mohan Roy opened a private school in Calcutta for imparting free English education. It was the first private institution of its kind started by an Indian.[2] He opened another school–Anglo Hindu School in 1822 in Calcutta for imparting free tuition in English to the boys.[3] He established Vedanta College in 1825, where oriental learning was taught along with the western arts and sciences.[4]

Native demand for English education is also reflected in the establishment of English schools at Bhawanipur (1800), Chinsura(1814). The work of Native School Societies and Native School Book Societies has already been mentioned before. Apart from these, many other schools teaching English were also established. Jai Narayan Ghosal started a school at Banaras in 1818 for teaching English, Persian, Hindustani and Bengali.[5] Rasik Chandra Mitra, a product of Hindu college, established Hindu Free College in Simla in 1831.[6] Around the same time, according to *The Calcutta Review*, six morning pathsalas were opened at six differed places.[7] In Calcutta, two charity institutions, Benevolent Institution and Hindu Free School were opened in 1831and1834 respectively.[8] English schools were also opened in different parts of Calcutta and other places such as Hughli, Burdwan, Midnapur, Dacca, Barisal, Santipur, Murshidabad, Rangpur, Allahabad, Agra and Delhi.[9]

A common feature of these schools was the emphasis on the study of English, as official efforts to provide English education materialized only after 1835. Natives' urgency to introduce the western knowledge was such that in the beginning even collaboration with the missionaries was risked. For example, Kalinath Raychoudhury and Baikuntha Raychoudhury placed the entire management of their institution under the control of Rev.

Alexander Duff. Ram Mohan Ray took the lead in collaboration with missionaries as he saw them as a promising agency for the dissemination of western knowledge. He appealed to the Church of Scotland Assembly to send more teachers. When Alexander Duff came to India in 1830 he received valuable support of Ram Mohan to start new English schools. Ram Mohan Ray did not share the belief of some his contemporaries that the study of the English language and literature would inevitable lead to the conversions. On the contrary, he believed that the roots of the indigenous culture and religion were deep enough to resist any such temptations. He exhorted students not to desist studying in missionary schools just because Bible was taught there. He gave them his own example that the study of sacred books of the different religions had not made him leave his religion.[10]

Native Attitude Towards English Turned More Mature and Cautious with Passage of Time

Native demand for the English education was not at the cost of neglect of vernacular languages. All the schools mentioned above also provided learning of vernaculars, Sanskrit and in some cases Persian.The traditional classical studies, in Sankrit or Persian, did not serve the purpose of mass education. Raja Ram Mohan Roy's memorandum to Lord Amherst in 1823 did not plead for replacing indigenous languages by English. Its central agenda was to introduce modern scientific studies in India. Raja Ram Mohan Roy did much to promote the Bengali language. He pioneered the translation of Upanishads into Bengali. Raja also promoted Bengali journalism through his paper *Samvad Koumudi*. His followers made efforts to translate scientific and literary works in English into Bengali. Ram Mohan Roy was clear in his mind about the priority of instruction of the children in their mother tongue over foreign language. In the seventh issue of *Samvad Koumudi,* he emphasized upon the necessity of having children instructed in the principles of grammar of their own language, previous to imposing upon the study of foreign language.[11]

Gradually the native approach towards the English became more cautious and mature. Collaboration with missionaries was avoided as the evangelising tendencies of Missionaries became more apparent. Besides, it was generally accepted that vernacular medium was best suited for disseminating the western knowledge. This realization is visible in the report of the Bombay Native Education Society for the year 1825-26: "English can never become the most facile and successful medium of communicating to the natives, as a body, the literature, science and morality of Europe."

Despite the fact that native public opinion had not asked for sweeping change of making English the medium of education, Government in 1835 went ahead and made English the medium of instruction. A letter to a Calcutta newspaper in 1837 voiced the Indian response to the 1835 policy in following words: "The knowledge which the Committee (of public Instruction) are labouring to disseminate ... may in course of fifty years give us fifty thousands tolerable scholars ... out of seventy million who compose this presidency; but the knowledge must be acclimated in India through the mother tongue before the nation can rise in the scale of civilization."[12] Similar sentiments were echoed by Jagannath Shankar Shet, a member of Board of Education in Bombay Presidency, in May 1847. Shankar Shet dwelled upon the impossibility of educating the masses through English and acknowledged the fact that "the encouragement which we provide to vernacular education is far less than what the real interests of native education demand."[13]

The level of native consciousness about the ongoing educational changes with regard to their interests is suitably reflected in a petition to the Court of Directors in December 1837. It was signed by 8,909 Bengali Hindus led by eminent Bengali scholar Ram Comul Sen. The petition boldly called upon the Court to introduce measures for the encouragement of Sanskrit and Bengali education and literature; to restore stipends to students of Sanskrit College;

and to restart the publication of oriental works. The petition displayed sharp insight when it referred to the negative fallouts of education policy on India. India, according to the petition, was being made sub-servient to English in economic, technical and academic domains. It referred to Lord Bentinck's resolution of March 1835 as "most injurious, opprobrious, subversive of our professions and religion and conducive to the unpopularity of the Government." The petition stressed upon the impossibility of teaching English to the masses as well as the expensive nature of English education. Learning of English was considered to be of no great advantage as only lower posts were offered to Indians. Overall seen, the petition was very assertive about the educational rights of the natives.[14] This petition displayed a radical shift in the public opinion about English vis-à-vis the native languages. Rather than blindly falling for the English, the educated class showed that it was conscious of the neglect of Sanskrit and Bengali. There is no doubt that English was seen as a gateway to the new knowledge and the new opportunities, but as this petition conclusively establishes, the native intelligentsia had their own conception of their educational requirements and was alive to the need of preserving their cultural identity.

Three decades after the above petition, Indian grievances against the English remained unaddressed. A petition co-authored by Sir Syyed Ahmad Khan on behalf of the British India Association in 1867 saw English as the 'greatest obstacle to the general and rapid propagation of useful knowledge in the country.' The petition also emphasized the fact that the present system of English education was responsible for a general decline in the knowledge, morality and culture of students. Petition demanded that vernaculars of the country be made the medium of instruction.[15] Government's response to their petition betrayed its poor opinion of the native vernaculars- that the vernaculars of the country do not as yet afford the materials for conveying instruction of the comparatively higher order contemplated by the British Association.[16]

Besides the demand for education through vernacular medium there were several other concerns. The quest for an education meeting the needs of the Indian society was taken up by various associations and individuals. In this context,the work of three associations is particularly relevant for their pioneering and significant contribution. They were: Tattwabodhini Sabha, Students Literary and Scientific Society and British India Association.

Tattwabodhini Sabha

Tattwabodhini Sabha, established in Calcutta in September 1839 by a group of Brahmos under the leadership of Devendranath Tagore, played an important role in the development of modern Bengali language and literature. To train youngmen in the principles of the Sabha and also to promote vernacular education, Tattvabodhini Pathsala was established on 13 June 1840.[17] Tattvabodhini Pathsala can be called as the forerunner of the national education institutions which appeared much later. Its curriculum included modern subjects like physics, geography and mathematics, which were taught through vernacular medium along with the teaching of ancient scriptures. Later, English language was also included in its curriculum. The Pathshala functioned up to 1848. Similar pathshalas were opened at Barrackpore and Suksagar in Bengal.[18]

Tattvabodhini Sabha actively promoted the researches in the ancient Indian history and culture. The objective of its Indological researches and studies was to revive the ancient Indian greatness, self- confidence, self-respect and patriotism among the Indians. The Sabha also contributed in the task of translation of Hindu scriptures. Sabha was also the first to prepare school text books in Bengali. Several luminaries of that age such as Devendranath Tagore, Ashvini Kumar Dutta, Iswar Chandra Vidya Sagar and Bhudeb Mukhopadhyaya were associated with the text book writing work at the Sabha. Akshoy Kumar Dutta also worked as teacher in Tattwabodhini Pathsala.

Students, Literary and Scientific Society

The work of Tattvabodhini Sabha was limited to Bengal. Eucational work in the western India was taken up by the Students, Literary and Scientific Society.[19] Society's objective was to develop intellectual and moral side of people through removal of illiteracy and spread of knowledge. To achieve its objectives, the Society adopted the methodology of reading and discussion of essays, lectures on physical and chemical sciences, and publishing of low priced literature to meet the requirements and taste of the people. The Society organized two vernacular branches in September 1848–Marathi Dhyan Prasarak Sabha and Gujrati Dhayan Prasarak Sabha. In 1851, another branch- Budhhi Vardhak Sabha for Gujaratis was organized. Society also published a monthly magazine called *Dhyan Prasarak*. The Society gave special attention to the cause of women education and opened in October 1849, six schools for girls of which three were for Marathi girls and rest were for Parsee girls. By 1854, two more girl schools were opened. In 1851, five boys' schools for Marathi and Gujrati boys were opened. In all these schools, English and vernacular studies were conducted side by side.

British India Association

British India Association in its petitions and agitations frequently took up the educational issues. It had demanded in 1853 the establishment of universities in three presidencies.[20] In 1857, the Association asked for the institution of professorship in Sanskrit and Arabic in Government institutions.[21] In 1859, they protested against the increase in tuition fee in the Government schools of Calcutta as a result of which the Government was forced to roll back the fees.[22] In 1867, the Association opposed the Government's move to levy a tax for the purpose of defraying the expenses of vernacular education and organized public meetings as part of its protest.[23] In 1870, the Association launched a powerful agitation against a resolution of Government which intended to reduce the Government's aid to Anglo-vernacular and oriental education. The Association regarded the Government's move as "fraught with the greatest injury to the educated interest of the country and to the prospects of progressing civilization."[24] The Association's appeal on the issue generated country wide support as a result of which forty-seven local meetings were held in different parts of India to protest against the Government's resolution.[25]

Regional branches of British India Association were also active in educational matters. In 1867, a petition by North West branch of the Association boldly questioned the ability of the official system of education in meeting the twin ends of mass education and modern education. According to the petition, great majority of the population were not at all covered by education. "The country", the petition read, "as a whole is in its original state of uncivilized ignorance and has tasted none of the advantages of learning and civilization." The petition also declared the objective of its movers with respect to education. This objective, in the words of petition, was, "not to revive the dead learning and refinement of Asia, but to supplant all this by the introduction of the truer and more recently acquired knowledge of Europe, while we desire to benefit not the few only, but the large mass of people."[26]

Sir Syyed Ahmad Khan, one of the movers of the above petition, had earlier petitioned the Government of North West province on the issue of education in 1866. He wanted that the landlords of Aligarh district to be accepted in a supervisory role over the education funds in the district because they are the ones who provide the funds as taxpayers.[27] This petition is one of the earliest instances when Indians demanded their right to control or supervise the education programmes because they funded the education by paying taxes.

Early Experiments: Hindu College Pathsala, Hindu HItharthi Vidyalaya, National School, Bhagwat Chatuspati, etc.

Besides some associations and societies, several experiments to satisfy the native educational aspirations also started in the middle of 19th century. An year before the establishment of the

Tattvabodhini Pathsala, the Hindu College Pathsala was founded by Prasanna Kumar Tagore in June 1839. It is with the establishement of this Pathsala that we got the first ever reference to the term 'National Education.'[28] Pathsalas's declared objectives were "to provide a system of national education, and to instruct Hindu youths in literature, and in sciences of India and of Europe, through the medium of Bengalee language."[29] Pathsala provided education up to the elementary level. It was under the control and direction of the Hindu College management. The biggest obstacle in the way of school was that its students were not able to get admission in any Government English school because Government schools imposed conditions of a fixed age limit and a certain proficiency in English. The proficiency in vernaculars acquired in Pathsala was not recognised by Government schools. Despite repeated requests the Government refused to raise the age limit.

Another school designed to promote Hindu education was Hindu Hitharthi Vidyalaya.[30] It was founded in Calcutta on 1st March 1846. Raja Radha Kant Deb was the President of the school committee and Devendranath Tagore was its Secretary. Bhudev Mukhopadhdyaya worked as head master of this school for sometime. The school did not charge any fee. It was opened to dissuade Hindu students from attending missionary free schools. Similar institutions were established at Panihati (in 24 Paragna), Krishna Nagar (Nadia), and Apurbapur (Hooghly).[31]

The work of Devendra Nath Tagore and his followers had deep influence on the evolving concept of national education. One of his followers, Akshoy Kumar Dutt, is credited with evolving, in 1856, the first ever comprehensive scheme of national education. It included compulsory education till the age of 15, technical and vocational education, mother tongue as medium of instruction at all levels, and use of culture for nation building besides other aspects. Highest emphasis in his scheme was on positivistic sciences.[32]

National School of Nabgopal Mitra, established in 1870, was a continuation of the tradition of Tattvabodhini Pathsala and Hindu Hitharthi Vidyalaya. Besides the focus on teaching elements of ancient Indian culture, National School paid special emphasis on instruction in chemistry, drawing, riding and use of fire arms. Native culture and technical education were also emphasised in the City College and other schools opened by Brahmos and Ramkrishna Mission in 1870s and 1880s. In 1895, Bhagwat Chatuspathi established by Satis Chandra Mukherji endeavoured to give a thorough training in the Hindu thought and life along with industrial training in a residential campus.

Natives' Evidences Before the Education Commission of 1882

The growing discontent of the native educated class with the official education polices is adequately witnessed in the evidences recorded before the Indian Education Commission in 1882. In these evidences we find the opinion of a large number of the contemporary learned individuals, associations, and reform bodies concerned with education. Luminaries who disposed before the Commission included Dada BhaiNaoroji, Syed Ahmad Khan, Jotirao Phule, R.G. Bhandarkar, Rajendralal Mitra, G.W. Lietner, Brojendra Nath Seal, V.S. Apte, Kristodas Pal and Sorabjee Sapurji Bengali. An immediate cause of the native discontent with regard to the official education policy was the Government's resolution of 8th February, 1882. The resolution in question indicated the intention of the Government to leave higher and secondary education to the private initiative and instead focus only on primary education. Native intelligentsia opposed the Government move. They argued that Government was already extracting high rates of taxes (Rs.3 ½ per person) as education cess out of which the Government was spending very little (8 paisa per person) on education. Secondary and higher education were already reeling under the fund crunch. Native intelligentsia asserted that if Government wanted to augment funds for primary education, it must not be done at the cost of secondary and higher education.[33] There was also an apprehension that higher education would pass into the hands of missionaries.

Evidences presented before the Education Commission of 1882 reflected a vest panorama of educational issues being thought over by the Indians. For example, V.S. Apte[34], a leading educationist in Maharastra, in his evidence before the Commission raised the following issues:[35]

1. Control of the higher education be left to the indigenous bodies.
2. A more liberal and less interfering system of grants-in-aid. Grant-in-aid policy favours the missionaries more than the native private enterprise.
3. Fears of missionaries taking over education.
4. Discrimination against Indians in Government services must end.
5. Vernacular books should be prepared only by the natives themselves.
6. Undue importance should not be given to English over vernaculars. 'It appears that the aim of the whole educational system is to send forth into world each year a lot of anglicised graduates instead of graduated natives.'
7. The present system of education instead of building character checks the development of national character. "The monotonously uniform system of instruction conducted upon English model and tastes, the removing of means by which students may be reminded of their nationality, even in innocent sports and games, the adoption of text books such as Morris History which magnify British influence and British power and lower and degrade Indian men and manners, are the points that can be cited."
8. The prevalent examination system encourages cramming.

Poona Sarvajanik Sabha in its evidence before the Education Commission stressed on utilising the indigenous school agency for the spread of primary education on a universal scale. 'Chief defect of the present system appears to us to be that it takes little or no account of the indigenous agency'.[36] The Sabha was of the opinion that content of the school curriculum must meet the special needs of the communities. Sabha criticized the neglect of technical education and demanded the establishment of new industrial schools and polytechnic schools to meet the requirements of the country.They also opposed the suggestion of Government to withdraw from the higher education.

Jotirao Phule (1827-1890), a radical social reformer and educationist of western India, in his evidence denounced the downward filtration theory and advocated a shift of focus to education of masses.[37]He termed the education policy of the government pro-higher class, leaving the masses 'wallowing in ignorance and poverty'. His evidence also emphasised on useful technical knowledge, lowering of fees, utilization of indigenous schools and universalization of primary schools.

The issue of decline of Sanskrit studies and plea for their restoration was also taken up. Shastris (Sanskrit scholars) of Poona deplored, how, the English authorities "tore up by the roots the long- nourished tree of Sanskrit learning".[38] Shastris of Ahmedabad also expressed the concern that "Hindu sciences and philosophy stand a chance of rapid disappearance."[39] Both these memorials pleaded with the Government to take steps for a revival of Sanskrit learning in India.

Indian National Congress Criticizes Government's Education Policy

British Government's intention to focus on primary education and leave the higher education to private initiative was seen by the politically conscious natives as a ploy to discourage higher education since the Government viewed the political consciousness as the work of educated class. With the establishment of Indian National Congress in 1885, Government's education policy was criticised consistently by way of the resolutions. Justice K.T. Telang reminded the Government of its 'duty of fostering and encouraging education' at the 1888 session of Congress. Herambchandra Maitra moved a resolution pleading the government to enhance financial allocation for 'all branches of education' at the 1891 session. At the 1892 session of the Congress, Brajendranath Seal while moving a resolution for more grants, especially for the technical education, made a sarcastic assessment of the British education policy in India:

"The recent educational policy may be briefly sketched thus- Higher education of the University as well as the secondary grade tabooed as regard State or Municipal aid; the attempted diversion of a large class of students from the academic or literary to practical or professional studies other than law, in the interests of the industrial development of the country, if not also with an ulterior political motive, combined with the non-provision of polytechnics or technological institutes, or even of commercial, industrial or agricultural schools of the secondary grade, to impart that very sound scientific and technical training which the Government is so very anxious to see diffused and extended in the material and economic interests of the country. An anxious and watchful regard for the intellectual improvement of the masses, combined with a strange apathy to that higher education, which, in the language of Mountstuart Elphinstone, is the light that must touch the mountain tops before it can pierce to the levels and the depths. And finally the non-expansion of the State system of elementary education for the masses, not because of the indifference of the people, but would fain saddle the Municipal and Local Boards with it; in one word, the practical denial of the responsibilities of the Government for any sort or degree of education whatever, in contravention of the theory and practice of all civilised states. This is the position to which we are reduced today in India."[40]

Dinsha Wacha, one of the founders of Indian National Congress, in a letter to Dadabhai Naoroji interpreted the resolution of 8th February, 1882 as the first effect of the Indian National congress. According to Wacha, the Government intended to reduce the number of educated natives. This was as futile, Wacha said, as trying to stem the Atlantic. Wacha rightly concluded that this policy of he Government "will give natives greater stimulus to promote higher education. It will teach them greater self- reliance."[41]

New English School

The self-reliance in education which Wacha referred to had already been attempted. Pioneer institution in this direction in western India was New English School. It was opened on 1st January 1880. Men behind this endeavour were V.S. Chiplunkar and his followers like B.G Tilak, G.G. Agarkar, V.S. Apte and M.B. Namjoshi. The intention of this group was to compete with the best Government high schools and missionary schools, while being rooted in indigenous values and patriotism. They also had a firm conviction that Government aid will deviate the school from its avowed aims and unique character. V.S.Apte's words, "in order that education may produce the highest beneficial results…it is absolutely necessary that it should be in the hands of the people themselves".[42] In an address presented to the President of Indian Education Commission, the founders of the School said: "we believe a nation that has not taken its education in its own hands cannot soon rise in literary, social or political importance; and it was with this thought that prompted us to open the New English School."[43]

The New English School started with 35 boys and by 1885 the strength of the school reached 1009. Pass percentage at the School touched 90 %.[44] Success of this school can be estimated from the praise it received from W.W. Hunter, President of the Education Commission of 1882, "this institution though not receiving any aid from the Government can rival and complete with success not only with Government High Schools in this country but may compare favourably with the schools of other countries."[45]

New English School was the first successful high school without the aid of the Government.[46] In this respect it was an inspiring example for the national schools which were established later. In this school, unintelligent cramming was discouraged and the habits of the intellectual self-help and independence were developed in its place.[47] The success of the New English School proved that natives could run the administration of educational institutions as efficiently as the Government or missionaries. Many other misconceptions were cleared too. The emphasis on teaching of vernaculars did not come in the efficiency of teaching of western sciences and literature. The School also proved that high quality education could be imparted in spite of the low fees. It also marked the beginning of a new phenomenon whereby well educated Indians instead of taking up Government employment gave their services to the national cause. Later years saw this kind of example being followed at large scale in national educational institutions. Teachers of this school exhorted students for patriotic public service. It is no surprises that the first demand for *swaraj* in Maharastra came out of this school.[48] Thus New English School prepared the ground for a education movement on national lines in the coming decades.

The managers and sympathizers of the New English School formed a society called Deccan Education Society in October 1884. Persons associated with society included Sir James Fergusson, Sir William Wedderburn, M.G. Ranade, R.G. Bhandarkar, K.T. Talang, B.G. Tilak, N.C. Kelkar, V.S. Apte, G.K. Gokhle, R.P. Paranjpe and D.K. Karve.[49] Under the auspices of the society, Fergusson College was inaugurated on January 2, 1885 in Poona. It was affiliated to the University of Bombay. The College showed good progress as its strength increased to 1108 in 1891 from 99 in 1885. The College and the Society soon became centres of educational and social activities of the nationalists. These activities alarmed the British Government. The Director of Public Instruction wrote a lengthy despatch regarding the affairs and constitution of the Society. The despatch referred to the association of some life members of the Society to certain political events. It saw such activities as against the original objects of the Society.[50]

British Government pressurised the Society to amend its constitution and suggested a new governing body which shall have considerable Government presence. This governing body had the power to appoint and remove all permanent members, manage all funds and decide other questions of management. The Deccan Education Society was forced to adopt these changes. Thus gradually the School and the College lost their distinctive features of providing education according to the national needs.

Nutan Marathi Vidyalaya

Exactly three years after the establishment of New English School, Nutan Marathi Vidyalaya was founded in Poona in 1st January 1883. It was founded by Krishna Govind Ukidwe, Damodar Sadashiv Karambelkar and others in the memory of Vishnu Shasti Chiplunkar. Like the New English School, vernacular medium was used to teach all the subjects in this school. Within one month of its opening, 350 students were enrolled in the school. In February 1888, promoters of the school handed over the School to the newly registered body Marathi Shikshan Prasarak Mandali. The objects of the body were to popularize and cheapen the education; to start new schools and to take under control already existing schools and to encourage the Marathi language as medium of teaching.[51]

Arya Samaj's Endeavours in Education

Educational reconstruction had started in North India before it started in Western India. Pioneer and chief promoter of educational reconstruction on national lines in North India was the Arya Samaj. Fundamental principles of the Arya Samaj gave important place to acquisition of knowledge and dispelling of ignorance. Arya Samaj recognized the fact that the development of an independent system of education must precede all attempts at reconstruction and readjustment of the basis of Indian society.[52] Hence, Arya Samaj's work in the field of education is unparalleled when compared to other socio-religious reform movements. Even before he founded Arya Samaj in 1875, Dayanand Saraswati had established '*Ved-Pathshalas*' at several places: Kasganj (1868); Jalesar (1868); Farrukhabad (1869); Mirzapur (1870), Chhalesar (1870) and Kashi (1873).[53] These *Vedpathshalas* taught *Vedas*, *Ashtadhyayi*, *Mahabhasya* and *Manusmriti*. The course of study was of six years. These *Pathshalas* attempted to revive the ancient system of *Gurukulas*.

After the establishment of Arya Samaj, Swami Dayananda started feeling the necessity of imparting modern scientific and technical training to Indian youth. He also corresponded with a professor in Germany to explore the possibility of sending Indian students there for training.[54] When this scheme did not materialise, efforts were made in the direction of establishing technical training facilities in India. Newsletters of Arya Samaj in 1882 and early 1883 emphasized the setting up of Vedic educational institutions which could also provide modern scientific education. After the premature death of Dayananda (30th October, 1883), a public meeting was called in Lahore on 8th November 1883 where it was decided to establish Dayanand Anglo Vedic School and College. The basic objective, according to Lala Lajpat Rai, was to avoid the limitations and short comings which an exclusively Sanskrit or an exclusively English education produced.

Dayanand Anglo Vedic High School Lahore started functioning on 1st June 1886. Lala Hansraj became the Head Master on the condition that he will not draw any salary from the institution. By 1895, the institution had become a post-graduate college. The chief aims of D.A.V. College Lahore were: to encourage, improve and enforce the study of Hindi, Sanskrit , Vedas, English literature and western science; to provide means for technical education; not to receive any assistance from Government; to provide teaching only by Indian teachers; and to provide free education.[55] The purpose behind the establishment of D.A.V. College, according to Lajpat Rai was two fold. First was to start an educational experiment as a purely indigenous enterprise. Secondly, to develop a spirit of self help and self reliance in the Indian society. Thus the men behind this experiment could visualize both the immediate needs and the future needs of the country. In meeting those needs it was important that Indians should develop self-dependence.

By 1914, D.A.V. College, Lahore had become the biggest educational institution in Northern India and probably second biggest in whole of India in terms of student strength.[56] By 1925, the College had grown into a huge institution. The following branches or departments were functioning in 1925:

1. Arts College imparting post graduate education.
2. Science College for B. Sc. Degree.
3. College of Hindu Medicine combining knowledge of *Ayurveda* and modern medicine.
4. College of Divinity.
5. Research department for research in ancient history and culture.
6. Industrial High School for vocational education.
7. A general High School.

3006 pupils were receiving education in all these departments under 110 teachers in December 1925.[57]

D.A.V. College at Lahore worked as a central institution with which many colleges and schools scattered all over the country were associated. Bhai Parmanand, a prominent Arya Samaj leader opened a high school on similar lines in British Guiana on March 30, 1910, with the help of founds collected there.[58] Later, Arya Samaj institutions were also opened at many places abroad to meet the educational needs of the Indian emigrants in Mauritius, Surinam, Singapore, USA, UK, Fiji, Burma (Myanmar), Kenya, Tanjania, Trinidad, South Africa, Uganda and Mozambique. In all these schools abroad, special emphasis was laid on Hindi and Vedic culture to strengthen the bond with Indian cultural heritage and indigenous roots.

Besides D.A.V.s' there were a large number of institutions run by Arya Samaj which included Gurukulas (ashram schools),

Sanskrit Schools (day schools), Upadeshik Vidyalayas (to prepare Arya missionaries), Dayanand Bal Mandirs, Arya Bal Niketans, Arya Public Schools, Shishu Mandirs, Vedic Nursery Schools and Model Schools. A table depicting the number of institutions being run by Arya Samaj all over India in 1925, except Assam is being given below.[59] This data also includes the ashrama schools associated with Gurukul Kangri.

S. No.	Province	No. of Institutions	No. of Students
1.	Punjab	350	36964
2.	U.P.	127	8991
3.	N. W. F. P.	22	3421
4.	Delhi	14	2433
5.	Bihar and Orissa	11	409
6.	Bombay	9	1429
7.	Burma	9	1045
10.	Madras	5	545
11.	Bengal	4	745
12.	Central Provinces	2	30
13.	Baroda	1	10
14.	Bhopal	1	70
15.	Hyderabad	2	200
16.	Punjab States	6	331
17.	Kolhapur State	5	1072
	Grand Total	**568**	**57695**

D.A.V. movement strived to fulfil the national requirements in the domain of education. The steady progress of this movement was the result of the single minded devotion and managerial skills of the persons associated with it. But D.A.V. movement failed to break all lies with government education system as D.A.V. Colleges were associated with the university. This handicap was avoided by another Arya Samaj group which believed that Gurukul education was best suited to meet the educational needs of India. Central institution of this kind of education was established in 1902 in Hardwar.[60]

Notes and References

1 J.K. Majumdar, ed., *Raja Ram Mohan Ray and Progressive Movements in India*, Calcutta, 1941, p. 104.

2 *Raja Ram Mohan Ray, Centenary Volume*, part II, Section I, pp. 44-45.

3 Ibid.

4 Dhanpati Pandey, *The Arya Samaj and Indian Nationalism (1875-1920)*, Delhi, 1972, p. 27.

5 Susobhan Sarkar, *On the Bengal Renaissance*, Calcutta, 1979, p. 18.

6 Ibid.

7 Ibid.

8 Ibid.

9 Ibid.

10 *The Father of Modern India, Commemoration Volume of Rammohun Roy Centenary Celebration*, Calcutta, 1935, p. 8.

11 V.C. Joshi, ed., *Ram Mohan and the Process of Modernization in India*, Delhi, 1975, p. 57.

12 Gautam Chattopadhyay, *Awakening in Bengal in Early Nineteenth Century*, Calcutta, 1965, p. XIX.

13 J. Richie, *Selections from Educational Records*, Part II, Calcutta, 1922, pp. 16-17.

14 *Great Indian Educational Debate*, op. cit., pp. 273-278.

15 Hafeez Malik, ed., *Sir Syyed Ahmed Khan's Educational Philosophy: A Documentary Record*, Islamabad, 1989, pp. 39-40.

16 Ibid, p. 49.

17 *Studies in History*, January-June 1987, Vol. III, no.1, p. 16.

18 Ibid., p. 23.

19 *Students' Literary and Scientific Society* (1848-49 to 1947-48), Bombay, 1950, pp. 1-6.

[20] V.A.Narain, *Proceeding of Indian History Congress, XXX, Bhagalpur,* 1968, p. 330.

[21] Ibid.

[22] Ibid.

[23] Ibid., p. 332.

[24] Ibid.

[25] Ibid.

[26] Hafeez Malik, op. cit., p. 39.

[27] Ibid. pp. 17-18.

[28] AmlesTripathi, *Extremist Challenge*, Calcutta, 1967, p.79.

[29] *General Report on Public Instruction in Lower Provinces of the Bengal Presidency for 1843-44*, p. 79.

[30] *Studies in History*, 1987, Vol. III, No-1, p. 27.

[31] Ibid.

[32] *Concept of National Education, Diamond Jubilee Seminar*, National Council of Education, 1967, p. 5.

[33] K.G. Pandit, *The Deccan Education society, 1885-1960*, Poona, 1960, pp. 24-25.

[34] Vaman Shivram Apte, b. 1858, d. 1892. One of the founders of Deccan Education Society, Poona.

[35] Malati G. Apte, *The Growth of National Education in India with special Reference to Maharashtra*, University of Bombay, 1953, pp. 227-242.

[36] *Report of Indian Education Commission*, Vol. 1, p. 451.

[37] Ibid., p. 141.

[38] Sabyasachi Bhattacharya et al., *Educating the Nation*, New Delhi, 2003, p. 179.

[39] Ibid., p. 180.

[40] Ibid., p. 68.

[41] Wecha to Naoroji, 17 July 1888, cited in Anil seal, *The Emergence of Indian Nationalism*, Cambridge, 1968, p. 20.

[42] Cited in Richard P. Tucker, *Ranade and the Roots of Indian Nationalism*, Bombay, 1972, p. 182.

[43] K.G. Pandit, *The Deccan Education Society*, Poona, 1935, p. 2.

[44] P.M. Limaye, *History of Deecan Education society*, pp. 5-6.

[45] Ibid., pp. 6-7.

[46] Richard. P. Tucker, op.cit., p. 181.

[47] P.M. Limaye, op. cit., p. 12.

[48] Richard P.Tucker, op. cit., p. 181.

[49] P. M. Limaye, op. cit., p. 181.

[50] Ibid., pp. 159-160.

[51] Malati G. Apte, op. cit., pp. 114-116.

[52] "The Educational Problem of Indian Nationals", *Modern Review*, January, 1918.

[53] *Manthan*, June 1985, p. 9.

[54] Ibid. p. 11.

[55] Lala Lajpat Rai, *Arya Samaj*, Calcutta, 1915, p. 183.

[56] Dhanpati Pandey, *The Arya Samaj and Indian Nationalism*, pp. 100-101.

[57] *Modern Review*, December 1925, p. 874.

[58] Home Political B, September 1911, pp. 3-7.

[59] *Modern Review*, December 1925, p. 875.

[60] Gurukul Kangri and its founder Swami Shraddhanand have been discussed in detail elsewhere.

6

Institutions of National Education

The emerging idea of national education, though in the air in the later part of the 19th century, could take practical shape only in the 20th century. As Sumit Sarkar has rightly observed, a political impulse was necessary to transform the idea of national education into a popular movement, and graft to its programme the militant slogan of boycott of existing education institutions.[1] Lord Curzon provided that impulse in the form of University Act of 1904 and the partition of Bengal (1905). During the Swadeshi movement, which started as a reaction to the partition of Bengal, repression of students made the boycott of Government schools a very popular programme. National education became one of the major plans of the Swadeshi movement. Congress, in its Calcutta session of 1906, passed a resolution in support of national education: "time has arrived for the people all over the country earnestly to take up the question of national education for both boys and girls, and organise a system of education, literary, scientific and technical, suited to the requirements of the country on national lines and under national control."[2]

Institutions of national education were gradually set up in several parts of India. Apart from spatial variations these institutions also displayed differences in terms of their educational philosophy and their nature. Some institutions followed the Gurukula ideal while some focused on technical education. Others laid emphasis on general education with a balanced amalgamation of Indian and western education. The nature of institutions varied from primary pathshalas to colleges and universities. Some of these institutions functioned independently but most of them were organised and controlled by National Council of Education, Bengal and Tilak Maharastra Vidyapith, Poona.

Despite the apparent differences, national educational institutions shared many common features. All of them, in their own ways, tried to establish an alternative system of education based on national requirements. As mentioned in the next chapter, their founders were convinced of the unsuitability of the official curriculum, both in terms of its colonial nature as well as its inadequacies like lack of technical education. The curriculum adopted by national educational institutions tried to incorporate as far as possible the indigenous educational philosophy, cultural heritage, moral and social values. Institutions for technical education emphasized on meeting the industrial and technological needs of the country and making the country self-reliant. As far as possible, vernacular languages were adopted as medium of instruction.

A key feature which distinguished the national educational institutions from other nationalist ventures in education (like Banaras Hindu University) was that they chose to remain independent of the official system of education. They not only rejected the official curriculum, examination system, certificates and degrees; but they also turned dawn all offers of the financial help from the colonial Government as it would have brought them under Government control.

National Educational Institutions in Bengal

Being the first to have come into contact with the English education, Bengal was the leading province in the terms of educational consciousness in India. By the beginning of the 20th century, the idea of national education had become popular among nationalist intelligentsia of Bengal. Curzon's reactionary steps in education had further underlined the urgent need for national control over education. Eruption of Swadeshi Movement with its message of *swadeshi* and boycott created suitable conditions for establishment of large number of national educational institutions in Bengal. For this reason Swadeshi movement has been called the foster parent of the national education movement. [3] It was the first movement in which students participated in large members. Colonial authorities tried to suppress the students with the help of various repressive measures such as Carlyle Circular and Lyon Circular. Carlyle Circular (10 October, 1905) threatened the school authorities that participation of students in political activities could lead to withdrawal of grants and scholarship and also disaffiliation of schools. [4] Lyon Circular banned the *Bande Matram* slogan and also warned that the boys of recalcitrant schools and colleges could be debarred from Government service. [5] Many students were expelled from the schools. Leaders of Swadeshi movement came forward in support of students. Their line of action was that if self-help could be applied in matters of economics, it could also be applied to teach the students. "Can we not found a University of our own", they asked.[6] As a result, the collection of funds started for the purpose of establishment of proposed national university.

To take up the cause of the students an Anti-Circular Society was formed on 4th November 1905. A conference organized by the Society resolved to found a national school for expelled students of Rangpur. As a result, the Rangpur National School came into existence on November 8, 1905 as the first national school during the Swadeshi movement.[7] This school was started with about 300 boys and 3 volunteer teachers. Anti-Circular Society also started a school for rusticated students in Calcutta at the residence of Krishna Kumar Mitra.[8]

The work of fund collection for National University received a boost with some big voluntary contributions, the prominent donators being: Brojendra Kishore Roy Choudhury (5 Lakhs), Maharaja Surya Kanta Acharya Choudhuri (2.5 lakhs) and Subodh Chandra Mallik (1 Lakh).

National Council of Education and Society for the Promotion of Technical Education in Bengal

To give proper shape and organization to the national education, a conference was convened on 16th November 1905. It was attended by nearly all the workers involved deeply with the question of national education such as Gooroo Dass Bannerji, Satis Chandra Mukherjee, Hirendra Nath Datta, Ashutosh Choudhary, Rashbehari Ghose, Rabindra Nath Tagore, Tarak Nath Palit, C.R. Dass, Surendra Nath Banerjee, Bipin Chandra Pal, Subodh Kumar Mallik, Brojendra Nath Seal, Abdul Rasul and Motilal Ghose.[9] The Conference adopted the resolution that "a National Council of Education should be at once established to organise a system of education – literary scientific and technical on national lines and under national control."[10] In its second meeting on 10th December 1905, the Conference setup a small Ways and Means Committee to finalise the scheme for a National Council of Education (N.C.E.). Its report was adopted in the third and final meeting of conference held on 11th March 1906, on this day the National Council of Education, Bengal was constituted. S. N. Banerji called the formation of N.C.E. as "the first constructive effort of the Swadeshi movement, the first fruit of that partition which was designed by its sponsors to weaken our political importance… the eldest and first born progeny of the Swadeshi cause." [11]

The report of the Ways and Means Committee summed up the scheme of national education to be taken up by the N.C.E.[12] The scheme proposed to impart literary, scientific and technical education on national lines and under exclusive national control. It sought to promote education in such branches which were best suited to develop the material resources and meet the pressing needs of the country. Moral and physical education were to be actively encouraged and funds were specially setup for denominational religious education. Vernacular languages were to be the medium of education with English being the compulsory second language. The functions of the Council also included establishing and affiliating institutions. Textbooks and periodicals were also to be prepared, printed and published by the Council. The course of studies adopted by the Council gave special importance to the literature, history, philosophy and other forms of knowledge associated with the country. At the same time, best assimilatable ideals of the West were to be imparted to the students. A conscious effort was to be made to inspire students with a genuine love for the country as well as to inculcate desire to serve the country. Along with the preparation of content, and guiding principles, the Council also planned to set up and run ancillary institutions like laboratories and libraries. The report also prepared a constitution and organizational structure for the N.C.E. The Council was registered on 1st June 1906. N.C.E played a leading role in organising and coordinating the activities of institutions of national education.

On the same day N.C.E. was formed (1st June 1906), a breakaway group from the N.C.E. registered another body for national education namely 'Society for the Promotion of Technical Education in Bengal' (S.P.T.E.). This group was led by Tarak Nath Palit and its other prominent members were Bhupendra Nath Basu, Nagendra Nath Ghose, Nilratan Sarkar and Manindra Chandra Nandy. S.P.T.E. group was opposed to the scheme of literary, scientific and technical education. This group wanted to focus solely upon the technical training whereas N.C.E. paid equal emphasis on both the theoritical and technical (applied) aspects of science. But S.P.T.E. did not take up theoretical aspects of science. Moreover, N.C.E. scheme also intended to take up issues neglected by the official system of education such as national ideals, cultural heritage, patriotic sentiments and mother tongue of the people. N.C.E. set up the Bengal National College and School and S.P.T.E. founded the Bengal Technical Institute.But despite these differences, N.C.E. and S.P.T.E. had many things in common. Both the groups had similar views about the neglect of science and technology by the British Government and its repercussions for India. Both the Societies had Rashbehari Ghose as President;

Many Bengali leaders were members of both organizations simultaneougly.

S.P.T.E. followed a three tier scheme of studies – primary, intermediate and secondary.[13] Primary stage was meant for training artisans and skilled labourers. Intermediate course was a three year course. In this course students were imparted practical training in various industrial tasks. They were also given lessons in elementary sciences and English. The secondary course involved four years of training to the students. Three branches of engineering-mechanical, chemical and electrical–were available for studies. The whole course had a close link with the contemporary Swadeshi thought.[14]

Bengal Technical Institute also had a manufacturing department where manufacturing and repairs of various articles and machines was undertaken. Many brilliant teachers and scientists such as Jagdish Chandra Basu, Prafulla Chandra Roy and Pramatha Nath Bose (the first principal of Bengal Technical Institute), were associated with the Bengal Technical Institute. Name of the Institute changed to College of Engineering and Technology after the merger of S.P.T.E. and N.C.E. Later on, College became the nucleus of the modern Jadavpur University.

Compared to S.P.T.E's limited programme of technical training, curriculum of N.C.E. was broad based and comprehensive. The scheme of education of N.C.E. provided for three broad stages: primary (three years), secondary (seven years) and collegiate (four years).[15] The ideal age of students for these stages was six, nine and sixteen years respectively. In the primary stage, elementary literary, scientific and technical knowledge was imparted through kindergarten system. Students were taught the use of simple tools, clay modelling and paper cutting etc. They were taught orally without the use of textboxes.

Secondary stage of N.C.E. aimed to prepare the students for a definite career. In this stage, various aspects of science were taught through laboratory method and workshop practice. In the last two years of secondary course, the student was given the choice of taking up either the secondary literary course or the secondary scientific course or secondary technical course. In the collegiate or 'proficiency' course, students had to specialize in literary, scientific or technical studies. There were provisions for further micro- specialisation and research.

According to Satis Chandra Mukharjee, the guiding spirit behind the N.C.E., the special features of the N.C.E. scheme included awakening of powers of observation and thought; vernacular medium of instruction; specialization during the collegiate stage; discipline; moral and religious education.[16] In Gooroo Dass Banarjee's view, the scheme sought "on the liberal side, to train students intellectually and morally so as to mould their character according to the highest national ideals, and on its technical side to train them so as to qualify them for developing the national resources of the country and increasing its natural wealth."[17] Bipin Chandra Pal called the scheme as "the realization of the national destiny".[18]

Bengal National College, established on 14th August 1906 was the model institution of N.C.E. Aurobindo Ghosh was its first principle and when he resigned in 1907, his position was taken over by Satis Chandra Mukherjee. Besides Aurobindo Ghosh and Satish Chandra Mukherjee, the teaching staff of the College included luminaries such as, Radha Kumud Mukherjee, Dharmanand Kosambi, Benoy Kumar Ghosh, and Dr. Bipin Behari Chakravarty. Besides regular teaching by the teachers, outstanding scholars were called upon regularly to deliver extension lectures. They included Rabindra Nath Tagore (literature), A.K. Coomaraswamy (art), Gooroo Dass Bannerjee (mathematics), Harindra Nath Dutta (*Upanishad*) and Surendra Nath Bannerji (history). The institution had three departments: literary, scientific, and technical. The manufactural section of the technical department was doing commendable work in 1909 as a feeder to many indigenous Industries.[19]

After working separately for four years, N.C.E. and S.P.T.E. amalgamated together on 25th May, 1910 on the condition that half of N.C.E.'s income would be earmarked for expenditure on technical education.[20] The combined institution from now onwards was called Bengal National College and Technical Institute. Its literary and scientific side come to be known as the Bengal National College and its technical and applied side was called as the Bengal Technical Institute.

Malda District Council of Education

While N.C.E. concentrated on secondary and higher education, another Council - Malda District Council of Education- took up the work of national education at primary level.[21] The Council was established on 6th June, 1907 by Prof. Benoy Kumar in collaboration with Bepin Behari Ghose, Radha Chandra Seth, Maulavi Mohammad Nur Bux and Prem Krishna Bhaduri. Malda District Council was a district level organisation working on N.C.E.'s line although not formally attached to it up till December 1909. The Council was an entirely representative body of Malda district, comprising the representatives of the municipalities and different sections of population. Malda District Council concentrated on dissemination of national education at primary level in the rural areas.

An important limb of the Malda District Council was its literary research department. Leading men of literature in Bengal were associated with it. According to N.C.E.'s report for the year 1911, the department was able to bring out several outstanding publications in history, linguistics and education.[22] The Council also took initiative in arranging for sending the bright students and teachers to the American universities for getting advance knowledge in modern arts, industries and sciences. Malda Council controlled several institutions imparting national education, a list of which is being given below.

S. No.	Place	Standard	No. of pupils on 31 Dec. 1912.	Year of foundation
1.	Malda	Sec. School (5th Std)	120	1907
2.	Malda	Night School	20	1908
3.	Kaligram	Sec. School (3rd Std)	125	1908
4.	Kaligram	Girls School	40	1909
5.	Dharampur	Sec. School (2nd years)	158	1908
6.	Dharampur	Gils School	8	1912
7.	Dharampur	Night School	15	1912
8.	Maltipur	Sec. School (2nd year)	45	1908
9.	Paranpur	Sec. School (2nd year)	80	1908
10.	Jadupur	Sec. School (2nd year)	50	1908
11.	Narottampur	Sec. School (Ist year)	70	1909
	Total		731	

National Schools in Bengal

During the Swadeshi movement, a large number of national schools were established in mofussil areas of Bengal. Most of the bigger schools were controlled and funded by N.C.E., but some schools were outside the N.C.E.'s influence. By October 1908, East Bengal had about 40 national schools with about 2500 to 3000 students.[23] Number of national schools in the province rose to 64 in June 1909.[24] Majority of the national schools were situated at districts or sub-divisional headquarters. Standard of these schools varied from primary to high schools. Curriculum adopted by most of the schools was on the lines prescribed by N.C.E. Bigger schools also included technical and vocational education in their curriculum. Some of the books adopted as part of curriculum by these schools were sometimes declared seditious by the Government. The strength of the national schools varied between 30 students and 250 students. Number of teachers also varied between 1 and 15 per school.

As mentioned earlier, Rangpur National School was the first product of national education movement during Swadeshi movement. The school was known to be anti-Government. By 1909, Rangpur district had three more national schools. Among them, Kurigram Middle English School (est:1908) and Khat Khatya National Pathshala were prominent for their association with political activities. In the Dacca district, Dacca National School (est: 1906) was the earliest as well as the largest. Students of this school were implicated in several cases of political violence against the state. Pulin Bihari Das, a teacher of this school was described as 'the most dangerous agitator in the province' and 'inspirer of secret samitis.'[25]

Other schools in Dacca district worth mentioning were: Mojpore National School (November 1907), Sanihati National School (February 1908), Pubdi National School (February 1908), Amteli National School (1909), Sonarang National School (April 1908) and Rautgao National School (December 1908).

Mymen Singh District had 8 national schools in 1908 to which three more were added in 1909. Prominent among these were Mymen Singh National School (April 1906), Harimohan Institute at Kishorganj (August 1906), Taraganj National School (1905) and Uthari National School (January 1908). Government suspected that most of the national schools in the district were associated with political activity of the extreme kind. Kali Prasanna Ghosh, the head master of Mymen Singh School was a very active political agitator. Most of the students and teachers of the school were volunteers of secret society known as Sadhna Samaj. Hari Mohan Institute was described as 'center of agitatation in Kishore Ganj'. An annual report of this school stated that objects of national education were 'patriotism, physical exercises and religion'.

Tippera District had the highest number of national schools in Bengal. Largest of them was Camilla National School. Other national schools in the district were: Chandpur National School (1906), Subahpur Middle English School, Kaitola Jatiya Bidyalaya, Chandla Middle School, Camilla Middle English School (July 1906), Deerghabhumi Middle Vernacular School (January 1908), Raniara Middle English school (November 1907), Chunta National School (November 1908), and three other national schools at Charpara, Bardia, and Faultai Bajar. The only national school in Noakhali district was Noakhali National School. The report of Director of Public Instruction stated that the political activity at this school consisted of 'political meetings, celebration of political or seditious events, visits of political agitators and secret meetings'.[26]

Rajashahi, Dinajpur, Jalpaiguri, Malda, Chittagong and Bogra districts also had one national school each: Adarsh Bidyalaya at Rampur Baolia (1908); Dinajpur National School (April 1906); Jalpaiguri National School (April 1907); Malda National School (June 1907); Bogra National School; and Jamal Khan National School (April 1908). Out of these, Dinajpur National School had openly celebrated 'Shivaji' festival in 1907. Some students and teachers of this school were charged with participation in the revolutionary activities. Activities of Jalpaiguri National School were also reported as 'very much Swadeshi and anti- partition'.

In Sylhet district the prominent national schools were, Sylhet National School (1906), Bamiachung National School (1907), Srimangal National School (1908), and Lakhi National School (1908). Two national schools of Pabna district were Pabna

National School and Baghmora National School. Farid Pur district in 1909 had national schools at Kamargram, Burihat, Dholgram, Manhigati, Panchuria, Nohakholi, East Manihari, West Manihari and Raghunathpur. Bakarganj district had 9 national schools, they were situated at Jhalashakti, Amrajuri, Brahmanandita, Nazirbari, Danadawat and Kachnakti.

West Bengal legged behind East Bengal in the number of institutions of national education. At the height of national education movement there were only 13 national schools in West Bengal.[27] Number of students studying in these schools, excluding these studying in Bengal National College, was 453 in 1910. Prominent national schools in the West-Bengal were: Kalna National School, Burdwan district; Garhbeta National School, Midnapur district; Dakshineshwar National School, 24 Paragna district; Santipur National School, Nadia distict; Jassore National School, Jassore district; Magura National School, Jassore district; Sanihati National School, Khulna district; and Khanjarpur National School, Bhagalpur District. Out of these, Garhbeta National School was called 'a centre of sedition' in the report of Superintendent of Police.[28] The schools at Santipure, Magura as well as Bandematram School at Jassore were also believed to have links with the extremist political activities. Bande Matram School was closed under the pressure of administration in June 1910. In 1910-1911, Magura National School also ceased to exist.[29] A new national school was opened at Amgram in March 1910. In the same year the school at Garhbeta changed its name to Chandra Kumar National Institution.

After the partition of Bengal was revoked in 1911, the Government reports on national schools present a unified picture of national education in the reunited Bengal. The number of national schools in Bengal in 1912 was 15. This number increased to 16 in 1913. The number of students decreased to 800 in 1913 from 1000 in 1912. According to the Report for the year1913[30], financial difficulties of national schools were increasing and the grants from NCE other sources were getting smaller and fewer, and teaching staff was being ill paid. As a result many national schools were forced to close. But the following national schools were still functioning at the end of 1913: Jhalakati National School, Baneshwar National Pathsala, Chaitainya National Pathsala, East Chand Khali National School, Sanihaṭi National School, English Bajar National School, Kaligram National School, Dharampur National School, Dangarpur National School, Santipur National School, Moyna National School, Maltipur National School, Chaitanya pathsala, and Chandpur National School.[31]

Apart from the above mentioned national schools, there were a large number of pathsalas (primary schools), providing national education in rural Bengal. They got little or no aid from N.C.E. and played lesser role in politics. In spite of these limitations they made the authorities extremely nervous as these pathsalas were breaching the traditional barriers present in the society like Hindu-Muslim; upper castes-lower castes; urban gentry-rural masses etc. These divisions of Indian society were used to be highlighted by colonial administration to counter balance the rising tide of Indian nationalism.[32] For instance, a pathsala in Dhalgram village in Faridpur district consisted entirely of the Namsudra caste students. Conveners of these pathsalas made considerable efforts to secure the Muhammadan pupils.[33] Thus these pathsalas were strengthening nationalism in a very effective manner in the areas which were not much effected by the mainstream nationalist forces.

The movement for nationalizing the primary education in rural Bengal developed first in Barisal. Swadesh Bandhab Samiti of Aswini Kumar Dutt controlled about 200 pathsalas. In Faridpur District 13 out of the 14 thanas had such pathsalas. District Association of Faridpur, led by Ambica Charan Majumdar, was running 25 primary national schools with about 1200 pupils.[34] Work of Malda Jatiya Shiksa Samiti has already been mentioned. *The Dawn* (of May 1910) listed another 35 national primary schools existing in 15 other districts of Bengal- 11 in Tippera, 4 in Mymensingh, 3 in Jassore, 2 each in Dacca, Noakhali, Bogra,

Pabna and Hooghly, and one each in Rangpur, Dinajpur, Nadia, Midnapur, Howrah, Khulna and Chittagong. The same issue of *The Dawn* also reported efforts for setting up national schools for girls in Mymen Singh and Rajshahi.[35]

But once the Swadeshi phase was over, the number of national education institutions came down drastically. Number of the affiliated schools with the N.C.E. declined sharply after 1910, as shown by the following table.[36]

Year	November of Schools associated with NCE
1907	10
1908	17
1910	18
1911	08
1913	06
1918	02 (Chandpur and Santipur)

Declining trend was also noticed in the strength of Bengal National College once the Swadeshi movement ceased. Ultimately, in 1917, the Bengal National College had to be closed dawn due to lack of students. In its place, another institution, the Bengal National Academy was started but it was also closed down for the same reasons in 1920. But Bengal Technical Institute continued to function despite difficulties.

In the wake of financial and other problems, a Reconstruction Committee was appointed in 1918. Recommendations of the Committee included: dedication of funds for commercial and industrial education; to focus on training students for organizing small scale industries on national lines; inclusion of subjects like commercial and economic history, geography and English in curriculum for technical education: and making Bengali the medium of education as far as practicable.[37] These recommendations were accepted and adopted. From 1918 onwards nearly all of the resources of N.C.E. came to be dedicated to the development of technical education. In the same year, National Education Week (8th April-15th April 1918) was celebrated. This week was devoted to the popularisation of national education though public meetings and articles in news papers etc.

The Non-Cooperation movement in 1920-1922, created conditions similar to Swadeshi movement. The call of boycott of educational institutions led to large scale boycott of Government schools and colleges. Like the Swadeshi days, hastily set up national schools came up to accommodate expelled students as well as those who boycotted the Government schools. Apart from the national schools, several new nationals universities such as Kashi Vidapith, Bihar Vidyapith, Gujrat Vidypith, Bengal Vidyapith and Jamia Milia Islamia also came up. The work of N.C.E. was also expanded again. But attempts to reopen the Bengal National College failed. Despite Rashbehari Ghose making N.C.E. the residuary legatee of his properties valued at Rs. 13 Lakh, adequate financial resources needed for its long-term smooth functioning could not be arranged. The number of national schools in between 1922 and 1947 associated with N.C.E. has been shown in the following table.[38]

Year	Number of national schools associated with N.C.E.
1922	17
1924	21
1925	22
1926	17
1927	15
1928-30	14
1931	13
1932	08
1933-34	07
1935-48	03

Bengal Technical Institute's Success against all Odds

Closure of the general wing (Bengal National College) notwithstanding, the technical wing of N.C.E. made steady progress after 1920. In 1921, Bengal Technical Institute (B.T.I.) became the first engineering college in India to start a chemical engineering course.[39] In 1925, University of Edinburg, of its own accord, granted recognition to the B.T.I. though it was still not recognized by the Government of India. In 1928, Bengal Technical institute was renamed as the College of Engineering and Technology, Bengal. The technical excellence of the college and the exigencies of Second World War compelled the Government to recognize the College. In 1939, the Defence Department granted recognition to graduates of the College in chemical engineering. In the same year, Post and Telegraph Department granted recognition to diplomas in mechanical and electrical engineering courses of the college. In 1941, a centre for training of war technicians was opened in the College at the instance of Government. In 1944, College ended its custom of awarding diplomas and started granting the degrees.

Rabindranath Tagore's Institutions

Education institutions established by Rabindra Nath Tagore occupy a distinctive place among the institutions of national education. They remained unaffected by the political movements. These institutions were a manifestation of the poet's ideas on national education. A brief description of these institutions is being given below.

Santiniketan

Santiniketan was established at Bolepur in Bengal in 1901. The school was patterned after the forest ashrams of ancient India, but many of the methods and much of content taught there were modern.[40] The objective of the school was to inculcate in student, the spirits of brotherliness, mutual effort, freedom, stimulation, devotion, communion with nature and service to mankind. The activities at the school were programmed to awaken the creative powers of the students and to promote their all round development.

Rabindranath Tagore introduced a unique teaching a methodology at *Santiniketan*. The teaching was conducted in open air, under the trees. Student-teacher ratio was kept vary small so as to encourage close interaction between teachers and taught. Very few books were used. Most of the teaching was conducted through question- answer sessions and by conversation among students and teacher. Study of nature in natural setting was emphasized. Students were grouped on the basis of different subjects they studied. They were also taught many fine arts and vocational crafts.

Sriniketan

Sriniketan, the agricultural school, was established at Surul village in 1922. The school aimed to teach agriculture and its allied industries for village reconstruction. Pupils at this school were provided with land, necessary equipment and other requirements like seeds and raw material. They worked under the supervision of manager of the school. The problems faced in raising different crops formed the topics of class room instruction. Besides farming, arrangements were also made for poultry farming, dairying, weaving, dyeing and carpentry. Whole process of learning was designed to be as self- supporting as possible. The overall emphasis was on learning by doing and utilisation of all profitable experience.

Along with the agricultural work, literary studies and fine arts were also a part of the curriculum. Students also trained the village folks in sanitation, hygiene, disease prevention, social bonding, cooperative-farming, and improved methods of agriculture and allied activities. Students of Sriniketan also organized cultural programmes and fairs. Overall programme of learning at Sriniketan was life centred and society centred.[41]

Lok- Shiksha- Sansad

Lok-shiksha-sansad was established in 1936 to promote the cause of mass education. This institution aimed to establish a number of study centres and examination centres. It started conducting examinations equivalent to Matriculation, Intermediate and B.A.. Curriculum included subjects like Bengali, elementary hindi, history, geography, mathematics, and general science. Lokshiksha Sansad also published cheap but quality text books for various subjects.

The Viswa-Bharti

Tagore established the Viswa-Bharati University in 1921 on the model of ancient Indian universities. Its motto- "*Yatra Vishvam Bhavati Ekam Nidam*," characterises its fundamental principles:

1. To give education on the basis of indigenous cultural ideals;
2. To bring the diverse cultures of the East into intimate relationship with one another;
3. Approaching the science and culture of the West from the standpoint of their unity; and
4. Developing universal brotherhood in order to achieve world peace.

The university was coeducational and residential. It attracted students from different parts of India and also from abroad. Students could choose and study diverse subjects according to their interest. By 1955, the University was maintaining the following departments:[42]

i. Vidya – Bhavana : School of research in literature and philosophy;

ii. Cheena-Bhavana : School of Sino- Indian studies;

iii. Shiksha-Bhavan : College for higher studies;

iv. Kala- Bhavan : Department of fine arts;

v. Sangit-Bhavan : School of music and dance;

vi. Sriniketan : Institute of rural reconstruction ;and

vii. Silpa-Bhawan: School of industries.

National Education in Western India

During the Swadeshi Movement a few national schools in Maharastra were started. Out of them, three schools, Samrtha Vidyalaya, Maharastra Vidyalaya and Amraoti National School are worth mentioning. A much more widespread growth of national educational institutions in western India took place during Non-Cooperation Movement. During 1921-22, these were about 189 national education institutions in Bombay province with about 17,000 students. In Central Provinces, 86 such institutions were imparting education to 6,338 students.[43] Akin to the National Council of Education in Bengal, chief coordinating, controlling and affiliating body in Maharastra was Tilak Maharastra Vidyapith.

Samartha Vidyalaya, Talegaon, Poona

The first national school set up in Maharastra was Samarth Vidhalaya. This school was established on 1st January 1906. Apart from Prof. Vijapurkar, Dr. Atma Ram Parandekar, Sakharam Ramchandra Bhagwat and Raja Ram Damodar Desai were instrumental in the establishment of this school.[44] The school was of secondary level.

The curriculum of the primary section of the Vidyalaya focused on writing and arithmetic. While in the secondary section, special emphasis was laid on religious and cultural studies. Study of Sanskrit and at least one vocation was compulsory for every student. Special attention was paid to the physical education and nutritional diet of the students. In the study of history, geography and modern languages, European knowledge was not neglected. Use of foreign articles was discouraged while the cult of swadeshi was promoted. The school gave due attention to effective teaching methodologies. Teacher-student ratio was kept small and cramming was discouraged. As far as possible, study of the nature was imparted in a natural environment. The founders of the school while selecting the teachers gave priority to their dedication to the cause of national education rather than their academic qualifications.[45]

The patriotic flavour of the education being imparted in Samarth Vidyalaya provoked the Government to launch a crackdown on the school. The British Government considered the Vidyalaya 'an organisation of uncompromising extremism'.[46] The Government was much alarmed by the reports that founders of this national school planned to convert the school in to a great Mahratta National University.[47] Government at first targeted Prof. Vijapurkar, its founder. Prof. Vijapurkar along with Prof. Vamanrao Joshi was prosecuted on charges of sedition and sentenced to three years of imprisonment on 21st September, 1909.[48] On 10th June 1910, Samartha Vidyalaya was charged with pernicious teaching, and a danger to public peace.[49] In the same year, Samartha Vidyalaya was declared illegal and was ordered to stop its activities.

After his release from the jail, Prof. Vijapurkar made efforts to revive the Samartha Vidyalaya. The Government agreed for revival of the school on three conditions: a new name for the school; no former teacher accept Vijapurkar to be re-employed; and school should not publish its own books.[50] Prof. Vijapurkar had to accept these conditions grudgingly. The school was restarted with the name 'New Samartha Vidyalaya' in 1918. The new school faced problems from various quarters since its beginning.Government made the charge that the school was still following its erstwhile nationalist ideology. On the other hand, other leaders of national education believed that by acceding to the Government's conditions, Vijapurkar had compromised with the principles of national education. As a result the new national schools that were established during Non-Cooperation Movement refused to have any an association with New Samartha Vidayalay. Due to all these problems the New Samartha Vidyalaya was closed soon after the death of Prof. Vijapurkar in 1926.

Maharastra Vidyalaya, Poona

Maharastra Vidyalaya acquired the character of a national school in the beginning of 1908 when it prescribed its syllabus on the lines prepared by N.C.E. Bengal.[51] Maharastra Vidyalaya was also recognised as one of the examination centres for N.C.E., though it was not affiliated to N.C.E.. The scheme of studies adopted by the school consisted of a 6 year course combining the literary education with scientific and technical education. Teaching of elementary classes was conducted with minimum use of books. A selective study of ancient epics was also imparted. Students were taught both theoretical and practical aspects of science. They were also taught fine arts such as drawing and singing and also vocational subjects like weaving and carpentry. The school was residential in nature. Special attention was given to their character development and physical development. In 1908, the average daily attendance of the school was 125. It had 8 teachers. Library of the school had about 1000 books.[52]

Amraoti National School

Founded during the Swadeshi Movement, Amraoti National School followed closely the curriculum of N.C.E. Bengal. Though the School was not affiliated with National Council, it got its students examined by the N.C.E. Bengal.[53] The Government was very suspicious of the nationalist activities at the School. According to Director of Criminal Intelligence, the School was of 'seditious nature'. According to his report, religious instruction imparted in School was associated with 'most extreme nationalism'. Government was also worried that the School that questions asked in the examination as well as the books prescribed by the School incite anti-Government feelings.[54]

Yeotmal National School, Yeotmal

Yeotmal National School was established in 1906 through the patriotic efforts of Dattopant Apte, Haribhau Pathak, V.G. Kelkar, Prithvigir Harigir and L.N. Ane.[55] *The Dawn Magazine* called this school as unique as it was solely financed and controlled by people of the same locality.[56] School charged fee only in its first year of existence and from the second year free education was imparted. Its eleven years long course of studies included literary subjects, fine arts and various crafts along with physical training. In August1908, School started a home for helpless students called Anathashram to provide them free education with shelter. The Yeotmal National School closed in the beginning of 1910.

Three other national schools which are known to have been started during the Swadeshi movement in Deccan were Poona National School, Tilak Rastriya Shala and Anatha Vidyarthi Grihaye. Poona National School was opened through the efforts of Bhaskar Balawant Bhopalkar and his brother Anna Saheb Bhopalkar. Rastriya Shala, Nasik was established by Bala Saheb Khare in 1906. Both the Schools proved to be short lived. Tilak Rastriya Shala at Nasik was revived again in 1921. Besides general academics and training of weaving, spinning and tailoring, the school also taught preparation of soap, menthol and peppermint.

Anatha Vidyarthi – Grihaye Maharastra Vidyalaya, Poona

Founder of this school was Sri Balukaka Kanitkar. He was inspired by the ideas of Chiplunkar and Lokmanya Tilak. This school was also established in the aftermath of Swadeshi Movement on 12 May 1909. Lokmanya Tilak himself was one of the supporters of this school. The purpose of Balukaka was to provide national education to poorer classes.[57] He had radical nationalist ideas on education and so wanted to impart political education along with general education. The curriculum of the school also included technical education. The school maintained a workshop and printing presses.

In 1915, Mahatma Gandhi requested the sponsors of the school to introduce weaving and agriculture in the school. The school adopted Gandhian programmes. Khadi became the dress of the school. Spinning wheel and handloom became the part of daily activities of school. During the Non-Cooperation Movement, the school changed its name to Swavlamban Rastriya Pathsala, Chinchwad on 3rd February 1921. Along with a new name, the school also adopted the larger curriculum of other national schools. Under the industrial education, weaving, press (printing), book-binding, tailoring and gold smithy were taught. Day-to-day life of school resembled simple austere life of a Ashrama. Students of the school also collected alms (*bhiksha*) once a week from nearby localities. Pathshala also organized a dispensary for public use.

Tilak Maharastra Vidyapeeth

Indian National Congress' appeal for the boycott of schools and colleges and establishment of national schools and colleges in 1920 had a very favourable impact in Maharastra. National educational institutions came up in all districts of Maharastra. An urgent need was felt to organise, coordinate and control such institutions. To deal with this problem, a meeting of public workers was convened at Vasai (Bassein) under the presidentship of Dr. Kurtkoti. It was unanimously decided at this meeting that a national university should be started for this purpose. The proposed national university came into shape, with the founding of Tilak Maharastra Vidyapeeth on 6th May 1921. Dr. Kurtkoti became the first Chancellor (Kulpati) of the Vidhyapeeth.

Objectives of the Vidyapeeth included running a system of education on national lines, without being dependent on government for financial assistance, chalking out a curriculum for developing national ambitions and making students self- supportive, recognizing and affiliating the already established national schools, establishing new ones, conducting examinations and conferring degrees, and promotion of higher research.[58]

Institutions which came under the control of the Vidyapeeth were of two categories. Some of them continued to carry out their own examinations, but got their examinations recognized by the Vidyapeeth. Other institutions got their examination conducted directly by the Vidyapeeth. Vidyapeeth also conferred degrees to the students though these degrees were not recognized by the

Government. Vidyapeeth also sponsored other educational activities related to national interests but neglected by the British Government including mass education, adult education and carrying out research in ancient Indian literature.

Subjects taught under the guidance of Vidyapeeth included study of mother tongues, classical languages, foreign languages, history and politics, religion and metaphysics, economics, trade and medical science.[59] Facilities for the study of many vocational subjects were also made available. Curriculum for the higher education in arts and commerce streams was of three years duration while technical subjects were to be studied for four years.[60]

There were three national colleges officiated to the Vidyapeeth: Tilak Mahavidyalaya, Poona; National Medical College, Bombay; and Vyapari Mahavidyalaya (Commerce College), Poona. The following national schools were also affiliated with the Vidyapeeth:

1. Tilak Rashtriya Pathshala, Poona
2. Swavlamban Pathshala, Chinchavad
3. Rashtriya Shala, Baramati
4. Tilak Rashtriya Vidyalaya, Satara
5. Tilak Rashtriya Pathshala, Nipani
6. Tilak Vidyalaya, Belgaum
7. Rashtriya Vidyalaya, Sholapur
8. Rashtriya Pathshala, Ahmadnagar
9. Rashtriya Pathshala, Mahad
10. Lokmanya Tilak Vidyalaya, Dipoli
11. Rashtriya Vidyalaya, Vengurle
12. Tilak Vidyalaya, Ratragiri
13. Lokmanya Shikshan Sansthan, Malvan
14. Rashtriya Shala, Bombay

15. Tilak Rashtriya Vidyalaya, Jalgaon
16. Tilak Rashtriya Vidyalaya, Bhusaval
17. Tilak Rashtriya Vidyalaya, Khamgaon
18. Tilak Rashtriya Shala, Akola.
19. Rashtriya Shala, Amraoti
20. Rashtriya Vidyalaya, Dharmangaon
21. Rashtriya Shala, Hinganghat
22. Tilak Rashtriya Shala, Varora
23. Tilak Vidyalaya, Nagpur
24. Tilak Rashtriya Pathshala, Shirdi
25. Tilak Rashtriya Vidyalaya, Shondurjan

To promote research in the Vedic literature a Vedic Sanshodhan Mandal (Institute for Vedic Research) was started in 1928. Mandal was later made an independent body. Major objectives of the Mandal were to spread Vedic learning; arrange for learning, teaching and publication of Vedic literature.

Tilak Mahavidyalaya

Tilak Mahavidyalaya started its functioning on 8th December, 1920, with 60 students under the chairmanship of Chintamanras Vaidya.[61] Objectives of the Vidyalaya were similar to those of its parent body, Tilak Maharastra Vidyapeeth. The college course included the study of English, Marathi, Sanskrit and other general subjects. Vocational courses like carpentry, weaving, indigenous medicine and commerce were also taught. In the beginning an engineering course was also started. Among all courses, the best progress was shown by Ayurvedic course, a four years course started in 1922. The department of Ayurvedic studies was able to establish and maintain a large and up-to-date hospital called Tarachand Ramnath Ayurvedic Hospital. Pharmacy of the department called Ayurveda-Rasa-Shala prepared medicines on a large scale. Ayurvedic department also undertook comparative studies of Western and Eastern medicine systems.

With the exception of Ayurvedic course, other courses run by the college faced numerous difficulties. But overall seen, the college made satisfactory contribution to the cause of national education. Students of the college were encouraged to participate in constructive social work. The college also organized public classes for imparting education in Ayurvedic first aid. The college opened Gram Seva Ashram in Jategaon- Khurd in the district of Poona for imparting training in rural development. Studies of indigenous culture and traditions were given the pride of place in Tilak Mahavidyalaya. Activities and environment of the college sought to make students self-supporting and national minded. Above all the college inculcated in to students the idea of sacrifice for national cause.

Due to the patriotic nature of the Tilak Mahavidyalaya, The Government of Bombay declared the college as illegal and forced it to close in 1932. Rastriya Shikshan Mandal again reorganized the Ayurvedic section and estabilished a new institution called Ayurvedic Maha Vidyalaya on 26th June 1933. Tilak Maharastra Vidyapeetha remained its parent body. The college and its hospital received grants from the Congress Government of Bombay. In 1939-40, the course of studies at the college was extended from four to five years. In 1948, the college introduced master degree in Ayurvedic studies.

Medical College, Bombay[62]

National Medical College was started by Dr. D.D. Sathya and some other patriotic minded doctors of Bombay on 4th September 1921. The College was affiliated to Tilak Maharastra Vidyapeeth. At first, this medical college started functioning in the premises of a small hired bungalow. A munificent endowment of B.Y.L. Charitable Hospital in 1925 for teaching purpose by Dr. A.L. Nayar proved to be very beneficial for the College. Dr. A.L. Nayar also contributed substantially for the construction of College building in 1927. On the basis of the academic excellence of the College, it was affiliated to College of Physicians and Surgeons of Bombay in 1926. National Medical College has the unique distinction of being the sole institution of Western medicine among the institutions of national education. It helped to demolish the official propaganda that without the support of the Government, specialized institutions like medical colleges will not be able to run successfully.

Tilak Vidyalaya, Nagpur

Tilak Vidyalaya, Nagpur was established on 3rd January 1921 by Sunder Lal Bhagwandin.[63] This school started with about 50 teachers and had four branches of studies: literary, scientific, technical and Urdu. There was a separate school for Urdu. Later a College of Finc Arts was also attached with this school. In 1929, the school was temporarily shifted from Bombay to Poona and finally to Nagpur where it was attached with Nagpur Tilak Vidyalaya. The school also had a residency (hostel). Both, teachers and students of the school played active roles in various Congress led movements such as Mulsi Satyagraha, Tenda Satyagraha, Shastra Satyagraha and Hyderabad Satyagraha.

Tilak Rashtriya Vidyalaya Khamgaon, Vidharbha

This school was established in January 1921 through the efforts of Dr. Bhan Saheb Parasins, Sheth Mohan Lalji Purwar and L.C. Purwar. The curriculum of the school included academic and vocational education along with yoga as compulsory physical education. Vocational studies at the school included fine arts like painting and sculpture. The school followed an independent curriculum of studies till 1940 and after that it followed the curriculum prescribed by Tilak Maharastra Vidyapeeth. Two students of the school participated in the Dandi March while about 60 students participated in Civil Disobedience Movement. In 1942 most of the teachers of the school were jailed for participating in Quit India Movement.

Tilak Vidyalaya, Yevale [64]

Tilak Vidyalaya, Yevale was established on 22nd May 1921 through the initiative of the local Congress leaders. The Vidyalaya adopted the programme of studies chalked out by Samratha Vidyalaya. The school laid special emphasis on physical development of the students through physical exercises and indigenous games like kho-kho, Alapatya, Malkhamb and wrestling. Teachers of the school adopted novel but effective ways of teaching different subjects. Poems about Tilak and sermons from *Gita* were regularly recited to the students. National days of importance, such as Ganapati festival, Shivaji and Tilak's anniversaries, were celebrated as festivals in the schools. Public lectures were also organized on important issues.

The school hosted the 6th National Educational conference in 1928. Active participation of students and teachers of the school in the ongoing political struggle led to closure of the school in 1932.

National School at Mahad (Kulaba)[65]

National school at Mahad (Kulaba) was started in January 1921. Teachers and students collected funds for the school on a weekly basis. Founds were also generated through sale of khaddar and handicrafts produced at the school. Teachers and students of the school had close association with Congress activities.

Rashtirya Pathshala, Ahmad Nagar[66]

This national school was also started in 1921. It functioned till 1932 and was again restarted in 1934. The school had a hostel for boys and teachers; gymnasium (Arogya Mandir Vyayam Shala); accounts division (Mohan Mudra Mandir) ; library (Saraswati Mandir with about 5000 books), science centre (Vigyan Mandir), and a workshop for vocational learning.

National Schools in Ratnagir District [67]

Ratnagir district of Maharastra had four national schools between 1921 and 1926. They were at Vengarle, Malvan, Dapoli and Ratnagiri. The school at Vengarle was established through the initiative of local merchants. Main spirit behind the establishment of national school at Malvan was S.K. Patil. The National School at Dipole was started through the efforts of Haribhau Gokhle, a local merchant. National school at Ratnagir got contribution from Tilak Swarajya Fund. All the schools had, besides the academic courses, vocational courses like spinning, weaving, gardening, painting, carpentry and book binding. All the schools had closed by 1926 for want of funds.

Tilak Rastriya Pathshala, Nipani[68]

The Pathshala started in 1921, was conducted in the style of an ashram. In 1930-32 nearly all the students and teachers of the pathshala participated in the civil disobedience. The school could not function after 1938 due to lack of funds.

Lokmanya Tilak Rashtriya Vidyalaya, Tumsar[69] (Central Province)

Was also started in 1921 by Shri A.M. Makade. The Vidyalaya experimented with self sufficiently through Khadi. It became a centre of political activity in 1942 during the Quit India Movement.

Apart from the national schools associated with Tilak Maharastra Vidyapeeth and Samartha Vidyalaya there were several other independent institutions imparting national education in Maharastra like Rayat Shikshan Sanstha, Satara; Khandesh Shikshan Mandal, Amalner; Pragya Pathshala Mandal, Vai; Sadhakashram, Andheri; and Vaishya Vidyashram, Sabwane. A brief account of these national institutions is being given below.

Rayat Shikshan Sanstha[70] was established by Bhaurao Patil at Satara in 1919. It aspired to disseminate national education among the masses and train the suitable teachers for this task. Another objective of the Sanstha was to train the village workers for the rejuvenation of rural industries for rural reconstruction. To meet there objectives, Rayat Shikshan Sanstha aimed to open a school in every village having a population of more than 300.

Sanstha also opened a hostel–Chhatrapati Sahu Hostel–for the poor boys. To meet the demand for properly trained teachers, a training school for primary teachers was opened in July 1935.

Khandesh Shikshan Mandal[71] at Amalner was earlier a Government recognized society. Some of its teachers attended the Nagpur session of Indian National Congress. They responded to the Congress' call for boycott of Government institutions and establishment of national institutions and converted their society into Rastriya Shiksha Society. Later, Society also opened an Arts college- Rashtirya Mahavidyalaya and also an Ayurvedic College. The excellent work of the Khandesh Shikshan Mandal could not continue for long due to its opposition to the official education system. Government officials were able to create a rift in the management body. Pro-Government members of the management body were able to pass a resolution giving up the national education.

Pragya Pathshala Mandal[72] in Satara district had its origins in a private school established by Pandit Narayan Shastri Manathe in 1903. In 1916, this school was converted into a public institution with nationalistic objectives. The aim of this institution was to prepare nationalist minded youth to educate people so as to preserve their self respect and pride in their national culture. Curriculum of the institution included grammar, *Nyaya*, Vedic literature, religious studies, english, history and economics. Texts such as *Geeta Rahsya, Panchadashi, Geeta Bhasya, Gyaneshwari, Dasbodh,* etc. were taught as part of the curriculum. The only limitation in the national nature of the institution was its castiest nature, only the Brahmin students were eligible for admission in this institution.

Another independent institution dedicated to imparting national education was **Sadhakashram** near Bombay at Andheri.[73] The institution focused on those students who left the schools associated with Government to serve their motherland. Curriculum of Sadhakashram laid more stress on the physical labour. Students of the ashram led an austere life. In the training that lasted for more than one year, students were taught the methods of agricultural work in the villages. Daily schedule at Ashram included spinning Charkha, cleaning the premises and cooking.

The distinctive feature of the national schools in Maharastra was their direct association with political movements led by Congress. Following figures related to participation of students and teachers in Civil Disobedience Movement in 1930 amply illustrate this fact.[74]

S. No.	Name of Institution	Number of Pupils Participated	Number of Teachers Participated
1.	Tilak Mahavidyalaya, Poona	25	4
2.	Tilak Rashtirya Pathshala, Nipani	11	3
3.	Tilak Rashtirya Vidyalaya, Satara	14	6
4.	Pragya Pathshala, Vai	36	N. A.
5.	Tilak Rashtriya Vidyalaya, Yevale	7	4
6.	Rashtriya Pathshala, Ahmadnagar	44	5
7.	Tilak Rashtirya Pathshala, Vengurle	6	1
8.	Vaishya Vidyashram, Sasvane	32	8 (including 2 females)
9.	Navin Samartha Vidyalaya, Talegaon	13	3

S. No.	Name of Institution	Number of Pupils Participated	Number of Teachers Participated
10.	Tilak Rashtriya Vidyalaya, Khamgaon	42	8
11.	Tilak Rashtriya Shala	8	10
12.	Tilak Rashtriya Vidyalaya Nagpur	35	8
13.	Tilak Rashtriya Shala, Poona	N. A.	3

National Educational Institutions in South India

Like the other parts of the country, the first national schools of south India came up during Swadeshi movement. National High School established at Ramchandra Puram in 1906 was perhaps the first national school in south India. It was the result of efforts of Perraju, a local leader who had donated his property to start this school.[75] In the next year another national school was established at Rajmundry during the visit of Bipin Chandra Pal there.[76] Funds for this school were raised with the help of public donations. Another school, called Desiya Vidyalaya was opened in Rajmundry in 1908.[77] All the three institutions at Rajmundry were affiliated to the National Council of Education, Bengal.

The largest institution of national education in Andhra was Andhra Jatheeya Kalasala. It had its origins in 1907 when some young men formed Swarajya Samiti. The Samiti aimed to start a national school at Masulipatnam. A public meeting organized by the Samiti on 17th November 1907 called for the creation of a model educational institution. This model institution later came to be known as Andhra Jatheeya Kalasala.[78] The meeting also called for setting up a body called Vidya Parishad or Andhra National Council of Education. Ultimate objective of the Council was to establish an Andhra National University.[79] As a result of hectic work in this direction, Andhara Jatheeya Kalasala was able to start its work in February 1910. Among its chief organizers were Subramania Iyer, Dewan Bahadur Krishna Swamy Row, K. Hanumantha Rao and B. Pattabhi Sitaramayya,[80]

Andhra Jatheeya Kalasala was located at Masulipatam. The institution had an extensive campus which housed a laboratory, library, workshop, machine and welding sheds, foundry, playground and an agricultural farm. The curriculum of studies at the institution aimed at coordinating various aspects of modern knowledge with the scheme of indigenous culture. The course of education included general literary instruction along with carefully graduated course in manual training, various arts such as drawing, painting and sculpture. There was also a separate section for agricultural studies. Emphasis, in all the courses, was on inculcating dignity of labour and spirit of fellowship. Moral and religious education was the dominating spirit of all life and work in the institution. Basis of moral and religious teaching were epics and the *Puranas*, biographies of national heroes and great men and celebration of national festivals. The day at institution began with Vedic mantra recital and the day closed with an epic story or bhajan recital. Vernaculars were given priority but the study of English was also encouraged for sympathetic appreciation of the western knowledge and culture.[81] Kalasala also ran a well equipped workshop to serve the needs of the local community. Various articles of use in home, industry and agriculture were manufactured and repaired here.

The swadeshi spirit in education found expression in the Hyderabad Karnataka in the establishment of national schools. Vittal Rao Devlankar, a leading pleader of Gulbarga estabilished a national school called Nutan Vidyalaya in Gulbarga in 1907.[82] In 1911 another national school came into existence in Chincholi. It was known as Osmania- Middle school.[83] Students of this school sung Vandematram and other patriotic songs despite the ban imposed by the Nizam Government. Students of this school also distributed revolutionary pamphlets printed in Hindi and Kannada.

During the Non-Cooperation Movement, a national school called Vidyananda Gurukula was established at Kukunoor on 27th July 1922. In this school, students were imparted education in Indian culture, Vedic science, extreme ideas of nationalism, Gandhian thought and concepts of Satyagriha. They were also taught the art of handling lathis. Library of the school was started with nationalist literature. Teachers and students of the school set up libraries and bhajan mandalis in different parts of the state to spread the spirit of nationalism.

A national school called Madarasa-i-Hamdard was established in Raichur in 1920 by Pandit Taranath.[84] Pandit Taranath was a leading nationalist of Hyderabad Karnataka. He also played a pioneering role in teaching the students the virtues of strikes and satyagriha as political weapons. One of the objectives of this school was to unite Hindus and Muslims.[85] Influenced by Taranath, Sirur Veerbhadrappa established a national school- Vishwantha National School-at Aador in 1932.[86] In the same year a national school for Harijans was opened by the followers of Taranath at Rajur.[87]

National schools of Hyderabad Karnataka produced thousands of volunteers for satyagriha aimed at liberation of the state from the oppressive rule of Nizam.[88] Many outstanding freedom fighters of Hyderabad Karnataka were the product of these national schools. Students of these nationals school look a leading part in many movements-Vande Matram movement, Join-Union movement and Bader movement, for integration of the Nizam State into Union of India.[89]

The National University at Adyar, Madras

The National University at Adyar was founded in 1918 by Annie Besant. In 1930 the school had about 100 pupils and 16 teachers.[90] Its aim was to provide national education based on ancient Indian system of education. The students lived in a small village of ten cottages. The life at school had several note-worthy features such as simplicity in living conditions, outdoor teaching, and close relationship between teacher and the taught.[91] Both, severe discipline and physical punishments was discouraged. Up to the eighth standard, vernacular was the medium of instruction. One period each day was given to nature study. Interestingly, boys were encouraged to keep pets so as to develop fondness for animals. Curriculum also included weaving, dying and carpentry so on to make students self sufficient. Students were encouraged to respect all religions. The daily morning prayers included a Sanskrit prayer, A Parsi prayer, a Muslim Prayers and a Buddhist prayer along with singing of Vande Matram.[92]

The Bihar Vidyapeeth

The Bihar Vidyapeeth, formally opened by Mahatma Gandhi on February 6, 1921, was one of the memorials of Non Cooperative Movement.[93] Under the auspices of the Vidyapeeth about one hundred primary level national schools and fifty secondary level national schools were started. One full fledged national college-Shri Rashtriya Mahavidyala, Patna was also opened. The Mahavidyalaya was started with the declared objective of "providing instruction to the students who were withdrawing from government aided and government controlled institutions and with a view to provide education on sound national lines to the young men of the province to prepare them for services to the country as also to give them instruction of a practical nature to enable them to earn their livelihood."[94]

Vidyapeeth prescribed syllabus for the college and conducted the examinations. Medium of instruction was Hindustani but other languages were also encouraged. Subjects taught under the Vidyapeeth were History, Philosophy, Economic, Hindi, Urdu and Bengali composition. A student had to take up one subject besides his own vernacular. There were 12 papers in each subject and course of study was of duration of 3 years.

The college had a first grade chemical laboratory while physics laboratory was in the making in July 1926. Annual reports of Vidyapeeth mention that many of the apparatus required for the laboratories were prepared in college workshop itself. College also had a good library. The college did not charge any fee for tuitions and lodging. Teachers employed here were very dedicated; they worked at very low salaries and made considerable personal sacrifice. Babu Rajendra Prasad who later became the first President of free India, also taught here for some time. Several ex-students of the Vidyapeeth started national schools. In a convocation address on March 20, 1926, C.Rajgopalachari compared the Vidyapeeth with other better privileged institutions in following words: " our Vidyapeeth in like a rag, as compared with the silken robes of royalty. But ours is a yellow rag that serves its purpose and clothes the naked *Sanyasi*, it is clean and is dear to us. No wonder that a few faithful toilers have struggled to build up and to keep up the Vidyapeeth inspite of falling off all around".[95]

The Gujrat Vidyapeeth

Gujrat Vidyapeeth was estabilished on December 16, 1920 in response to a resolution passed in the fourth session of the Gujrat Political Conference regarding the spread of national education.[96] Under the auspices of this Vidyapeeth colleges were started at Ahemdabad, Bombay and Surat. Besides these three colleges, the following schools and institutions also began functioning:

1. Puratatva Mandir – School for the study of oriental philosophy.
2. Adhyapan Mandir – A teacher training college.
3. Vinay Mandirs – 41 High schools.
4. Kumar Mandirs– 54 Primary schools.
5. Kumari Mandirs– 2 girl schools.
6. Three schools for untouchables.
7. One night school.[97]

The objectives of Gujrat Vidyapeeth were similar to those of Tilak Mahrastra Vidyapeeth. Important place was given to khadi in the course of education and other educational activities were correlated with it. Removal of untouchability and unity of people belonging to different faiths were long term objectives of the educational programmes of the Vidyapeeth. The Gujrat Vidyapeeth, like the national education movement in general, strived for best of the East and the West in its curriculum.[98]

Kashi Vidyapeeth

During the Non-Cooperation movement (1920-22), 137 national education institutions had been set up by July 1921 in the United Provinces only. Of these institutions the Kashi Vidyapeeth was most prominent.[99] Kashi Vidyapeeth was the result of almost single handed efforts of Shiv Prasad Gupta of Banaras, a member of the royal family of Banaras. He was deeply affected by the nationalist currents since childhood and had a deep desire to contribute to the national education movement. This desire was further deepened when he undertook the visit to western countries and Japan in 1913-1914. The educational systems which he witnessed abroad inspired him to take up education through mother tongue and free from foreign control. After returning to India he started correspondence in this regard with several leaders who were working in the field of education.[100] Meanwhile, Non-Cooperation movement created suitable conditions for the starting of new national education institutions. Shiv Prasad Gupta met Mahatma Gandhi in 1920 and discussed the establishment of a university in Kashi (Banaras). Shiv Prasad promised to donate ten lakh rupees towards this object. Gandhiji together with Shiv Prasad persuaded Dr. Bhagwan Das, a prominent scholar, to take up this work.[101]

As a result, the Kashi Vidyapeeth was established on *Basant Panchami*, 10th February 1921. Mahatma Gandhi inaugurated it and the inaugural ceremony was attended a by large gathering of nationalist leaders including Jawahar Lal Nehru, Abul Kalam Ajad, Motilal Nehru and Jamna Lal Bajaj.

The declared objectives of Kashi Vidyapeeth were as following: cultivation and development of Indian culture; compositeness of diverse people residing in India; service of mankind and universal brotherhood along with independence and love for the nation;

promotion and popularisation of ancient knowledge; and imparting of the highest level of education through the Hindi in Devnagari script.[102] Dr. Bhagwan Das was appointed the President, Chancellor as well as Acharya of the Vidyapeeth. Many teachers with patriotic bent of mind devoted their life to the Vidyapeeth such as Acharya Birpal Singh, Acharya Navendra Dev, Acharya Kripalani and also the great Hindi writer Premchand. Initially, Vidyapeeth taught upto the B.A. level. The curriculum covered four years. Devanagari Hindi was the medium of education. First year of the curriculum was dedicated to the study of Hindi and English. Specialization could be achieved in subjects such as Hindi literature, Mathematics and Philosophy (both Western and Eastern). The curriculum was further revised and enriched after 'National Education Conference' (1923) convened at Vidyapeeth gave its report.[103] In all courses of studies, nationalistic view point was emphasized wherever possible. Teachers and students of the Vidyapeeth lived in a homely atmosphere. They interacted freely among themselves on the basis of mutual respect and love. No fees were charged from the students till 1947. Deserving students were given scholarships.

Activities of the Vidyapeeth were not confined to academic field only. The students and the teachers of the Vidyapeeth have a glorious record of participation in the freedom struggle. During Non-Cooperation movement, students and teaches of Vidyapeeth led by Acharya Narendra Dev, toured the country side popularising the ideals of national movement. Many senior teachers of the Vidyapeeth were arrested when they issued the appeal to boycott the visit of Prince of Wales in December 1922. Banaras Hindu University, on the other hand, organized a reception in the honor of Prince of Wales. Teachers and students of Vidyapeeth openly participated in Civil Disobedience movement. As a reaction, the Government declared the Vidyapeeth unlawful during the period from February 1932 to February 1934. Police occupied the premises of the Vidyapeeth during this period. From 1934 to 1940, education and fight for independence were carried on simultaneously. In 1937, many teachers of Vidyapeeth such as Babu Sampurnanand, Acharya Narendra Dev, Acharya Birbal and Professor Ram Sharma were elected to the Assembly. Academic activities were once again disrupted in 1940 when Mahatma Gandhi launched Individual Satyagraha. After the launching of Quit India movement in 1942, police again occupied the Vidyapeeth premises. Vidyapeeth was declared unlawful again till 1944. Academic activities could only resume in 1945.

Prem Mahavidyalaya, Mathura

Prem Mahavidyalaya or the 'Free Industrial and Arts National College', Vrindaban, was established by Raja Mahaendra Pratap on 24th May 1909.[104]

Raja Mahaendra Pratap conceived the idea of a technical institution on national lincs after visiting the western countries. The industrial progress attained by the West as a result of solid foundations in technical education there, made Raja realize the incompleteness of education provided by the British Government in India. The Prem Mahavidyalaya as 'India's first free technical institution'[105] was born with the blessings of Madan Mohan Malviya. The occasion of inauguration of the institution was publicised by Raja as the birth of his son Raja Mahendra Pratap gave five villages from his Jamindari with a net income of Rs. 33,000 per monthly to the institution. The institution had elaborate arrangements for teaching smithy, carpentry, tailoring, sculpturing, carpet weaving, short hand and type writing, mechanical engineering, textiles, printing press and ceramics.[106] Besides these subjects of technical nature, general subjects such as Hindi, English, Political Science and Economics was also taught. Raja himself used to take the English classes.[107] The teachers employed in the institution were committed and dedicated. The institution played an important role in inculcating national consciousness in and around Vrindavan. Students and teachers of the Mahavidyalaya actively participated in political movements. The British Govenemnt tried to sieze Prem Mahavidyalaya in 1921 but could not be successful due to intervention by Sir Tej Bahadur Sapru. But in 1932, Mathura District administration declared the Prem Mahavidyalaya as threat to public peace and institution remained closed from 1932 to 1937.[108]

Gurukula Kangri, Hardwar

Origins of Gurukula Kangri lie in the dissatisfaction within a section of Arya Samajis regarding the establishement of D.A.V. College. This group was unhappy with D.A.V. institutions' neglect of Sanskrit, Vedic learning and other essential texts. As mentioned earlier too, D.A.V. was not entirely independent of the British education department's control. The radical step of remaining completely independent of the Government education system was achieved by Arya Samajis who were in favour of a Gurukula on Vedic lines. This group led by Mahatma Munshi Ram (later became known as Swami Shraddhanand) founded Gurukula in 1902.

Objectives behind the establishment of Gurukula were laid down by the Arya Pratinidhi Sabha in December 1900[109]:

1. *Vedas* are the highest form of knowledge. Without their proper study, knowledge is incomplete. To study the *Vedas* Gurukula is a necessity.
2. It is patriotic to study the Sanskrit. India's education system cannot be called national unless her schools teach the Sanskrit.
3. We must study modern scientific knowledge, like the Europeans do, in our vernaculars (i.e. not in English).
4. Examination system as laid by official education system is a hindrance to real learning. Gurukula shall not follow the official examination pattern.
5. Education at Gurukula shall be free.
6. Gurukula shall take up researches in Indology to counter the European bias.
7. Celibacy of the students is a necessary condition for learning.
8. Separate education for boys and girl students.

9. Total time for education must be 18 years, out of which 12 years should be for school education and rest 6 years for higher education in college. English should be taught from 9th class onwards.

According to Swami Shraddhanand, the declared aims of the Gurukulaa were manifold as well as liberal. They included rejuvenating ancient ideals like *Brahmacharya*. Indian philosophy and literature was to be resuscitated through researches and enriched further by assimilable elements of western thought. The Gurukula sought to produce good citizens as well as preachers of the Vedic religion. The highest ideal of Gurukula education was to benefit the humanity by re-establishing the best elements of Vedic thought and civilization. But this could be possible only when the Vedic institutions were moulded and shaped to suit the altered environment of modern times.[110] These objectives, as summed up by Swami Shraddhanand, clearly convey that the concept of education of Gurukula was not conservative but progressive and flexible.

The response of Gurukula to the British education policy impressed even Ramsay Macdonald, the former Prime Minister of England. After visiting the Gurukula he observed that "every one in India is unhappy regarding results of that (Macaulay's) Minute, but no one, so for as I have yet seen, save the founders of the Gurukula, has translated this unhappiness into a experiment."[111]

The Gururkula had its humble origins in the form of a Vedic Pathsala at Gujranwala in 1900. In 1902, the institution was transferred to village Kangri near Haridwar on the lands donated by Munhsi Amar Singh. From here onwards, its name became Gururkula Kangri. Initially the Gurukula was run in hutments made up of dry fodder. The living conditions became better gradually. The premises of the Gurukula was relocated permanently in Kanakhal near Haridwar after Kangri faced heavy floods in 1928.[112]

Students' daily regime at the Gurukula was very orderly and strict. Pupils had to get up at 4:30 in the morning, perform morning prayers, daily bath in Ganga and perform regular physical exercises. After that they went to school for studies, had lunch and again went to study after a break. Evening was the time for games and physical exercises. Students then again studied till nine in the evening and then went to bed. All students lived together without any caste or class distinction. In the initial years, students could not visit their homes during vacations. The effect of this disciplined yet cheerful regime on students can be best described in the words of Lord Maston, the Governor of United Provinces : "here we have abandon of ascetics devoted to their duty and working in the wilderness following the tradition of the ancient *rishis* combined with the most modern scientific methods and a set of strong physique; and obedient, loyal, truthful and develop, extraordinarily happy and extraordinarily well fed students."[113]

Till 1935, the Gurukula at Kangri had three college. The College of Divinity focused on study of Vedic literature along with comparative study of religions. The Arts College taught literature, Indian philosophy, history, chemistry and economics. Medical College followed the Ayurvedic school of medicine. But necessary additions were derived from the Allopathic system, particularly the surgery, in a scheme crafted by Kaviraj Gannath Sen. In 1935, a pharmacy for manufacturing medicines was added. For all the courses Hindi was the medium of studies. English was taught as secondary language. The greatest focus of Gurukula studies was on character building through religion. Above all, special care was taken to maintain a truly national environment. In this task too, religion was used to promote national feelings.[114] Students of the Gurukula were made to feel that they were heirs to a great and ancient civilization. The teaching of Hindu ethics, religion, traditions and metaphysics strengthened this feeling.[115] Vedic education thus indirectly promoted national feelings. About the nationalist credentials of the Gurukula, Gandhiji declared unambiguously:

"Gurukula is a truly national, self governing and self governed institute."[116]

A large number of Gurukulas based on the model of Gurukula Kangri were founded and maintained by the Arya samaj. Important among such Gurukulas were situated at Indraprastha (Delhi), Vrindaban, Baidyanath Dham (Bihar), Hoshangabad (Central Provinces), Daily (Meerut), Chittor, Sikandrabad (U.P.), Jwalapur (Near Haridwar), Dehradun (Kanya Gurukula), Gujranwala, Farrukhabad, Badayun, Potuhar, Mathura, Deolali, Rawalpindi, Derabuddhu (Multan), and Narsinghpur (Central Provinces).[117] In all these institutions clothing, boarding, books and tuition were provided free of cost.

Jamia Millia Islamia

Jamia Millia Islamia was founded at Aligarh on 29th October 1920 during the Khilafat and Non-cooperation movement in response to Gandhiji's call to boycott the Government supported educational institutions. It was also a revolt against the anglophile environment at Aligarh University. English professors, English content in curriculum and English ideals and lifestyle at Aligarh inspired a contemporary poet to sarcastically remark:

"Paida hua the app to Lundun ke wastey

Badqismati se baap ko Hindi bana diya"

(You were born for London, but misfortune made your father an Indian)[118]

Among those who responded to Gandhiji's call in support of national education were Shaikul Hind Maulana Mahamud Hasan, Maulana Mohammad Ali, Hakim Ajmal Khan, Dr. Mukhtar Ahmad Ansari, Abdul Majeed Khwaja and Dr. Jakir Husain.[119] These eminent personalities, along with others founded the Jamia Millia Islamia and nurtured it. While inviting the students of Aligarh for non-cooperation and exerting them to set up a national institution, Gandhiji compared the move with building a new house or planting a tree. For this purpose, the place needed to be "first dug up and levelled". It was "therefore, necessary to remove the British and their system of education so that we may manage our education according to our wishes and national needs."[120] Hakim Ajmal Khan was the first Chancellor of Jamia while Maulana Mohammad Ali became the first Vice-Chancellor. For the first five years of its existence, Jamia functioned in Aligarh. For administrative reasons it was shifted from Aligarh to Delhi in 1925.

Like the other national institutions of the time, Jamia too had to struggle hard to continue functioning because of financial difficulties. It is said that in its infancy, Jamia's only definite resources were its "unlimited dreams, fervent determination and enthusiastic nationalism."[121] In keeping with the highest ideals of national education, Jamia refused to seek recognition at the hands of the Government.

The declared objectives of Jamia reflected the general spirit of the national education. The education of youths was to be based on their cultural heritage but that did not reject useful elements of other cultures. It sought to inculcate the spirit of service, of tolerance, of self control and self respect. Jamia aimed at building character as well as overall personality of the growing minds. Its education aimed at preparing the coming generations to meet the future needs of the nation. [122]

After the initial difficulties, Jamia progressed steadily. Later on, it adopted the Basic Education of Mahatma Gandhi for its elementary classes. Jamia never hesitated to adopt the latest teaching methods and courses. By the time of independence, Jaimia had grown to have a residential University College imparting higher education in many branches of learning, a residential High School, a centre for primary and adult education, Jamia Chemical Industries, Urdu Academy, a monthly magazine in Urdu, and a book depot with largest stock of Urdu books in India.[123] Jamia's academic excellence invited students from all parts of India and also from abroad.

Notes and References

1 Sumit Sarkar, *The Swadeshi Movement in Bengal*, 1903-1908, New Delhi, 1983, p. 157.

2 B. PattabhiSitaramayya, *History of Indian National Congress*, Vol. I (1885-1935), Bombay, 1969, p. 85.

3 Benoy Kr. Sarkar, *Education for Industrialisation*, Calcutta, 1946, p. 245.

4 Home public A, August 1906, No. 269.

5 Sumit Sarkar, op. cit., pp. 160-161.

6 *The Telegraph*, October 25, 1905, cited in Haridas Mukherjee and Uma Mukerjee, *Origins Of National Education Movement*, Calcutta, 1957, p. 26.

7 Haridas Mukarjee and Uma Mukherjee, op. cit., pp. 29-30.

8 Sumit Sarkar, op. cit., p. 162.

9 Haridas Mukherjee and Uma Mukherjee, op. cit., p. 37.

10 Ibid.

11 *N.C.E. Bengal, A History and Homage*, Calcutta, 1956, p. 5.

12 Home Political A, February 1908, pp. 102-103.

13 Sumit Sarkar, op. cit., p. 166. But Haridas Mukherjee and Uma Mukherjee mention only two stages – intermediate and secondary.

14 Ibid.

15 See Appendix IV.

16 *N.C.E. Bengal, A History and Homage*, op.cit., pp. 69-70.

17 Haridas Mukharjee and Uma Mukaharjee, op. cit. p. 63.

18 Ibid.

19 Sumit Sarkar, op. cit., p. 168.

20 *N.C.E. Bengal, A History and Homage*, op. cit., p. 12.

21 Haridas Mukherjee and Uma Mukherjee, op. cit., pp. 122-123.

22 Ibid., p. 125.

23 Home Political A, March 1909, Nos. 10-11.

24 Home Political. A March 1911, No. 5.

25 Home Pol. A, March 1909, Nos.10-11.

26 Ibid.

27 Home Pol . A, March 1911, No. 6.

28 Ibid.

29 Op. cit., Home Pol. A, June 1912, No. 14.

30 Home Pol. B, November 1914, No. 235.

31 Ibid.

32 Sumit Sarkar, op. cit ., p. 179.

33 *Dawn* of January, May 1910 mentions that out of 650 students studying in 15 Pathshalas in Bakar Ganj district about 177 were Namsudras and 50 were Muslims, cited in Ibid., p. 180.

34 Ibid.

35 Ibid., p. 181.

36 Data mentioned in table has been compiled from *N.C.E. Bengal, A History and Homage,* op.cit., p. 17 and Haridas Mukherjee and Uma Mukherjee , op. cit., p. 114.

37 *N.C. E. Bengal,* op. cit., p. 29.

38 Ibid., p. 19.

39 Ibid.

40 William J. McKee, *New Schools for Young India*, Chapal Hill, 1930, p. 85.

41 *Manthan*, March 1985, p. 67.

42 Syed Nurullah and J.P. Naik, *History of Education in India*, Calcutta, 1955, p. 738.

43 K.K. Chaudhary, *Maharashtra and Indian Freedom Struggle*, Bombay, 1985, p. 72.

44 P.S. Apte (ed.), *Maharashtrantil Rastriya Shikshanaya Itihasa*, Poona, 1958, p. 33.

45 Malati G. Apte, *The Growth of National Education in India with special Reference to Maharashtra*, University of Bombay, 1953, pp.163-166.

46 Home Pol A, June 1910, 41.

47 Ibid.

48 Malati G. Apte, op. cit., pp. 168-169.

49 Ibid.

50 Ibid. p. 175.

51 Haridas Mukherjee and Uma Mukherjee, op. cit., p. 130.

52 Ibid., p. 131.

53 Home Pol. A, June 1910, Nos. 28-41.

54 Ibid.

55 *Maharastrantil Rastriya Shikshanacha Itihas*, op. cit., pp. 3-9.

56 *Dawn Magazine* (July, 1909) cited in Haridas and Uma Mukherjee, op.cit., p. 132.

57 Malti .G. Apte, pp. 234-35.

58 Ibid., p. 207.

59 *Maharastranteel Rastriya Shiksanacha Itihas*, op.cit., p. 140.

60 Ibid., p. 142.

61 Ibid., p. 155.

62 *University of Bombay (1857-1957): Centenary Souvenir*, Bombay, 1957, pp. 100-101.

63 *Maharastranteel Rastriya Shiksanaya Itihas*, op.cit., p. 204.

64 Ibid., p. 221 and Malti G. Apte. op. cit., pp. 242-244.

65 *Maharastranteel Rastriya Shiksanaya Itihas*, op. cit., p. 129.

66 Ibid., pp. 189-191.

67 Ibid., pp. 227-230.

68 Malati. G. Apte. op. cit., pp. 227-230.

69 Ibid., 269.

70 Ibid., pp. 301-303.

71 *Maharastranteel Rastriya Shiksanaya Itihas*, op. cit., p. 241 and Malati G. Apte, pp. 238-41.

72 *Maharastranteel Rastriya Shiksanaya Itihas*, op. cit., p. 249 and Malati G. Apte, pp. 289-91.

73 Malati G. Apte, op. cit., pp. 204-206.

74 Ibid., p. 214.

75 Y. Vaikuntham, *Education and Social Change in South India: Andhra 1880-1920,* Madras, 1982, p. 105.

76 Ibid.

77 Ibid.

78 *Indian Review*, March 1914, p. 197.

79 Ibid.

80 Haridas Mukherji and Uma Mukherjee, op., cit. p. 134.

81 Indian Review, March 1914, op., cit. p. 196.

82 B.C. Mahaleswarappa '*Swadeshi Spirit through National Schools in Hyderabad Karnatka,* , *PIHC*, 56th session, 1995, p. 557.

83 Ibid.

84 Ibid. p. 559.

85 Ibid.

86 Ibid.

87 Ibid.

88 Ibid.

89 Ibid., p. 560.

90 William, J. Mckee, op. cit., p. 94.

91 Ibid., p. 95.

92 *Modern Review,* July 1921, pp. 11-14.

93 *Modern Review,* July 1926, p. 25.

94 Ibid.

95 Ibid., p. 30.

96 Malati G. Apte, op.cit., p. 288.

97 Ibid.

98 Sir P.C. Ray while inaugurating the Gujrat University elaborated on this aspect of national education in particular context of Gandhiji. He said that "the immense faith that Mahatma Gandhi did have in the ancient forms of culture did not made him blind to the great changes that have actually occured through the flux of time" (*Indian Review*, March 1923, p. 202).

99 Sumit Sarkar, op. cit., p. 222.

100 *Manthan*, March 1985, p. 84.

101 *Kashi Vidyapeeth Heerak Jayanti Abhinandan Granth, Varanasi,* 1983, p. 417.

102 *Manthan*, March 1985.

103 The Convenor of the conference was Acharya Narendra Dev and it was presided by Dr. Bhagwan Das. It was attended by representatives of almost all the institutions imparting National Education in India. See the report of the Conference in Appendix V.

104 *Raja Mahendra Pratap Janma Shatabdi Smarika* edited by Braj Bihari Lal Sharma, Part I., Vrindavan, 1986, p. 59.

105 Ibid., Part II, p. 21.

106 Ibid.

107 Ibid ., Part IV, p. 19.

108 Ibid., Part I, p. 60.

109 Satyaketu Vidyalankar, *Arya Samaj Ka Itihas*, Vol. III, 1983, pp. 177-178.

110 Lala Lajpat Rai, *A History of Arya Samaj*, Bombay, 1967, p. 144.

111 *Gurukula Kangri Viswa Vidyalaya Diamond Jubilee*, Haridwar, 1960, p. 14.

112 *Manthan*, June 1985, p. 14.

113 *Gurukulaa Kangri Viswavidyalaya*, op. cit., p. 13.

114 *Modern Raview*, October 1926, pp. 298-301.

115 Dhan Pati Pandey, *The Arya Samaj and Indian Nationalism*, Delhi, 1972, pp. 105-106.

116 *Modern Review*, October 1926, pp. 298-301.

117 Dhan Pati Pandey, op. cit., p. 106.

118 Cited by Mohammad Talib, "*Jamia Millia Islamia : Career of Azad Talim*" in Knowledge Power and Politics, ed., Mushirul Hasan p. 158.

119 *Prospectus of Jamia Millia Islamia*, 2004-05, p. 3.

120 Mohammad Talib, op. cit., p. 159.

121 Ibid., p. 160.

122 Nurullah and Naik, op. cit., p. 736.

123 Ibid., p. 737.

7

Pioneers of National Education in India

The credit for developing the idea of national education and undertaking bold experiments on the ground is shared by many remarkable individuals. Each of them had a unique notion of what constituted the national education and how it could be achieved on the ground. The diversity and the intensity of thought on the subject of national education points to the richness of the concept. It also signifies the importance of the question of national education in the contemporary nationalist discourse. Seen in a holistic manner, the difference or the variation among the opinions of the ideologues is mainly concerned with the definition and the means by which national education programme could be implemented. But at the same time, there was a tacit consensus on the broad parameters of the national education. Pioneers of national education had a common goal; to evolve a system of education along the national lines, under the national control and serving the national interests. They all agreed that education system imposed by British in India promoted colonial interests and hence it went against the national requirements. The official system must be replaced with an alternative education system serving the Indian national interests. All of them also agreed that knowledge is not static but living and growing. Hence the national education must include a judicious mix of the ancient Indian educational ideals and the modern education of the West including the teaching of science and technology. Thus national education movement became an essential aspect of the national reconstruction as well as an important ingredient of the Indian freedom struggle.

A brief account of the main ideologies of the national education movement is being given here.

Akshoy Kumar Dutt (1820-86)

Akshoy Kumar Dutt has the distinction of being the first Indian to evolve a scheme of national education.[1] Born on 13th July 1820, in district Nadia in Bengal, he received his early education in a Christian school.[2] Besides Bengali, Sanskrit and English, he had the knowledge of Greek, Latin, Habrew and Greek. He was nominated as a member of Tattva Bodhini Sabha in 1839. Later, Akshoy Kumar Dutt became the editor of Tattvabodhinini Patrika and serialized articles on diverse facets of the Indian culture and history. He also wrote on botany, geology, geography, theology and philosophy as well as socio-economic problems of the day. He joined Brahmo Samaj on 21st December 1843 and questioned the infallibility of Vedas.[3]

Although a versatile genius, Akshoy Kumar's most foresighted, original and brilliant ideas came up in the field of education. Akshoy held out a well reasoned out plan for the adoption of Bengali as the medium of instruction in all stages of learning. He clearly saw the impossibility of educating the millions of Indians through English and adduced several reasons in favour of the vernacular. "First, knowledge gained through English was coterie knowledge; the rest of the country derived no benefit from it. Secondly, it fostered the spirit of xenophilia, with the resultant hatred of one's own culture, country and people. Thirdly, the cost of education through English was four times heavier than that conducted through the vernaculars. Fourthly, in reply to the objection that there were no good text books in Bengali it might be said that the works of such masters as Bacon, Locke, Newton, Laplace and Humboltz could be translated into the native tongue."[4] The imaginative ingenuity of Akshoy Kumar Dutt on the question of education is manifested best in his work *Dharamaniti* in which he explained his comprehensive scheme of education, starting from the elementary to the higher stages. Some of the important points of this scheme are as under.[5]

- Provision for compulsory education till the age of 15 (starting from the age of two).
- For the majority of students, there should be provision for technical and vocational education, instead of theoretical university education.
- Schools of technology as well as of agriculture should be established.
- Medium of English is a vehicle of denationalization and promotes distaste for culture, language and people of the country.
- Physical training of children should never be neglected.
- Textbooks on history should not glorify the life and careers of despots, war-maniacs and enemies of humanity such as Caesar, Alexander and Napoleon. 'Characters of such conquerors are to be depicted in such a way as to create an aversion to war, enviousness and greediness in the minds of the readers.'
- Relative importance of various subjects, in the order of their importance, is as follows: arithmetic, algebra, trigonometry, geography, natural history, chemistry, anatomy, physiology, physics, history, economics, psychology, principles of religion, theology, literature, painting and other arts.

Rabindra Nath Tagore (1861-1941)

Early writings of Rabindra Nath Tagore leave no doubt that he believed in the national regeneration through self-reliance and service to the nation.[6] He also expressed his deep distrust of the motives of the British rulers.[7] These ideas are reflected in his educational philosophy as well. He was of the opinion that if education is placed in the Government's hands, it will use that education to fulfil its own interests. Tagore emphasised, "we can impart education according to our desire only if we take education in our own hands."[8]

Tagore's conception of the ideal education is brought out in his first writing specifically dealing with education - '*Siksar Herpher*'

– "Our Education and its Incongruities" (1893). In this essay he pointed out the defects of the existing educational practices. This essay eloquently pleaded for a system of education conducted in congenial surroundings and joyful spirit. It also made a case for a realistic education which would adequately serve the fundamental needs of India. The essay formulated Tagore's conception of the ultimate aim of education as the all round development of an individual.[9]

Mother tongue was an important ingredient of Tagore's scheme of education. According to Tagore, foreign language places a big obstacle before the power of expression and the flowering of originality. He felt that a common medium of mother-tongue could remove the class barriers, and rural-urban divide. Moreover, the science could not be accessible to general population unless scientific education was imparted through the mother tongue.[10]

Tagore participated actively in the movement for national education in Bengal. He addressed a number of meetings of students during the Swadeshi movement. In these speeches he enthusiastically advocated the principle of educational self-determination. He exhorted the students to leave the Government schools and join the national schools. He also praised the student community for their self-sacrifice for the cause of nationalism. He was one of the founder members of the National Council of Education (N.C.E.), Bengal.

Tagore enunciated his own conception of national education in an article-*Siksa-Samsya*– "The Problem of Education" (1906). National education, Tagore wrote, evolves through the "accumulated endeavours and cherished ideals and traditions of the people of the land."[11] Thus Tagore considered national education to be organically linked with the life of a nation. To formulate any scheme of national education it was necessary to identify the ideals and traditions mentioned above. According to Tagore, the Gurukula system of education conducted in the forests of ancient India has inspired the educational practice through the centuries. So the ideal institutions of the national education should follow that system. At the same time he cautioned that the ancient education system cannot be and should not be imitated blindly. Such a system must include the European sciences as subjects of study. But at the same time, the foreign ideals, morals and values need to be forsaken and they should be replaced with indigenous ideals, traditions and culture. It is interesting to note that Tagore, though being a founder member of N.C.E., did not agree with the system of education and principles adopted by the National Council. He considered the N.C.E. to be working on foreign model. He expressed his disagreement: "no truly national system of education in India could be based on any imitation of a foreign model."[12]

As regards the Gurukul or the Ashram ideal, Tagore was of the opinion that teacher's home away from cacophony of the civilization provides the ideal environment for education. Nature was the key resource of his pedagogic strategy. Nature was the best teacher. It awakened the creative powers of the child as well as his sense of freedom. Tagore concluded, "learning to see fire, air, water, land, and the whole universe as pervaded by a universal consciousness is true education."[13] But Tagore admitted that such ideal schools cannot be expected to spring up in large numbers in modern conditions. One single ideal institution will be sufficient to inspire and guide the national education movement. Tagore experimented with his concept of education at Santinikatan Ashram at Bolpur in Bengal. Later he followed it up with a university named Vishva Bharati.

Vivekananda (1863-1902)

Vivekananda considered national education as a vital tool for national regeneration. He was convinced that if India is to rise again, it will have to take education in its own hands.[14] Main challenge for education in India, according to him, was to alleviate the oppressive physical and social conditions as well as moral degradation of Indian people. The task of social, moral and material reconstruction could be accomplished only if Indian youth internalises the philosophy of Vedanta along with western science. Vivekananda regarded education 'as the manifestation of the perfection already in man'. It is not synonymous with information. In his opinion, the British education system focussed on imparting information (by cramming) and awarding degrees on the basis of the capacity to recall information. Such kind of education being foreign in content was weakening students mentally and physically. Colonial education, according to him, teaches "that we are nobodies, seldom are we given to understand that great men were ever born in our country. Nothing positive has been taught to us. We do not even know how to use our hands and feel. We master all the facts and figures concerning the ancestors of the English, but we are sadly unmindful but about our own. We have learnt only weakness."[15]

Grave implications of foreign control over education led Vivekananda to realize the urgent necessity of national control over education. He exhorted the fellow Indians that "we must have a hold on the spiritual and secular education of the nation, you must dream it, you mush talk it, you must think and your must work it out, till then there is no salvation for the race."[16]

Vivekananda's ideas on national education can be summarised as following:

- Education is the training of mind. It is life building, man making and character.
- Education must help the common mass of people to equip themselves in the struggle for life.
- Education must provide means for developing one's physical and moral strength.
- Religion is the core of education.
- Education should inspire every Indian to take pride in his glorious heritage. At the same time he should be able to imbibe the positive values in the western knowledge system, particularly the values of science and technology.[17]

Vivekananda was the pioneer in advocating the use of education to lift the masses. He considered the lack of education as the main cause of rampant poverty in India. According to him, education was the key to political and social progress.

V.S. Chiplunkar (1850-1882)

Vishnu Shastri Chiplunkar was the first in Maharastra to create the suitable conditions for the national education movement. Born in Poona in 1850, he studied under Professor William Wordsworth in Deccan College. After finishing his B.A. Chiplunkar became a teacher in Poona High School in 1873. At the age of twenty-four in 1874, he started *Nibandhamala*- a periodical in Marathi. In the very first essay of the *Nibandhmala* he pointed out the following disadvantages of the foreign domination: "foreign domination has resulted in all round deterioration, politically, economically and socially; our learning is superficial and we have lost our faith in religion. We have lost the sense of initiative whether in individual or public life."[18] In the same essay he gave an indirect hint that the discontent of the people might lead to revolution. In January 1880, he founded *Kavyetihasa Sangraha*, a periodical designed to rediscover and publish the classics of Sanskrit and Marathi poetry. In the same year he founded the *Chitrashala Press* to publish nationalist works.[19] His writings have had a decisive influence on modern marathi prose style.

In 1872, Chiplunkar wrote that Government education made students unpatriotic and destroyed their moral fibre.[20] In 1879 he resigned from the Government service, pleading "supreme disgust of the drudgery of a Government school life" as the final cause of the break.[21] Shortly afterwards he established a new high school. But the Government aid for his school was minuscule though mission schools received aid in abundance. Chiplunkar resolved to open a new school entirely independent of the Government. He called upon teachers with patriotic fervours willing to work for minimal pay. Chiplunkar attracted young graduates including Tilak, M.B.Namjoshi, and V.S.Apte to join him. Together they opened the 'New English School[22] in January 1880. The school drew praise from even the British officials. Chiplunkar and his associates attacked Government schools for their emphasis on English language and culture. Chiplunkar also condemned the lack of moral training in Government schools and the poor moral examples set by teachers. Teachers of the New English School exhorted students to use their education for patriotic public service. This school was the first successful high school without the aid of the Government. Chiplunkar set an early example to be followed later by Vijapurkar during the movement for national education.

V. G. Vijapurkar (1863-1926)

The ground prepared by V.S. Chiplunkar in Maharastra was used by V.G. Vijapurkar to plant the first sapling of national education in the form of Samartha Vidyalaya. Vijapurkar was born on 26th August 1863 in a lower middle class family. Though he was able to pass matriculation examination only in his second attempt but he was placed fourth in the Bombay Presidency. He graduated with Sanskrit as a special subject from Deccan College, Poona. Here he was a favourite student of renowned orientalist Dr. R.G. Bhandarkar. He post graduated from Kolhapur College, again with Sanskrit as a special subject. He worked as a fellow and as a lecturer in several colleges till 1905. He was extremely simple and modest and believed in self less work and social service. Ideologically he was influenced by the bhakti saints of Maharastra, Kabir, Edmund Burke, *Gita* and *Bible*. He also condemned child marriage and bigamy.

Vijapurkar based his nationalism on the ideas of Swadeshi, boycott and national education. He believed that the struggle for independence must start with basic changes in the educational pattern, boycott of foreign goods and militant journalism. He was convinced that western education through the medium of English dissociated the students from Indian traditional life and culture. Moreover, education school should become the vehicle of industrial development. He suggested that primary and secondary school education should be oriented towards the development of the small scale industries.

Vijapurkar was expelled from the service in September 1905 from Raja Ram College, Kolhapur by Kolhapur Darbar for inciting the students to revolt.[23] To give shape to his ideas on national education, he started the Samartha Vidyalaya on 1st January 1906.[24] Samartha Vidyalaya was declared an illegal organization by British Government on 10th June 1910 and ceased to function after that.

Vijapurkar was a prolific writer and edited several magazines. He was the editor of *Granthamala*, a Marathi journal from 1894 to 1906. From 1906 to 1909 he was the editor of *Vishwavritta.* While editing *Vishwavritta* in January 1909, Kolhapur state prosecuted him on the charges of sedition and sentenced him to three year imprisonment. From 1898 to 1908, Vijapurkar edited *Samartha,* a semi-political weekly from Kolhapur. Apart from writing on social and political situation, he published articles on defects of then prevalent education and his ideas of reform in it. He was particularly concerned about the lack of national sentiments even in colleges such as Deccan College and Fergusson College. Foreign language, according to Vijapurkar, was a waste of energy. The official system of education, Vijapurkar was convinced, did not pay attention to the religious and moral education and behaviour.

Unfulfilled life long aspiration of Vijapurkar was to establish the Bhartiya Vishva-Vidyalaya.[25] Its blueprint was based on the best ideals of western education and ancient Hindu culture. Ancient ideal of *Dharma-Artha-Kama* was to be the goal of education provided here. It was to have 6 faculties: Vedic Pathshala; Ayurvedic Pathshala; faculty of *Sthapathya* (architecture); *Veda* and *Arthshastra* (engineering and economy); faculty of agriculture; faculty of fine arts; and faculty of languages (Indian and foreign both). Vijapurkar called for contributions in this grand project from all people and groups in society. The Vishva-Vidyalaya was to focus on higher education. For primary education, at least one school in each village was to be established. For secondary education, a network of secondary schools was to be established. Samartha Vidyalaya was to be one of many such secondary schools.

Swami Dayananda (1824-1883)

Arya Samaj as the pioneer of national education in North India has already been discussed. Swami Dayananda had the vision to see education as the vehicle of social reconstruction and national regeneration. One of the ten fundamental principles of Arya Samaj declares that 'ignorance must be dispelled and knowledge diffused'.

Dayananda's educational philosophy has been discussed in the second chapter of his book *Satyartha Prakash*. Salient points of his educational philosophy are : compulsory and free education in the state of *Brahmacharya* in *ashram* environment; equal opportunity of education for all persons irrespective of caste, creed, colour, sex or status; and state should take the responsibility to provide education.[26] Dayananda was not against the study of western sciences, he considered science and technology necessary for the national development.

Dayananda propounded an ambitious all round scheme of education. The full period of training for male students covered twenty-two years of studies in the following manner:

I. Phonetics, Panini's grammar, and Patanjali's *Mahabhasya* – 3 years

II. *Nirukta* of Pingala – 4 months

III. *Nirukta* of Yaska – 8 months

IV. *Manu Smriti*, *Ramayana* and portions of *Mahabharata*- 1 year

V. The six Darshaanas and ten *Upnishads*- 2 years

VI. All the four *Vedas* and *Brahmans* – 6 years

VII. Medical science – 4 years

VIII. Science of music, arithmetic, algebra, geography, geology and astronomy – 3 years

IX. Science of government- 2 years. [27]

In order to implement his ideas in education, Dayananda established six Ved-Pathsalas in United Provinces by 1873.[28] Through these Pathsalas, he attempted to revive the Vedic system of Gurukulas. Dayananda also made efforts to provide European technical knowledge to Indian students. In this connection he corresponded with Prof. G. Vize of Germany. He first planned to send Indian students to Germany for training. When it was found impossible to send students abroad, he made efforts to call teachers from abroad to provide training in India. He was also not against the English language but in his opinion, a student should first master his mother tongue and Sanskrit before he learns English or any other foreign language. After his death in 1883, his followers established Dayanand Anglo Vedic College and School. Another group of followers established Gurukul Kangri as the first national school.

Sister Nivedita (1867-1911)

Sister Nivedita, originally Margret Noble, was an Irishwoman by birth and a teacher by profession. While in England she had participated in the Irish movement, by being attached to 'Free Ireland', an Irish revolutionary organization. In November 1895, she attended some lectures by Swami Vivekananda which proved to be the turning point in her life. She was deeply impressed with Swami Vivekanand's ideas and accepted him as her Master. She came to India three years later and was initiated into *Brahmacharya* and renamed Nivedita. She realised that the primary need of the hour was to unshackle India from the bondage of colonialism. She began taking an interest in Indian politics and made a sharp defence of Indian culture. British Government constantly watched her movements and imposed censorship on her correspondence several times. After the death of her master in 1902 she resigned from the Rama Krishna Mission. For the rest of her life, she worked tirelessly for freedom and emancipation of India. Her memorial set up after her death in 1911 sums up her love for her adopted country: "Here Reposes Sister Nivedita, Who gave her All to India".

Sister Nivedita made a special contribution in the field of girl education on national lines. She set up Nivedita Girls School at Calcutta. Her efforts also paved the way for the foundation of a number of other educational institutions including a College run by the Ramakrishna Sarda Mission, Dakshineswar. Nivedita School was established in November 1898 with the encouragement of Swami Vivekananda and the blessing of Sarda Devi, the consort of Sri Ram Krishna. It provided instruction in English and Bengali languages. Handicrafts taught at the school had a special bearing on the revival of Indian industries. The object of incorporating handicrafts in the curriculum was to enable 'every pupil her own living, without leaving her home'.[29]

Nivedita tried vigorously to infuse love for India and its heritage in the minds of her pupils by taking them to museums and places of historical interest and sacrifice. She introduced spinning in her school and made the prohibited '*Vande Matram*', the daily morning prayer.[30] Her school also celebrated the release of Swadeshi leaders from imprisonment in January 1910.

Sister Nivedita was well aware of the short comings of British education system in India and its ill effects on national life. She was convinced that a nation cannot became great unless it has the right kind of education system.[31] Without a system of national education India will be doomed and forgotten.[32] She said that education must represent the aim and ends of a nation. Such an education must be integrated with the social life of that nation.[33] Moreover education must evoke the national sense among the peple.[34] Nivedita emphasized that the books for Indian students must be written by Indians themselves because a foreign mind cannot appreciate the indigenous sense of religion, aesthetics and customs.[35]

Sister Nivedita also wrote a book on the subject of national education- *Hints on National Education in India*. The book analyses the need and form of national education to be imparted in India. Essays in the book focus on:

- Need for developing a structure of education so that Indian life could be better understood.
- Importance of three elements of education: acquisition of knowledge, relation with the society and complete human development.
- Emphasis on training of the heart as well as the mind.
- Utility of education in national development and national ideals as different from western ideals and culture.
- Right kind of education for the Indian women.
- Methods of training of youth for social work particularly the manual training as part of the general education in India.

Sir Gooroo Dass Bannerjee (1844-1918)

Gooroo Dass Bannerjee received education at Hare School, Presidency College and Calcutta University. He had a brilliant academic and professional career. He post-graduated in Mathematics with University Gold Medal in 1864 and became Bachelor of Law in 1865. He started his professional career by becoming a lecturer of Law at Behrampur College and after same time became a High Court advocate. He qualified for the Doctor of Law in 1876 and became Tagore Law Professor in 1878. In 1879 he became the fellow of Calcutta University and in 1887 became a member of Bengal Legislative Council. He became a Judge of High Court in 1888. Sir Gooroo Dass Bannerjee has the distinction of becoming the first Indian Vice-Chancellor of a university. He worked as Vice-Chancellor of Calcutta University during the period 1890-1893. He was reappointed to the same post in 1902 but resigned after a year. He was also a member of the Indian University Commission appointed in 1902 by Lord

Curzon, and wrote his famous note of dissent. Gooroo Dass Bannerjee retired voluntarily from the post of High Court Judge in January 1904. In the same year he was knighted by the British Government. He was chosen as the President of 'Dawn Society'. He was also a member of National Council of Education. He also served on the Managing Committee of Benaras Hindu University (1915). He was actively associated with Indian Association for the Cultivation of Science (est. 1876). He was also a member of Literary Academy of Bengal, Sahitya Parishad and Bharat Dharma Mahamandal.

As the Vice-Chancellor of the Calcutta University, Gooroo Dass Banarjee tried to democratise the constitution of the University. He also attempted to introduce Bengali as a medium of instruction of higher studies. In both these attempts he was unsuccessful in the end. Failure of his sincere efforts to introduce minor changes in the university pattern made him deeply suspicious of the British intentions in education. He realized that only an alternative system of education on national lines could provide the solutions to Indian educational problems. With this conviction he joined National Council of Education as a member in 1906. He wrote profusely on the question of national education. His writings include, besides numerous articles in the press, two booklets on the subject – *A Few Thoughts on Education* (1904) and *The Educational Problem in India* (1914).

Gooroo Dass Bannerjee was of the view that introduction of western education definitely had some beneficial effects on India. But he was opposed to its introduction at the cost of traditional education of India.[36] He made it a point that English loving sections of Indian society must be made aware of the fact that English education system was harming the country. Gradually he became convinced that the system of education the British had introduced was a millstone round the nation's neck.[37]

In his second and third convocation addresses as the Vice-Chancellor of the Calcutta University, Gooroo Dass Bannerjee spelt out the disadvantage of English as medium of instruction: it overtaxes the energy of Indian student, cramps his thoughts and fails to awaken much original thinking.[38] Regarding the inadequate female education he pointed to the neglect of 'one of the highest useful functions of the university'.[39] He considered the lack of technical education as the main reason behind India becoming an importer of all manufactured commodities.[40]

Gooroo Dass Bannerjee gave sound rationale for the Indianisation of the universities. His 'note of dissent' in the report of University Commission boldly stated that "it is Indian youth who resorts to them, and that their requirements and difficulties, their habits and modes of life, and even their sentiments and susceptibilities should receive due consideration, and for that purpose educated Indians should be represented on the senate."[41] In his opinion, the time was ripe to Indianise the education system. Western system could not be expected to solve Indian problems because circumstances and requirements of the West are different from India. Policy makers being foreign to India and its problems, had an incorrect diagnosis. For this reason Indian control over education was mandatory.[42]

Gooroo Dass Bannerjee also dealt with the question whether the nature of education should be national or cosmopolitan. In his speech on the occasion of inauguration of the Bengal National College he said that assimilation of best foreign ideals is desirable in the later stages of mental growth. But in the earlier stages, such assimilations is not possible and any attempt to force it will retard instead of accelerating the mind.[43] In the same speech he defined the national education. He called it as an "education on national lines and attaching special importance to knowledge of the country, its literature, arts, history and its philosophy."[44]

Mahatma Munshi Ram (Swami Shraddhanand) (1856-1926)

Munshi Ram, popularly known as Swami Shraddhanand was born at Talwandi (District Jallundhar, Punjab). In 1882, he listened to Swami Dayananda and was drawn to him. He converted to Dayanand's views after he read the *Satyartha Prakash.* Shortly afterwards he joined Arya Samaj at Lahore. Due to his background as a successful lawyer, his hard working nature and sincerity of purpose, Munshi Ram soon became an important leader of Arya Samaj. He became President of Representative Assembly of the Arya Samaj in Punjab in 1889.

After the establishment of Dayanand Anglo Vedic School in 1886 in Lahore, ideological differences over the question of education cropped up in Arya Samaj. Munshi Ram belonged to the group which objected to 'Anglo' part of the education being imparted at the D.A.V. School. This group was in favour of purely Vedic education and wanted to open a gurukula instead of a college. When the Arya Samaj split in 1893 into the college section and the gurukula section, Munshi Ram was acknowledged as the leader of the later section. But before this, he had, in association with Lala Devraj of Jullundhar, ventured in the field of girl education. He had been shocked to find that missionary girl schools were blantanly promoting Christian teachings. He wrote articles under the title "Adhura Insaaf" in his paper *Sadharama Pracharaka* to make people conscious of the need of female education on the lines laid down in the *Vedas*. After much effort, Kanya Mahavidyalaya, Jullundhar, as a residential school for girls on Hindu ideals was founded.

After the split in Arya Samaj, Munshi Ram focused his energies on educational work. To vindicate his stand on education, he first left his law practice and then left home in 1899. He publicly vowed that he would not return till he had collected Rs.30,000, a sum considered sufficient to start a Gurukula. The Gurukula was first started in Gujranwala (Punjab) in 1900 but later shifted to Haridwar in 1902. Cynics had hoped that he would attract no student to such an outlandish scheme of education. Out of first four students who joined the institution in 1902 two were his own sons. To fully devote himself to the cause of Gurukula, he become the Governor Director of the institution and continued in that position till 1917.

Gurukula was a living embodiment of the ideas and ideals of Mahatma Munshi Ram. Many eminent visitors to the Gurukula called it as the only true national institution in the field of education. Gurukula did not remain confined to ancient ideals of education; it slowly picked many new and scientific approaches. It remained committed to the ideals of the national education and spurned the offer of financial assistance by the Government. Gurukula under Mahatma Munshi Ram experimented with the use of Hindi as medium of instruction even at the college level and in technical studies (Pharmacy).

Last phase of Mahtma Munshi Ram's life (became Shraddhanand an 12 April 1916, when he adopted *sanyas* or renunciation) was devoted to nationalistic activities in the political field. In 1918 he organised famine relief work in Garhwal. In 1919 he entered active politics against Rowlett Act. In the same year he became the first Hindu to be invited to address from Jami Masjid. In 1922, he became the president of Shuddhi Sabha (to welcome back converted Hindus in to the Hindu fold). Last years of his life were spent in the cause of uplift of depressed classes and reconversion to the Hindu fold before he was assassinated in Delhi by a Muslim fanatic in December 1926.

Satis Chandra Mukharjee (1865-1948)

Historians of national education movement and also the contemporary accounts leave no doubt that 'Satis Chandra was the soul of the national education movement'.[45] In the words of Benoy Kumar Sarkar, "From 14 November 1905 (the date of Ashutosh Choudhary's manifesto appealing for boycott of Calcutta University) to 14 August 1906 (the date of formal inauguration of Bengal National College) the history of the national education movement is virtually the biography of Satis Mukherjee".[46] He was greatly responsible for transforming the ideology of national education into a concrete programme. Rabindra Nath Tagore in a speech (February 1906) observed that "Satis Babu is one of the main props of the movement for national education which is now going on in the country; in fact it is he who has inspired it."[47] Even after the formation of National Council of Education (N.C.E.), Satis Chandra Mukherjee continued to play an important role in various capacities such as a Secretary of N.C.E; as a lecturer in National College (1906) and as its principal (succeeded Aurobindo Ghosh in 1907-1908). His journal *Dawn* established in 1897, is the richest source on ideology and factual details of national education movement.

Early in his life Satis Chandra Mukharjee was influenced by the positivism of August Comte but later he became an ardent admirer of the Hindu way of life. He was also fully alive to the necessity and the usefulness of all other systems, secular or religious, Eastern or Western. In his professional career, Satis Chandra Mukharjee was a lecturer of history though he was also registered as a barrister.

Like the other pioneers of national education, Satis Chandra Mukharjee also reached the conclusion that education reconstruction on the national lines cannot be successful unless it was outside the official control. He viewed the national education as a part of constructive Swadeshi. His correspondence with Sir George Birdwood[48] further clarified what an ideal education for India could be. Sir Birdwood, suggested that instruction of western science and technology should be retained and promoted. But literary, artistic, philosophical and religious education of India must never be surrendered rather it should be strengthened and extended, for the "first thing to do is to take the whole of your higher education into your hand".[49] The crux of Birdwood's suggestion was that if India was to regain her place in the world, she must control her own education.

Satis Chandra had become conscious of the serious deficiencies in the prevalent system of university education in India as early as 1893-94.[50] He was not content with a mere theoretical discussion of the educational problem. In an attempt to preserve the indigenous traditional values in education, Satis Chandra Mukharjee established a unique institution known as Bhagavat Chatuspati based on *asram* ideals. Bhagavat Chatuspati aimed to give "a thorough training in Hindu thought, life and manners" along with knowledge of western sciences.[51] In1897, Satis Chandra started *Dawn* magazine and continued to edit it till its last issue in 1913. It carried articles on religion, philosophy, history & culture, and science besides education. In July 1902, Satis Chandra Mukherjee established the Dawn Society as a reaction to the report of the University Commission. Dawn Society was intended to remedy the defects and deficiencies of the existing system of university education and to be an institution for the cultivation of patriotic and nationalistic impulses.[52] The Society, through weekly classes, regular lectures and public meetings, inspired and trained students and intellectuals to deliberate and work for an independent system of national education. Much before the Swadeshi movement started, Dawn Society was contributing to the growth of the Swadeshi spirit in educational, cultural and industrial fields. It was Down Society's work which laid the foundation of National Council of Education. Satis Chandra had directed his energies towards that end through the Down Society, since July 1902. When the countrywide movement for national education began around October-November 1905, the Dawn Society became its most active centre.

Satis Chandra paid special attention to the deficiencies and short comings in the prevalent system of university education. One of his earliest articles on the subject was "Principles of University Education in the East and the West". In this article he compared the ends and ideals of education in the West with that of ancient India. Ancient Indian ideals of education included perpetual regulation of conduct and intellectual growth of the student; whereas the ends in the case of western education were materialistic in nature. Moreover, the modern universities in India themselves were bad copies of their western counterparts so there were double defects in Indian universities.[53] In a lengthy paper, published in *Dawn* (April – June 1902) entitled "An Examination into the

Present System of University Education in India and a Scheme of Reform", Satis Chandra analysed virtually every aspect of university education and suggested a scheme of reform. The problems discussed in the paper included: tendency of cramming, examination reform, dominance of college by the university, lack of originality in the products of university and neglect of research. He concluded in the same article that character of the university in totality cannot be changed under the present or existing system of education. According to Satis Chandra, the incorrigibility of official education system stemmed from the fact that political and administrative objects were working behind the educational policy. He wrote that Government's policy was not to impart either true western knowledge or true eastern knowledge. Instead the Government policy was to direct "the ambitions and aspirations of educated Indians along a narrow line of thought, along the line merely of seeking official patronage, or professional advancement."[54] Satis Chandra's view was that the best assimilation of both higher eastern and western thoughts was necessary in the interest of national advancement. He complained that the foreign education did not enable Indians to become self-reliant, self-sacrificing and patriotic. This education was not preparing the Indians to successfully take on the challenge of great industrial competition. He posed the question – "must we still stand by with folded hands until the doom of extinction overtakes us?"[55]

Satis Chandra Mukharjee was worried by the fact that foreign education has made Indian culture and history foreign to Indian students. Indigenous achievements in arts, literature and science were not known to Indian students. They were not able to appreciate the greatness of Indian cultural and social traditions. In his opinion, these unfortunate effects were the result of conspicuous absence of Indian themes in college curriculum. Satis Chandra Mukharjee saw national education as a medium for rousing national consciousness. This idea was explained in an article- "The Birth of National Idea or the Awakening of the National Sense in a People."[56] Essence of the article is that prolonged foreign domination leads to moral and intellectual enslavement of a whole people. People under foreign domination acquire the slave's habit to think individually and not in collective capacity. The basis of nationality is found in deep seated love for the people and land of the county. This deep seated love can be created by intimately knowing the people, their customs, their religions, geography etc. Along with these, intelligent study of past brings out our ancient ideals and personality. Without knowing our people and our past intimately, we cannot become a nation.

D.K. Karve (1858-1962)

D.K. Karve devoted his entire life to the cause of women upliftment. He hailed from a very poor background and after facing various hardships he became a graduate in 1884. He started his career as a teacher in a girls' school at Bombay. In 1891, Gopal Krishna Gokhle called Karve to Fergusson College to join as a professor. Karve worked with Fergusson College and Deccan Education Society till 1914. In December 1893, Karve founded Widow Remarriage Association with other founder members at Wardha. He was also a cofounder of Balikashram, dedicated to the cause of widow education. In 1899 he opened the Widow's Home in Poona with the object of providing them opportunities in various professions such as medicine and education and thus making them self-supportive.[57]

Karve's work of women upliftment was centred on women education. A small beginning in this direction was made with the founding of Mahila Vidyalaya on 4th March 1903.[58] Mahila Vidyalya became a landmark in modern education for women on national lines. The objectives behind this initiative were to chalk out special curriculum for women in India; to prevent early marriage of girls and to arrange for free education of a few poor lady students.[59] The school became residential in 1911.

Karve was the founder of India's first women's university. Inspiration for this grand project came from Japanese Women's University which had been started in 1900. In August 1915, Karve recieved a pamphlet about this University and conceived the idea of a Women's University in Maharashtra. He expounded this scheme in his Presidential address at the Social Reform Conference held in Bombay in December 1915. His efforts in this direction came to a successful end on 6th July 1916 when the University started working. Karve became the first Principal of the College. Six girl students were enrolled in College in the first term.[60]

Karve ran the University on the principles of national education. Mother tongue was the medium of instruction at the graduate and post-graduate levels. Due attention was given to the special needs of Indian women in the curriculum. Later, Karve received a munificent donation from Sir Vithadas Thackarsay. This is how the Woman's University came to be known as Shrimati Nathibai Damodar Thakersay Women's University (S.N.D.T. University).[61]

Even after the establishment of S.N.D.T. University, Karve kept on working tirelessly for the cause of education. In 1928, at the age of seventy, Karve toured western countries for 15 months to collect funds for the Women's University. In 1936, he founded the Maharashtra Village Primary Education Society for general education. Society started several schools in villages of Maharashtra. In the last years of his life, Karve turned to fight the caste inequalities. He founded Samaj Samata Sangh in 1944 and the Caste Abolition Society in 1948.[62]

Karve's contribution to national educational movement is special for being the first one to work for female education under the ambit of national education. By focusing on the special needs of the Indian women Karve made the idea of national education more progressive, liberal and inclusive.

Lala Lajpat Rai (1865-1928)

Lala Lajpat Rai pursued the problem of Indian's national education throughout his political career and wrote extensively as it. He wrote a book on the subject called *The Problem of National Education in India*. This book analysed the concept of national education and also assessed the different efforts made in the direction of national education. Lajpat Rai was associated with the founding and functioning of several educational institutions of Arya Samaj. In particular, he was associated with the D.A.V. College, Lahore for more than twenty five years. He was appointed the Chancellor of Punjab Qaumi Vidyapeeth, a national university. Lala Lajpat Rai had earlier established the Tilak School of Politics in December 1920 with the objective of evolving a band of life members to be trained in different departments of national work.[63] With the starting of Non-Cooperation movement, Tilak School of Politics was practically suspended in favour of the National College, Lahore (under the auspices of Punjab Qaumi Vidyappeeth).[64] British Government became very suspicious about Lala Lajpat Rai's education activities. Government officials believed that real purpose of these activities was to teach Swadeshi and Swaraj.[65]

Lajpat Rai regarded education as a vital aspect of national life. He wrote that we can not afford to have loose and confused ideas about aims and methods of education. The future of India depends upon it. He stressed on devoting all the mental energy possessed by the people to understand the idea of national education.[66] Lala Lajpat Rai's educational thought was deeply influenced by American educational thought and particularly Herbert Spencer. It has been rightly said that Spenserian concepts formed the context in which the study of Dewey and his contemporaries encouraged Lala Lajpat Rai to develop a fuller version of an educational alternative for India.[67] The essence of this influence was that, to become free and great, India must strive for the economic development through technical skills. The key to economic progress and technology lies in education. As a result of the influence of American educational thought Lala Lajpat Rai was opposed to spiritual conception of education, denominational education and some other aspects of Gurukul education. Lala Lajpat Rai viewed the emphasis on spiritual education as a tendency towards negation of realities of life which according to him, was "the fundamental basis of our whole national weakness."[68] He considered education as an effective tool to solve real life problems such as 'misery, poverty, disease, ignorance and slavery of every kind.'[69] According to him, the bulk of students must study the sciences so that India could keep pace with the fast progressing world. Majority of the population must be engaged in agriculture, industries or business to ensure high production levels. Only a few people need to study Sanskrit, that too for the purpose of research and culture.

Lala Lajpat Rai was against the Gurukula ideal of education for other reasons too. He believed that Gurukula system aimed at too strict a mechanical discipline. Education provided in the Gurukul kept students isolated from real conditions of life. Also, the idea of separate education for boys and girls was regarded as outdated by the Lajpat Rai. In his opinion Gurukul system did not equip the students to face the challenge of the modern world.

Besides criticizing the Gurukula, Lajpat Rai also criticized sharply other contemporary institutions claiming to impart national education.[70] He rejected denominational education by calling it 'narrow and sectarian' and hence not national. He noted that Hindu College (Bananas Central Hindu College) and Aligarh College besides being denominational failed to dissociate themselves from the Government university examination system. National Council of Education in Bengal, according to Lajpat Rai, was the only 'truly national' institution. The reasons he gave in favour of his assessment were that National Council was free from sectarian tinge; it took cognisance of economic needs of the country; and it ignored university curriculum and as well as state aid. Lajpat Rai also analysed the causes of decline of institutions of national education. According to Lajpat Rai, the opposition to the state and lack of financial resources were the major causes for the decline of these institutions.

Any scheme of national education for India, as Lajpat Rai saw it, must suit the specific needs and requirements of India as a nation. India could not stick solely to its ancient ideals. At the same time it could not copy the education system of any western nation. "Our aim", he wrote, "is not to be English or American or Japanese. We want to be Indians but modern, up to date, progressive Indians proud of our past and aspiring to a greater future. Our scheme of National education should be chalked out with this end in view."[71] The principles of national education as envisaged by Lajpat Rai included higher technical education, physical education and education for patriotism.[72]

Patriotism or nationalism, according to Lajpat Rai, was above the love of a region, creed or religion. He favoured Hindustani as the national language. But he also said that it should not in any way affect the provincial vernaculars which should be the media of instruction at primary level in each province.[73]

Aurobindo Ghosh (1872-1950)

A scheme of national education, according to Aurobindo, in its endeavour to create a nation, can neither afford to cut off the nation from its past, nor ignore the modern scientific knowledge. Writing in 1908 in *Bandematram* weekly, Aurobindo spelled out his conception of national education:

"We must...save for India all that she has stored up of knowledge, character and noble thought in her immemorial past. We must acquire for her the best knowledge that Europe can give her and assimilate it to her own peculiar type of national temperament. We must introduce the best methods of teaching humanity has developed, whether modern or ancient. And all these we must harmonise into a system which will be impregnated with the spirit of self-reliance so as to build up men and not machines-national men, able men, men fit to carve out a career for themselves by their own brain power and resource, fit to meet the shocks of life and breast the waves of adventure. So shall the Indian people cease to sleep and become once more a people of heroes, patriots, originators, so shall it become a nation and no longer a disorganised mass of men ... National Education must therefore be on national lines and under national control."[74]

As the principal of National College, Aurobindo told his students that purpose of national institutions was not to provide information or careers but "to build up sons for the Motherland and to work and suffer for her". He exhorted them to study "for her sake; train yourself body and mind and soul for her sake... work that she may prosper; suffer that she may rejoice."[75] So Aurobindo saw national education as the embodiment of patriotism of highest form.

Aurobindo's association with the national education continued during his self imposed exited from politics (after 1907). In particular he was upset with the near failure of national educational institutions set up during the Swadeshi movement. He analysed the weakness of national educational movement in series of writings in '*Karma Yogi*' in 1909. He held responsible the leaders of the national education movement for the lack of progress towards the national education. Aurobindo felt that they could not fully grasp the meaning of national education nor create conditions for its success.[76] Their conception of national education did not take into consideration the Indian psychology. Mere inclusion of some Indian content could not make any scheme 'national'. "The so called national education", wrote Aurobindo, "was neither 'Indian' nor national, it was merely a revised edition of European education system."[77] At another place, Aurobindo wrote, "To tag on the word " national" to a school or college or even a council or Board of Education, to put into the hands of an indigenous agency mostly of men trained in the very system we are denouncing, to reproduce that condemned system with certain differences, additions, subtractions, modifications of details and curriculum, to tag on a technical side and think we have solved the problem does not really change anything."[78]

After analysing the weaknesses of the education scheme of N.C.E., Aurobindo set out to explore what ideal national education should be. This process involved three logical and sequential steps: what is an ideal education; can education be national; and what national education should be in the Indian context.

Aurobindo's approach towards the education was a blend of nationalism and spirituality. Aurobindo did not consider western conception of education as ideal because, in his opinion, it was based on insufficient knowledge of human psychology.[79] The purpose of the true education according to Aurobindo, is to bring out the best out of man in terms of body, mind and soul, as an individual, as a citizen of a nation and as a part of humanity.[80] Moreover, European perception of an individual was in the terms of him or her being a social, economic and political being, but Aurobindo saw man as a spiritual being with a national identity. In his words "the basis of a man's nature is almost always, in addition to his soul's past, his heredity, his surroundings, his nationality, his country, the soil from which he draws sustenance, the air which breathes, the sights, sounds, habits to which he is accustomed."[81] Aurobindo gave three principles to explain his conception of ideal education:

- Nothing can be taught. Teacher's function is to suggest and guide only;
- Mind should be consulted in its own growth;
- Third principle of the education is to work from near to the far, from which is to that which shall be.

After identifying the fundamental texts of ideal education, Aurobindo sought to prove that education must be nation specific i.e. education cannot be universal. He called the argument as 'an old and effete superstition' that mind of man is the same everywhere and can be passed through the same educational process. He argued that minds and souls of the individuals have infinite variations. These variations with their similarities and uniqueness must be seen along with minds and souls of nations. Thus education for different nations must be different.[82]

Having proved the need for a nation specific education, Aurobindo applied the concept of national education on India. For him, India had a spiritual conception of life which is absent in the West.[83]

Aurobindo applied the ancient Indian notion of soul or spirit on individual, nation and also the humanity. His conception of an ideal education meeting the needs of individual, nation and humanity can be best expressed in his own words: "it must be an education that for the individual will make its one central object the growth of soul and its powers and possibilities, for the nation will keep first in view the preservation, strengthening and enrichment of the nation-soul and its dharma and raise both into powers of the life and ascending mind and soul of humanity."[84] Thus Aurobindo's concept of national education when applied to individual, nation and humanity was collaborative in nature not conflictive.

Accepting the need for national education and its philosophical foundations in context of India was only the first step towards the national education. Aurobindo accepted the ground reality that the work of objectifying the method and form of education was yet to be done. But was under no illusion that a true scheme of national education cannot be solely based on ancient knowledge only. "It should be up to date in form and substance and modern in life and spirit", he said. It should prepare India for the future, not being faithful merely to the past. At the same time, in Aurobindo's opinion, it cannot follow the West in totality as the material civilization of West is itself in the process of dissolution.

Annie Besant (1847-1933)

Annie Besant was among the most prolific writers and speakers on the subject of national education. She was deeply concerned about the effects of foreign education on the Indian youth. She wrote that foreign learning in a foreign medium will 'emasculate national life' and 'kill the national character.' The alien education, according to Annie Besant, enforces foreign habits, foreign manners, foreign dress, and foreign religion. Unless indigenous effort is made, national spirit will decay.[85] So if India was to rise again as a nation, replacement of foreign education by a system of national education was necessary. Annie Besant deliberated on the characteristics of national education in a number of her writings. In order "to be national", Mrs Besant felt, "education must be controlled, shaped and carried by Indians. It must hold up Indian ideals of devotion, wisdom and morality. National education must promote Indian nationalism. It should contain Indian literature, Indian history, and Indian achievements in science, arts, politics and economics. National education must develop and promote national temperament and national culture. India should not try to become another England but a mightier India."[86]

The content of the national education as conceptualised by Annie Besant included both Indian and western learning, but the former was to be given priority over latter. She made herself clear on this subject in a letter published by the *Bengali* on 9th January 1906: "(national education) must be founded on Indian ideals and enriched not dominated by the thought and culture of the West".[87] She further explained that Indian literature, Indian history, Indian philosophy, Indian psychology and Indian medicine are to be taught as primary, while the western subjects and sciences are to be taught as secondary.[88]

Unlike most theorists of the national education in India, Annie Besant did not ignore the female education. She was able to see that female education as being imparted in India was more suitable for western women rather than for Indian womanhood. The course of studies suggested by Annie Besant for Indian women included arithmetic, science of daily life (diet, nutrition, first aid etc.), music, embroidery, *Bhagwat Gita* and stories of India's great men and women etc.[89] Purpose of female education should be to make women fit to be '*Lakshami* of the house' and one who can make

Indian home, the centre of spirituality and strength of the national religious life.[90]

To give shape to her idea of a national university, Annie Besant proposed a scheme before the Government in 1908. The proposed university was to 'impart education on national lines and under national control, not in opposition to, but standing apart from the Government system of collegiate education'.[91] It was to rely on voluntary support. The principle feature of the university was the inclusion of teaching of religions and morality as an integral part of true education. The Governing Board was to consist of leading lights of all the great religions of India. Most controversial point of the proposal was that Annie Besant sought a 'Royal Charter' from the British Government. The reason for British Government's refusal to do so is evident in Secretary of State's note of 11th December 1906: "her (Mrs Besant's) influence is bound to have political consequences and her religious teaching ...I believe (is) deliberately meant to promote the idea of an Indian nation which is spreading gradually and which may in course of time assume a form averse to British rule".[92]

Most of the leaders associated with national education movement did not support Annie Besant's move of seeking Royal Charter for the proposed university. They believed that it was akin to seeking official patronage indirectly. In their view Mrs. Besant went against the basic principles of national education movement. The *Modern Review* expressed their stand on the issue: "those who are for national education do not want a royal charter. It means control by aliens. It is a delusion and a snare. He who grants a boon can also deal a blow .... A national university must do without these favours."[93]

Despite this setback, Mrs. Besant continued her efforts in the field of national education. In 1915, she established a National College at Madan-Palle in south India. In 1917, she started the Society for the Promotion of National Education. Finally in 1918, a National University was established by her at Adyar in south India.

Bal Gangadhar Tilak (1856-1920)

Early in his political career, Tilak became convinced that solution to all problems of India lay in education. Along with Agarkar, Chiplunkar and Namjoshi, Tilak was instrumental in the foundation and running of New English School, Deccan Education Society and Fergusson College. Later, national education became an integral part of his programme of popular resistance.

Tilak saw no difference between the struggle for Swaraj and national education movement. For him the ideals of both Swaraj and national education were similar. He said that "national education is only a branch or a means to the attainment of self government and those who demand home rule for India cannot but jealously support a movement for the establishment of national education in this country."[94] According to him, national schools would be an ideal place to spread the nationalist message that Government was responsible for the poverty of the country and it wanted to keep the people in bondage.[95]

National education, Tilak said, must provide what the Government does not provide in its education. Through national education Indian people will be able to know about their country, their religion, their morals, the present conditions of their nation, their past, and also their rights and obligations as citizens.[96]

Tilak expected national education to fulfil India's educational requirements like patriotism, religious education, indigenous medium of education, and industrial education.[97] Moreover, to be truly national education, it must make the students capable to earn their livelihood independently of the Government.[98]

Tilak played an important part in preparing the ground work for national education movement in Maharashtra. In December 1906, Tilak discussed national education and establishment of a national university with leaders of Bengal. After returning to Poona, Tilak published a note in *Kesari* inviting pecuniary assistance for the establishment of national schools all over the Maharashtra.[99]

This note was signed by M.G. Deshmukh, D.A. Khare, V.G. Vijapurakar and Tilak himself. As a first step towards establishment of national schools in Maharastra, Vidya Prasarak Mandali was founded. Tilak and Vijapurkar toured the mofussil towns to promote the scheme of national education. Soon a number of national schools were started in Maharashtra. Most of them except the Samartha Vidylaya proved to be short lived. Tilak himself started a fund-gathering campaign for this school through speeches and collected a sum of fifty thousand.[100]

Notes and References

1 K.N.Pannikkar, *Presidential Speech, IHC Proceedings*, Aligarh, 1975, pp. 370-371.

2 *Modern Review*, October, 1970, pp. 308-10.

3 Ibid.

4 Arabinda Poddar, *Renaissance in Bengal: Quests and Confrontations, 1800-1860*, Simla, 1972, pp. 162-168.

5 *Concept of National Education in India*, Calcutta, 1970, p. 5, Arabinda Poddar, op. cit., pp. 163-165.

6 His Articles in '*Bharti*' projecting this theme are 'Cenciye Bala' – "Shouting" (1883), 'Jihva Asphatan'- "Bragging with tongue" (1883), Hate Kalame- "In Deeds" (1884) and National Fund (1883), cited in Himanshu Bhushan Mukherjee, *Education for Fullness*, Bombay, 1962, p. 14.

7 Examples of such writings are "Englishmen and Indians" (1893), '*Ingrejar Atankar*' – "The Englishmen's Dread" (1893), *Savicarer Adhikar*' – "Right to Justice" (1894), '*Rajnitir Dvidha*' – "Political Scruple" (1894) cited in ibid., p. 16.

8 Ibid., p. 31.

9 Ibid., p. 18.

10 Ibid., p. 16.

11 Ibid., p. 35.

12 Ibid.

13 Ibid., p. 36.

14 J.C. Aggarwal, *Basic Ideas in Education*, Delhi, 2001, pp. 203-204.

[15] *Swami Vivekanada's Complete Works*, vol.V, Calcutta, 1970, pp. 247-248.

[16] Swami Vivekanada, *Complete Works*, op. cit., vol. III, p. 301 and vol. IV, p. 362.

[17] Amiya Kumar Majumdar, "Swami Vivekananda and National Education", *Concept of National Education in India*, N.C.E. Bengal, op. cit., p. 22.

[18] B.B. Majumdar, *History of India Social and Political Ideas from Ram Mohan to Dayananda,* Calcutta, 1967, pp. 166 – 167.

[19] Richard P. Tucker, *Ranade and the Roots of Indian Nationalism*, Bombay, 1972, p. 179.

[20] N.C. Kelkar, *Life and Times of Tilak*, New Delhi, 1987, p. 85.

[21] N.C. Kelkar, *Indian Worthies*, Bombay, 1906, p. 144.

[22] The School has been described in detail elsewhere.

[23] Malati G. Apte, The Growth of National Education in India with special Reference to Maharashtra, 1963, pp. 166-167.

[24] Samartha Vidyalaya has been dealt in detail in next chapter.

[25] Malati, G. Apte, op. cit., p. 158.

[26] V.S.Rao, "Educational Activities of Arya Samaj" in *Concept of National Education in India*, op. cit., p. 83.

[27] B.B. Majumdar, op. cit., p. 204.

[28] Already mentioned in the third chapter.

[29] B.N. Pandey ed., *A Centenary History of the Indian National Congress (1885-1985)*, New Delhi, 1985, p. 212.

[30] B.N. Pandey ed., op. cit., p. 213.

[31] Siter Nivedita, "The Educational Problem in India", *Dawn*, February, 1904, p. 217.

[32] Ibid.

[33] Ibid.

[34] Ibid.

[35] Ibid. p. 218.

[36] Upendra Chandra Banerjee ed., *Reminiscences, Speeches and Writings of Gooroo Dass Banarjee,* Calcutta, 1927, p. 8.

37 Bhola Chandra Chatterjee, *Indo-British cultural Confrontation*, Calcutta, 1979, p. 93.

38 R. K. Dassgupta, 'National Education', *Concept of National Education*, op. cit., p. 13.

39 Bhola Chatterji, op. cit., p. 109.

40 Ibid.

41 Ibid., p. 132.

42 Gooroo Dass Bannarjee, *A Few Thought on Education*, Calcutta, 1904, p. V.

43 R.K. Dass Gupta, op. cit., p. 14.

44 Ibid.

45 *Dawn* Magazine, March 1906, Part III, pp. 35-40.

46 Benoy Kumar Sarkar, *Education for Industrialization*, Calcutta, 1946, p. 75. Also quoted in Haridas and Uma Mukherjee, *Origins of National Education Movement*, Calcutta, 1957, , p. 39.

47 *Origins of National Education Movement*, op. cit., p. 309.

48 Sir George Birdwood (1832-1917); born in India; Anglo-Indian official of Bombay Medical Service; Secretary of Asiatic and Horticultural Societies; authority on industrial arts of India; sympathiser of Indian renaissance.

49 Sir George Birdwood's letter to the *Dawn* dated 9th September 1898, cited in 'Dawn', June 1899, pp. 324-326. See Appendix II.

50 Op. cit., *Origins of The National Education Movement*, p. 10.

51 *Dawn*, June 1899, cited in Sumit Sarkar, *The Swadeshi Movement in Bengal*, 1903-1908. p. 155.

52 *Origins of National Education Movement*, op. cit., p. 14.

53 *Dawn*, September 1898, pp. 207-213.

54 *Origins of the National Education Movement*, op. cit., pp. 10-11.

55 *Dawn*, February 1898, p. 354.

56 The *Dawn*, November 1905, pp. 9-15.

57 Ganesh.L. Chandaverkar, *Maharishi Karve*, Bombay, 1985, pp. VIII-XI.

58 Ibid., p. XI.

59 D.K. Karve, *Looking Back*, Poona, 1936, p. 83.

60 Ganesh L. Chandravenkar, op. cit., p. XII.

61 Ibid., p.XII.

62 Ibid., p. XIII.

63 *The People*, Lala Lajpat Rai Number, 13 May 1929, p. 46.

64 Ibid.

65 Home Political. Deposit, November 1908,No-7. pp. 2-4.

66 Lala Lajpat Rai, *Problem of National Education in India*, New Delhi, 1966, pp. 31-32.

67 Krishna Kumar, *Political Agenda of Edu*cation, Delhi, 1991, p. 155.

68 *Problem of National Education in India*, op. cit., pp. 38-39.

69 Ibid., p. 41.

70 *Manthan*, January, 1986, pp. 49-50.

71 *The Problem of National Education in India*. op. cit., p. 106.

72 Ibid., pp. 119-120.

73 Ibid., p. 170.

74 Sri Aurobindo's editorial note on the concept of a National University in the *Bande Matram*, 1 March, 1908, quoted in Sabyasachi Bhattacharya et al., *Educating the Nation*, 2003, p. 11.

75 M.P. Pandit, '*Sri Aurobindo*', New Delhi, 1983, p. 98.

76 Ibid., p. 99.

77 *Brain of India*, Pondicherry, 1955, pp. 7-8, cited in *Manthan*, June 1985, p. 56.

78 *Sri Aurobindo and the Mother on Education*, Pondicherry, 1956, pp. 1-2.

79 *Sir Aurobindo and the Mother on Education*, ibid., p. 10.

80 Ibid. IInd Ed. (1960), p. 11.

81 Ibid., Ist Ed., 1956, pp. 10-11.

82 Ibid., pp. 5-6.

83 "India has seen always in man the individual a soul, a portion of the Divinity wrapped in the mind and body a conscious manifestation in nature of the Universal self and spirit."

84 *Sri Aurobindo and the Mother on Education* IInd ed. 1960, op. cit., p. 13.

[85] *Problem of National Education in India*, op. cit., p. 28.

[86] Ibid., pp. 28-29.

[87] Home Education B, February 1908, No- 23.

[88] *Dawn*, November 1905, p. 26.

[89] *Dawn*, June 1897, pp. 124-125.

[90] Ibid., p. 125.

[91] Home Education B, February 1908, No. 23.

[92] Ibid.

[93] *Modern Review*, April 1908, p. 367.

[94] *The Mahratta*, 7th April 1918 cited in *Samagra Lokmanya Tilak*, Vol. VII, p. 338.

[95] Dhananjay Keer, *Lokmanya Tilak: Father of our Freedom struggle*, Bombay, 1959, p. 263.

[96] Malti G. Apte, op. cit., p. 140.

[97] *Bal Gangadhar Tilak: His Writings and Speeches*, Madras, 1919, pp. 81-89.

[98] Malti G. Apte, op. cit., p. 140.

[99] Government of Bombay, *Source Material* etc., vol II, p. 217, cited in B.R. Sunthankar, *Maharashtra 1858-1920*, Bombay, 1993, p. 404.

[100] Dhananajay Keer, op. cit., pp. 282-283.

8

Basic Education: Gandhian Concept of National Education

By the 1930s, it was becoming increasingly clear that there was something wrong with the various schemes of national education and their application. Barring a few, most of the institutions of national education proved to be short lived. Fate of the national educational institutions was, by and large, dependent on the political movements. Students had to revert back to the Government backed schools and colleges once the national educational institutions collapsed. The biggest cause for collapse of institutions of national education was the growing financial difficulty in maintaining the institutions in the absence of any government aid. These institutions were dependent on support from public. In the absence of vigorous political movements, public contribution used to get slackened. Moreover, the diplomas offered by national educational institutions had few takers because these diplomas and certificates failed to get their holders jobs with the Government or admission in the higher courses as they were not recognised by the official universities or the departments of education.

Besides financial difficulties and problem of employbility, national education movement was still grappling with some fundamental issuues crucial to its genesis. As we have seen, Rabindra Nath Tagore and Aurobindo Ghosh had charged National Council of Education with adopting a largely western model of education in which only the content was Indian. Significance of the 'national' part of national education was not yet properly understood. The national education was not yet geared up to solve the numerous challenges before the nation.

The ideologies of national education movement had on their minds mainly the problems of paucity of technical education, foreign medium and imposition of colonial culture. But other pressing educational issues such as the neglect of mass education and poverty were avoided. At the height of the national education movement (in 1908), *Modern Review* pointed out that "national education movement has done almost nothing for the masses. The nation dwells in huts and hovels. To call a movement national which practically ignores these dwellers in huts and hovels is a misnomer."[1] Other glaring problems not addressed by institutions of national education included economic backwardness of the society, education of rural society, widening gap between rich and poor, communal problem, practice of untouchability, and lopsided development. In Gandhiji's words, "national schools, to be worth the name in terms of swaraj, for the attainment of which they were brought into existence, must be conducted with a view to advancing the national programmes in so far as it was applicable to education institutions."[2] Gandhiji wanted the national schools to become places where practical lessons in 'patriotism, useful toil and giving' could be imparted.[3]

The above mentioned shortcomings of national education movement were addressed by Mahatma Gandhi in his educational thought. Gandhiji's thought on education dealt with the issues which were fundamental to the Indian life such as poverty, unemployment, rural backwardness, character building, social inequality, communal harmony and also the physical, mental and spiritual development of the students. Real education, according to Mahatma Gandhi, must enable a person and the society to deal with the practical problems of life. The concept of national education, without Mahatma Gandhi's contribution, would have been limited merely to Indian control, vernacular medium, technical education and cultural nationalism. Gandhiji expanded the horizons of the concept of national education. He made it multi-dimensional and more complete so as to fulfil the needs of individual, society, and the nation.

Mahatma Gandhi's views on education were refined and vetted by some prominent educationists in 1937, in a scheme known as 'Wardha Scheme' of basic national education. Basic education marks the culmination of the process of development of the concept of national education. It has been rightly observed that, the period from 1937 to 1947 i.e. the period of growth of basic education, witnessed more fundamental thinking on the question of national education, than any other period before and after.

Mahatma Gandhi was convinced that foreign education was promoting the foreign rule. He used to say that foreign rule started in the field of children's education.[4] System of education introduced by the British in India was alien to Indians in every sense. It had no connection with indigenous surroundings. It did not meet the requirements of the country in any way. He declared that unless these foreign ideals were repudiated there could never be any national education.[5] The official system was 'conceived and born in error', he said, because the rulers considered the indigenous education system as 'worse than useless'.[6] In his opinion the objective behind introduction of education was sinful because the intention of the Government was to dwarf the Indian body, mind and soul.[7] All these factors led Gandhiji to call the prevalent education system as a national tragedy of first importance.

To Mahatma Gandhi, most bitter foreign element in the entire education system was its foreign medium. He was of the view that foreign medium had enslaved and emasculated those came under its influence.[8] Foreign medium put undue strain on the Indian children's mind. Lack of proper understanding made them crammers and imitators. Hence they are not able to do original work or think originally. They could not use their learning to teach the others. They could not identify themselves with the masses and hence they became foreigners in their own land.[9]

Mahatma Gandhi appreciated the usefulness of English language in the realm of ideas, knowledge and literature. In his opinion the treasures of English language could be easily passed on the Indian students through good translations. Gandhiji emphasized the fact that Indians could not grow on foreign ideas, however great they may be. Indians, he said, must build on their own heritage. They could flourish best by using their own ideas, literature, and shortcomings even if they were inferior to their English counterparts.[10] By neglecting their vernaculars, Indians were impoverishing themselves. He compared the neglect of vernaculars to 'national suicide'.[11] He concluded that without getting rid of the infatuation for English, swaraj cannot be attained.[12]

Gandhiji was very concerned about the fact that western education was further widening the rich-poor and rural-urban divides. Educated people had come to despise those who laboured with their hands. Moreover, the reluctance for manual work caused loss of self reliance and led to ill-productivity and unemployment. Gandhiji considered it a crime to make the education wholly literary and hence made students unfit for manual work in a country where more than eighty percent of the population was agricultural and another ten percent industrial.[13] The crime became more grievous when India saw herself as inheritor of a rural civilization.[14] He also observed that British education system had encouraged the decay of village handicrafts and hence was responsible for growing poverty of India.

Besides elaborating on foreign nature of education and its harmful effects, Gandhiji also analysed other evils of the English education system. He was convinced that this system of education could not prepare the students to face practical challenges of daily life. The wholly literary nature of education could not draw out the best in men in terms of body, mind and spirit. He categorically stated that literacy was not the end of education nor even the beginning.[15] Gandhiji emphasised that system of western education promoted materialism in place of spiritualism, competition instead of cooperation and violence in place of non-violence. Such kind of education did not build character. It did not prepare the students for fighting the social evils nor it trained them for the service of society.

In has been rightly said that Mahatam Gandhi 'touched nothing that he did not radically attempt to reform.'[16]

So while expressing his dissatisfaction with the official education system, Mahatma Gandhi was also evolving a revolutionary, yet a very simple alternative. True to his style, his scheme of education was worked out to become an integral part of his philosophy of regeneration of India. The ideas constituting his scheme, though implemented in 1937, were taking shape since the time he wrote '*Hind Swaraj*' in 1909.

Mahatama Gandhi had a very comprehensive conception of education. He wrote that he believed in the ancient aphorism[17]: "education is that which liberates".[18] According to his explanation, knowledge included all training that is useful for the service of mankind and liberation meant freedom from all kinds of servitude, external and internal. Such kind of education can not be a linear activity. It must address itself to the head, heart and hand, symbolizing a harmonious development of body, mind and spirit in order to develop an integrated personality. Such integration, emphasized Gandhiji, could best be affected though a life centred and activity centred education. Education imparted in this way will enable the student to solve correctly the problems of life in every department.[19] Gandhiji did not approve of studying various subjects in a compartmentalised way. He believed that different branches of knowledge must be studied in an interactive manner through a harmonious use of physical, mental, and spiritual faculties.

In Gandhiji's scheme of things, manual activity precedes the development of reading and writing skills. Once the child learns to operate a simple tool, his literary skills will develop very fast. He will write words artistically and he will read meaningfully. Taught in this way, the whole training will come naturally to student and it will be quicker and cheaper.[20] Gandhiji had two basic objectives behind craftwork. Firstly, the craft work was to act as the focus of integration of knowledge of the various subjects involving body, mind and soul. Secondly, teaching of the craft skills will lead to self-sufficiency of the students and they could also take it up as a career.

The best forms of manual productive work, according to Gandhiji, were village handicrafts. In his opinion, education in all stages must be imparted through the village handicrafts. Even in the cities, medium of education must be the village handicrafts. Gandhiji was confident that, use of such handicrafts will bring about a silent social revolution.[21] Such an education will prepare a healthy moral basis of the relationship between the cities and the villages. To Gandhiji, cities were the exploiters of village products, without paying them back adequately. Also, the urban folks viewed village based manual labour with contempt. By learning through rural handicrafts, even the city people will understand and appreciate the manual productive labour. Gandhiji visualised the revolutionary concept that the activity based learning would be able to eradicate class difference without class conflict, or colossal capital investment or the evils of large scale industrialization.[22]

Mahatma Gandhi saw education as the training of men's thoughts and emotions in relation with their environment and ethos. Seen in this light, only the mother tongue can be the best medium of instruction. Moreover, mother tongue expresses best the community's psyche and its emotional and intellectual needs. Gandhiji summed up the significance of mother tongue poetically: "I must cling to my mother tongue as to my mother's breast, in spite of its shortcomings; it alone can give me the life-saving milk."[23] Mahatma Gandhi was not against learning other languages but he emphasized that they must not be learnt at the cost of mother tongue. In this context, he expressed himself beautifully in a letter to Rabindranath Tagore : "I do not want my house to be walled in all sides and my windows to be stuffed. I want the cultures of all lands to be blown about my house as freely as possible. But I refuse to be blown off my fact by any."[24] Gandhiji welcomed the study of foreign languages with the condition that mother tongue must not be neglected. One should be able to express his best thoughts in his or her mother tongue. Gandhi deprecated the apprehension that it would need a lot of work to enable mother tongue to become medium of technical education. He said that people who made such suggestions were unaware of the rich treasure of expressions and idioms buried in the dialects of our villages.[25]

Spiritualism was a fundamental feature of all Gandhian programmes and his educational programme was no exception to it. For him an education without its spiritual aspect might even be harmful to the society.[26] Mahatma Gandhi related spiritualism in education to character building and self realization. He believed that character building of the youth will lead to an ideal society.[27] Teachers were expected to play a leading role in building characters of young people by their own example. Thus teachers must themselves rigorously practice the virtues which they want their students to imbibe.[28] Religious studies were also an integral part of his scheme of education. Gandhiji was of the opinion that the study of tenets of different faiths must be compulsory. Students should be trained to cultivate the habit of understanding and appreciating the doctrines of various religions in a spirit of reverence and broad mindedness, so as to understand the essence of religion.[29]

Mahatma Gandhi viewed education as a lifelong process. Education must not be confined to children of school going age. Adult education was an important aspect of his educational programme. Adult education was needed to mitigate the mass illiteracy which he termed as Indian's 'sin and shame.'[30]

Gandhiji explained that literacy campaigns must not focus at knowledge of 3R's only. Instead they should focus on the knowledge of practical utility such as village arithmetic, village geography, village history, hygiene and other useful form of knowledge.[31] Thus Gandhiji targeted ignorance more than illiteracy. According to him, a villager had no use for a dry knowledge of alphabet. He would accept more cheerfully the knowledge which finds a place in his daily life.

Gandhiji had realized that the biggest obstacle in the way of education in India was the lack of finances. So he put forward the concept of self-financed education. He said that the problem of lack of education in India was so colossal that it cannot be solved in a single generation, if the education is made dependent on outside (Government donation etc.) support. Besides, the majority of the people were so poor that they could not spend anything on education of their children. In such circumstances, Gandhiji's suggestion was that children from the very beginning should pay for their education by their work.[32] The simplest handicraft suitable for everyone was spinning. In Gandhiji's words, introduction of charkha would fulfil three purposes. It will "make education self-supporting, train the bodies of the children as well as their mind, and pave the way for a complete boycott of foreign yarn and cloth. The children thus equipped will become self-reliant and independent."[33] Self supporting education would also help in reducing the burden of taxes and thereby help in combating the poverty.[34]

The year 1937 was a landmark in the evolution of Gandhiji's ideas on national education. On September11, 1937, Gandhiji admitted that uptill now he was in the favour of manual training along with intellectual training in his scheme of national education. Now he had come to realize that manual productive work must be the "principle means of stimulating the intellect."[35] By giving priority to the manual training over the intellectual training Gandhiji achieved the final break with traditional education. The same year witnessed the assumption of power by Congress in seven provinces. Provincial autonomy provided by the 1935 Act designated education as a transferred subject. Congress leaders wanted to utilize this opportunity to establish a system of national education. Hence the question of national education received serious attention under favourable circumstances.

But soon the grand opportunity of educational reconstruction faced a threat in the form of financial difficulties of the Congress ministries. There was a strong popular demand for the introduction of a universal, free and compulsory primary education. But the implementation of this demand required large sums of money. The provisions in the provincial budgets were small and fresh taxation would have gone against the public opinion. The situation became more difficult, when, under Gandhiji's influence Congress ministries discarded revenue from the sale of alcohol and opium. In such a situation, Gandhiji's proposal of a self-supporting education became all the more relevant. Gandhiji sensed that right time had come to launch his scheme of basic national education. He wrote that "what I have seen through the glass darkly for the last 40 years, I have begun to see clearly under the stress of circumstances."[36]

Gandhiji's views on national education were discussed by a conference of educationists in Wardha on 22nd and 23rd October 1937. Called as the first conference of national education, the conference was attended by workers in national education from all over the country including the education ministers of seven Congress ruled provinces. The conference passed the following resolutions: free and compulsory education be provided for seven years on a nationwide scale; the medium of instruction must be mother tongue; process of education throughout this period should centre around some form of manual and productive work; all training be integrated to the central handicraft chosen with regard to the environment of the child; and remuneration of the teachers should gradually be covered by this system.[37] The conference also appointed a committee under the Presidentship of Dr. Zakir Hussain to prepare a detailed curriculum on the lines of above resolutions. The committee submitted its report to Gandhiji, Chairman of the Conference, in February 1938. In their report, the committee explained the principles and objectives of the scheme of 'basic national education' in terms of the recognized principles of education and psychology. It worked out a detail curriculum for a number of crafts and made valuable suggestions regarding the administration and examinations.

In the opinion of the committee, productive craft work is the most effective way of providing a balanced education. Seen from psychological perspective, it balances the intellect and practical elements of experience and saves the child from burden of purely academic and theoretical instructions. From the social point of view, such a scheme of education will help in breaking the existing prejudices between manual and intellectual workers. Educationally, the knowledge acquired through this method is more concrete and reality based. The committee also recommended that while teaching the students, the stress must be on the principles of co-operative activity, planning, accuracy, initiative and individual responsibility. The committee defined the objective of basic education as to produce self-reliant, efficient citizens, upholding the dignity of labour with a keen desire for social service in a co-operative community.[38] At the same time the committee also pointed out the danger of stressing the 'self supporting education' at the cost of intellectual, social and moral benefits of craft- training. The committee noted that this point must be constantly kept in mind while training the teachers and supervisory staff.

The idea of basic national education was formally adopted by Congress at its Haripura session in February 1838. The resolution adopted here read that "the Congress attaches the utmost importance to a proper organisation of mass education and holds that all national progress ultimately depends upon the method, content and objective of education that is provided for the people. It is essential, therefore, to build up a national education of a new foundation and on nation-wide scale." At Haripura, Congress also authorized the promotion of an All-India Education Board to work out a programme of national basic education. This Board was established in April 1938, under the name Haindustani Talimi Sangh with headquarters at Sevagram, Wardha. The Sangh was to act as a nodal and a guiding agency for the basic education. It was to affiliate institutions, supply the literature, prepare the curricula, arrange for the apparatus and train the manpower. Sangh was also given the task to experiment and explore further the concept of basic national education in the light of Gandhian principles.

Within a month of its organization, Hindustan Talimi Sangh established the first institution of basic education, the Vidya Mandir Training School at Wardha to train the teachers. Gradually, further steps were taken towards the introduction of basic education on experimental basis by Governments of Central Provinces, United Provinces, Bihar, Bombay and Kashmir. These steps included setting up of special boards, establishing trainings schools, new schools and converting traditional schools into basic schools. Some of the earlier institutions of national education also collaborated in the efforts to expand basic education. Jamia Millia Islamia and Andhra Jateeya Kalasala opened training courses in basic education in August 1838. Tilak Maharastra Vidhapeeth and Gujrat Vidyapeeth cooperated with the Bombay Government in the training of teachers and introduction of basic education in the schools affiliated to them.

By the end of first year of basic education, ten training centres were engaged in training teachers for basic education.[39] During the second year (1939-40), three new training centres were opened in Central Provinces, Bombay and Madras. Large numbers of new basic schools were opened and many primary schools were gradually converted into basic schools when trained teachers became available.[40]

After the completion of two years of basic education, a conference was held at Poona to take stock of the situation. Some of the important decisions taken by the conference were: English should be taught in schools only after seven years of regular education; work of basic education must be continued without interruption even in the case of any political change; teaching should be correlated not only to the basic craft but also with the child's physical and social environment; in the choice of the basic craft the predominant occupation of the people in locality should be taken into account besides the marketing factors.[41]

The progress of basic education received a setback when the Provincial Congress Governments resigned in 1939. Consequently, many of the Basic Schools started by the provincial governments were closed while most of the others were allowed to continue in a state of suspended animation. In April 1940, the Vidya Mandir Training Institute was also closed. The situation became worse in the period of 1942–1945 due to Quit India movement. But despite the adverse situation, the work of basic national education was not discontinued. Some of the institutions started by Gandhiji and his co-workers continued to work in difficult circumstances. Some patriotic Government officials and teachers of the Basic Schools resigned from the Government service and carried on their work in national Basic Schools. Governments of Bihar, Orissa, Bombay and Kashmir did not back out completely from the programmes of basic education. Prominent non-Government institutions which continued to operate in this period were Basic School and Basic Training School conducted by Jamia Millia Islamia, Basic School near Poona conducted by Tilak Maharastra Vidyapith, and Basic School and the Basic Training School at Seva Gram conducted by the Hindustani Talimi Sangh.[42]

The soundness of the underlying principles of basic education impressed even the Government backed education bodies. Central Advisory Board of Education in 1944, while preparing the plan for post-war educational development, praised and adopted the concept of basic education in principle. The Board, however, did not endorse fully the self-supporting aspect of the basic education scheme.[43]

After the release of national leaders, a Conference on National Education was called at Sevagram in January 1945. It reviewed the progress of Basic Education since its inception and chalked out programmes for the future. Most significant achievement of the Conference was the widening of the concept of Basic Education. Till now the scope of Basic Education was limited to primary education (from the age of seven to fourteen). In the words of Mahatma Gandhi, "Nai Talim or New Education has extended its scope today to the whole span of life from the movement of conception to the hour of death."[44] From now onwards, Basic Education was to cover pre-basic, post- basic and adult education. Hindustani Talimi Sangh was instructed to draw full- fledged schemes for each of these three segments of Basic Education. Apart from enlarging the scope of Basic Education, the Conference adopted a resolution which called for making Basic Education a means for creating a 'new way of life' from hitherto limited concept of a 'revolution in education'. Moved by K. M. Mashruwalla, the resolution called for making educational institutions of villages the producers of articles of use, besides being of true educational value. It was expected that an adult pupil in village could earn enough to defray his cost of education. If implemented, this step would lead to a double revolution in economy and education. Villages will become the centres of production. Production itself will increase leading to substantial increase in wages and income. It will lead to rural development in the right sense. The cause of education itself will be benefited as there will be enough incentive for the poor to send their children to school. According to the Resolution, Nai Talim should give technical feedback for improvement of technology and decentralization of small scale industries apart from making them economically viable.[45]

The year 1946 saw the return of Congress Governments giving a new impetus to the cause of Basic Education. In the same year a Conference on Basic Education was called by B.G. Kher, the Education Minister and Prime Minister of Bombay. The Conference declared that Basic Education was past its experimental stage and should be introduced in the provinces. It recommended the exclusion of English till the passing of basic stage. Moreover, physical well being of students including nutritional diet, medical care and hygiene must be made an integral part of the national education. This Conference marked the large scale extension of Basic Education. In 1949 the total number of Basic institutions in the country was 269. They included both, schools for teaching the students and teacher training centres.

Notes and References

1 *Modern Review*, July 1908, p. 81.

2 *Young India*, 7th August 1924.

3 Ibid.

4 *The Selected Works of Mahatma Gandhi, Vol. VI*, Ahmedabad, 1968, p. 514.

5 *Young India*, 20th March 1924, cited in M.K. Gandhi, *Towards a New Education*, Ahmedabad, 1953, p. 26.

6 *Young India*, 27th April, 1921.

7 Ibid.

8 *Selected works of Mahatma Gandhi,* Vol. VI, op. cit., p. 526.

9 *Young India*, 5 July 1928, cited in *Selected Works of Mahatma Gandhi*, op. cit., Vol. VI, p. 528.

10 *Harijan*, l July 1938, cited in ibid., p. 517.

11 *Young India*, 21st June 1928, cited in P.D. Kaushik, *The Congress Ideology and Programmes*, 1920-47, Bombay, 1964, p. 160.

12 *Young India*, 2nd February, 1921, cited in ibid.

13 Ibid.

14 *Young India*, 17th November 1929, cited in D.P. Nayar, *Towards a National System of Education*, Delhi, 1989, p. 133.

15 *Harijan*, 31st July 1937, cited in *The Selected Works of Mahatma Gandhi, Vol. VI*, op. cit., p. 507.

16 T.S. Avinashilingam Chettiar, *Indian Year Book of Education*, 1964, Second Year Book, Elementary Education, p. 58.

17 *Sa Vidya ya Vimuktay.*

18 *Harijan*, 10th March 1946, cited in *Selected Works of Mahatama Gandhi*, Vol. VI, op. cit., p. 503.

19 *Harijan*, 23rd May 1936, cited in D.P. Nayar, op. cit., p. 138.

20 Ibid., p. 140.

21 *Harijan*, 9th October 1937 cited in *Selected Works of Mahatma Gandhi, Vol. VI.* op. cit., p. 512.

22 Ibid.

23 *Harijan*, 25th August 1946 cited in D.P. Nayar, op. cit., p. 144.

24 *Young India*, 1st June 1921.

25 M.K. Gandhi, *Towards a New Education*, op. cit., p. 54.

26 M.K. Gandhi, *The Story of my Experiments With Truth*, Vol. II, Ahmedabad, 1959, p. 201.

27 *Young India*, 26th December 1929.

28 *Young India*, 14th October, 1928.

29 *Young India*, 6th December, 1928, cited in *Selected Works of Mahatma Gandhi,* Vol. VI. op. cit., p. 519.

30 *Harijan*, 18th February 1939, *Towards a New Education*, op. cit., p. 69.

31 *Harijan*, 22nd June 1940, cited in Ibid., p. 70.

32 *Young India*, 15th June 1921, cited in *Towards a New Education*, op. cit., p. 40.

33 Ibid.

34 Ibid., p. 41.

35 *Seven Years of Work*, Eight Annual Report of Nai Talim (1938-46), p. 5.

36 *Educational Reconstruction*, Hindustani Talimi Sangh, Wardha, 1939, (3rd ed.), p. 7.

37 Mahatma Gandhi, *Basic Education*, Ahmedabad, 1951, p. 26.

38 *Education Reconstruction*, op. cit., pp. 120-126.

39 *Seven Years of Work*, pp. 5-6.

40 Ibid., pp. 7-8.

41 *One Step Forward*, Hindustani Talimi Sangh, Wardha, 1948, pp. 217-219.

42 *Seven Years of Work*, op. cit., pp. 13-21.

43 Central Advisory Board of Education, *Post War Plan of Educational Development in India*, 1944, p. 12.

44 *Seven Years of Work*, op. cit., p. 22.

45 Ibid., p. 27.

9

Conclusion

Education is the process in which the knowledge, the character and the behaviour of the young are shaped and moulded. Education is the channel through which intellectual traditions, values, cultural heritage and aspirations of a society are transferred from one generation to another for refinement and preservation. However, under the British rule, education was made a means to strengthen the colonial hold over India. British tried to weed out everything which could help in making India a nation and resist the foreign rule. As a first step, indigenous education was made to perish and in its place, a carefully formulated foreign education was imparted to a select class of people. By cutting off the intimate link between the native society and indigenous system of education, colonial rulers attempted to purge the elements of cultural nationalism, identity and values present in Indian society for thousands of years. The new (colonial) education system was designed to impose foreign culture, foreign ideals, foreign ways and foreign religion in a foreign medium. The idea was, 1. in Lord Macaulay's famous words, "to form a class who may be interpretors between us and the millions whom we govern–a class of person Indians in blood and colour, but English in tastes, in opinions, in morals and in intellect."

Rise of the national consciousness in 19th century led a section of native intelligentsia to realise the implications of a foreign education as well as the colonial motives behind it. They also realized that India was being denied the real advantages of western education. In course of time it became clear to them that to save the national interests, education must be under national control. With this realization they endeavoured to develop an alternative system of education based on national requirements in order to achieve the national goals. Ironically, the foreign content of colonial education also proved to be transmitter of western ideals of nationalism and democracy and helped to regenerate the national consciousness in India. National consciousness in turn created national aspirations with a vision for a self-dependence and prosperous nation in all aspects of national life. In order to translate this vision into reality, a set of conditions and requirements was to be fulfilled. These conditions and requirements included revival of native cultural identity, self belief and economic regeneration of India through industrialization and literacy. Official education system, a tool of British imperialism, could not be expected to meet Indian national requirements.

The idea of national education rests on the premise that education system of a country is not a growth in the vacuum. Education of a country characterises the elements which constitute the identity, culture and nationality of its people. The concept of national education was based on the realization that the education must the controlled, shaped and carried on by the Indians themselves. Education must convey and promote the native cultural ethos and the national heritage. It must help in economic regeneration of the country through manual, scientific, technical and agricultural training, Moreover the education should be accessible to all sections of the society tresspassing the fault-lines of caste, class or gender.

Thus, the idea of national education that evolved was a product of national consciousness. It was a programme of national regeneration through educational reconstruction. Education acted as a tool for achieving national destiny. Thus, it can be said that it was a national movement in the domain of education.

From the previous chapters, certain conclusions can be extracted. Firstly, the concept of national education was a product of rising national consciousness. It was a manifestation of the emerging realisation about the colonial educational motives vis-à-vis Indian national requirements.National education movement was a programme of national regeneration through educational reconstruction. It was also a form of expression of resistance to the colonial cultural onslaught. The programme of national education became an integral part of the Indian freedom struggle during the Swadeshi movement and Non-Coperation movement.

Secondly, the concept of national education was evolved and refined through the efforts of many pioneers although each of them had a different approach depending upon individual ideology as well as the stage of struggle for Indian independence. The variations in the opinion of its ideologues were mainly concerned with the curriculum and means of implementation. These variations were inevitable since so many enlightened individuals were involved. Multi-dimensional views only enriched the concept of national education. Besides the apparent differences they shared many commonalities. All pioneers saw the urgent need for national education and also the ends to be achieved through it. They all agreed that education of the nation must be along national lines, under national control and must serve the national interests.

Thirdly, the thinkers conceptualised national education as an inclusive concept in place of an exclusive or a parochial one. They were against the colonial aspects of English education but not against the English or the European learning. They appreciated the western learning for its many fold benefits. They did not confine national education to ancient Indian learning, but they emphasized that western educational elements must not be adopted at the cost of Indian learning and vernacular languages. A broad consensus prevailed amongst the pioneers that national education must consist of a judicious mix of eastern and western educational systems.

Fourthly, the national education comprehensively covered all the aspects needed to improve the individual personality and national development: physical, moral, cultural, material and even spiritual.

Even the engineering students had to attend compulsory lectures on history and culture of the nation.

Fifthly, along with a balanced growth of mind, the stalwarts of national education strived to achieve excellence in their respective fields. Bengal Technical Institute, Gurukul Kangri and Santiniketan received accolades for the excellence they achieved. Apart from the excellence achieved by individual institutions, the movement for national education had several achievements as a whole. Popularity of the national education forced the Government to concede certain Indian demands in education. The Government was compelled to pass primary education acts for greater spread of education: Bombay Primary Education Act, 1918; Madras Primary Education Act, 1920; Bengal Primary Education Act, 1919; and Bengal (rural) Primary Education Act, 1930. The curriculum of secondary schools and university education was changed to include more Indian content. Mother tongue was made the medium of instruction at various levels of education. Technical and vocational education was provided on a larger scale then before. Study of vernacular languages was introduced in some universities. Regarding Basic Education, the British Government was favourably inclined to it after the end of World War II.

Students and teachers of national educational institutions actively participated in various political movements. Many of the political leaders and revolutionaries were product of national schools and colleges. 2. Glorious example of National College, Lahore is worth mentioning here. This college produced virtually the entire Punjab cadre of revolutionary party during the 1920s. Bhagat Singh, Sukhdev, Bhagawati Charan Vohra and Yashpal were students of this college. Bhai Parmanand of the Ghadar movement fame and Jayachandra Vidyalankar, an ideologure of revolutionary movement, were teachers in this college. National schools and colleges became synonymous with patriotism and anti-Government activities. The patriotic environment of national schools and colleges imbued a whole generation with the spirit of selfless dedication for the nation.

Lastly, the concept of national education and also its application, in its initial phase had several shortcomings. These shortcomings were brilliantly exposed and remedied by Mahatma Gandhi in his scheme of Basic Education. Basic Education can be called as the culmination of national education movement. Rooted in Indian soil, basic education endeavoured to address the body, mind and soul of learners as well as nearly all the problems of Indians society. Tragically, the ideals of national education were quickly forgotten once the real opportunity of restructuring the education on national lives arrived in the form of independence in 1947. Institutions of national education which had carried on with distinction against all odds during the colonial rule gradually submerged their distinct identity in the post-independence official system. Scheme of basic education was enthusiastically taken up in the beginning but soon it got entangled in the official red-tape and shared the fate of other constructive programmes of Mahatama Gandhi. All this leaves several questions unanswered. Why was national education not considered fit to be adopted as an ideal model for the whole country? Why was the feasibility of national education never really tested? Why the independent India professed colonial pattern of education with cosmetic changes? Unless these questions are answered, the debate on an ideal system of education for India will not lead to any meaningful conclusion.

10

Appendix I

G.W. Leitner, former Principal of Government College, Lahore and founder of Anjuman-i-Panjab presents a critique of the British system of education in India and suggests drastic reforms in it, in his answers to the questionnaire of the Education Commission, 1882.

Ques.2: (a) Do you think that in your province the system of primary education has been placed on a sound basis, and (b) is capable of development up to the requirements of the community? (c) Can you suggest improvements in the system of administration, or (d) in the course of instruction?

Ans. 2: (a) I do not think that in the Panjab the system of primary education has been placed on a sound basis. No such system can be said to be placed on a sound basis that ignores, or tends to suppress, indigenous education, both of which charges can be pressed against the system adopted by the Educational Department. To correctly ascertain the number and character of indigenous schools is, in itself, a task, which has not yet been accomplished by the department during the 26 years of its existence; and yet it is only one *preliminary* to their incorporation in a scheme of State education. These indigenous schools, being outside our present system, were never fostered by us. It was easier to start schools of our own, and to obtain credit for doing so, than to develop an institution which at every stage would have involved the consideration of local circumstances, if not prejudices, as well as the acquisition of a knowledge of languages and subjects out of the pale of official recognition. Yet the department would not have had any large number of schools to start with had it not converted many of the indigenous schools into Government schools by buying over their teachers, destroying indigenous schools as such, and establishing alien schools on their ruins. Urdu, which our officers knew a little, was made the current vernacular, whereas, incidentally with Persian, it was already being perfected in the numerous schools in which Persian was taught before our advent. The mahajani schools supplied and still supply the wants of the trading class, when contented with its profession; yet they were, as a rule, ignored. The Arabic, Sanskrit, and Gurumukhi schools were so identified with religious teaching, that a Government which derives its taxation from all denominations ignored them on the plusible, if economical principle of religious neutrality—a principle which should merely mean abstinence from religious proselytism, but not the subversion of all religious feelings by the introduction of a secular system, which is so pernicious, even in countries like France, where the best education is still given by clergy.

Nor was "religious neutrality", which, as in Prussia, should denote the impartial distribution of State funds to the religious teaching of all denominations alike, a sufficient excuse for the resumption of grants of rent-free land to the indigenous schools of all sects, whereby the endowments of education were swept away, which might have been converted to nobler use in course of time with a little more tact, patience, and knowledge than we displayed. Nor was "religious neutrality" an excuse for not giving grants to religious schools (especially if these schools also taught subjects of secular knowledge), in accordance with the Despatch of 1854, or for so construing the grant-in-aid rules as to make them inapplicable to indigenous schools in 1859, when the second Education Despatch left them to be taken care of by the "educational cess", not a hundredth part of which was devoted to indigenous schools, although raised for that purpose, as understood at any rate by the agricultural population. So the endowment having been destroyed the private teachers impoverished or swept away, the educational cess applied to other purposes, a disbelief in Government took possession of the thinking among the masses; whilst apathy took the place of the former veneration for learning, and ambition for employment was rendered synonymous with participation in the new system of secular instruction. How far it is suited to the wants of the people may be inferred from the fact that the Urdu language is taught for three years in primary schools, when either it is the vernacular of the people and they already know it, or it is not the vernacular and thus becomes a quasi foreign language. In how many schools and colleges in England is English taught as a subject of study; and since when? Eighteen months to Urdu would be ample, and the remaining eighteen months could either be devoted to Persian for certain classes of the community desiring it, in addition to branches of elementary general knowledge, or else to those branches only where Persian was not required. Instead of this, we find Urdu grammar actually dragged into the fifth year, whilst the whole nation is being sought to be converted into proletariat of munshis, in vain seeking for Government employment, by Persian being taught up to University standards in schools. Nor is the mental discipline which, linguistically, is alone possible by the study of a classical language (Arabic or Sanskrit) obligatory in any school up to the Entrance standard, so that even the better classes of the population are deprived of the religious and moral associations of their fellow-countrymen, in proportion as they avail themselves of our schools, whereby they ceased to be acceptable, if humble, pioneers of enlightenment in their homes, and merely become alienated from the rest of the community....

(b) Primary education is capable of development up to the requirements of the community, provided the community is allowed to judge for itself of these requirements; and no Educational Department, certainly as now constituted, presumes to judge for it. Local committees, consisting of official and non-official Europeans and Native members, can alone keep up the interest of the local public in local institutions. The personal influence and position of the teacher, if a good man, will rise when he is the pivot of the educational aspirations of these committees and of the wishes of the parents of his pupils. On many festive occasions, an educational gathering, if not darbar, should take place. The teacher would become an advisor of the community, and be, in his turn, controlled by it. The local committee, with educational panchayats in every village, would know, far better than any inspector, whether the teacher was painstaking, led a moral life, etc., and they also could constantly inspect the school buildings, and ascertain whether they were maintained in the proper sanitary condition. District inspectors, to test the teaching in the schools and to report to the local committees *at the very time* of the inspection may, for the present, still be retained, at least till the local committees and educational panchayats acquire a better knowledge of the proper inner working of a school, or till the tehsildars, who are now relieved of judicial work, are ordered by Government to make the inspections of schools a part of their official duty, whilst, if the "primary" examinations are to be maintained, they should be conducted by independent examiners in the district if not by the University itself. If indigenous *education* is to be saved from destruction, and to be developed; if a sound system of education at all is to take the place of the present routine of unsound *instruction*—then the official department, which has nearly destroyed popular *education*, should be abolished; the whole present educational machinery being decentralised and localised in favour of educational self-government below and a Government above for general (very general) guidance and discriminating encouragement....

The greatest blow, therefore, that, in my humble opinion, could be dealt to the true civilisation of this province is to *extend* the *present* denationalising system of primary instruction, Which will destroy all self-help throughout the province, and which will spread the petulant disaffection, now chiefly confined to high schools and colleges, to every village in the Panjab. Instead of 100 babus, clamorous for Government employment, we shall have 100,000 *declasses*, anxious for any change, such as are fostered by the official educational system of France.

If, however, the organisation of the educational department is to be in any way maintained, I would urge the abolition of the Directorship of Public Instruction – a costly, but useless, appointment—where it is not actually injurious to education....

If, therefore, the burden of the expense of primary education is to be, increasingly, borne by the people, all that is good in their own associations must be utilized, and should not be supplanted by a new code of obligations based on a little understood foreign civilization. Instead of impoverishing and alienating the Native priesthood, it should be identified in its feelings and interest with the maintenance of the State, when we shall find that the co-operation of the maulvis, pandits, and bhais with the wealthier of their co-religionists and with the Government will very soon cover the country with a network of schools extending to every village and every section of the community, and when it will be *our* fault if these schools do not add subjects of useful secular instruction to their religious curriculum.

Appendix II

Sir George Birdwood's Letter to Satis Chandra Mukherjee

India Office. Whitehall, S.W.

9th September, 1898

Dear Sir,

My wife's illness greatly pre-occupies me still and I am myself in very weak health having suffered from three attacks of influenza this year, but I cannot let this mail pass without writing and thanking you most cordially for your kind courtesy and kind thought in sending me a copy of the *Dawn*, containing the deeply interesting article 'In Memoriam' of the late Mr. Gladstone. The whole number interests me and it is a source of unfeigned pleasure to me to find the educated Hindus in India supporting, of their own inspiration and with their own independent means, a periodical of this description. I hail with delight any symptom of the spontaneous revival of the indigenous and traditionary, literary and artistic and philosophical and religious life of India—India of the Hindus. With almost equal satisfaction I note the growing attention which the Hindus, at least those who have come to England, are giving to the industrial development of their wonderful country, wonderful for its untold natural wealth, and for the strong, and I hope and pray, imperishable spiritual individuality of its great historical people. Once you take into your own hands the task of developing the reproductive resources of India and of extending its international commercial relations, the prosperity and wealth of the country will advance by leaps and bounds and that necessary material basis be provided which will ensure the maintenance - as by a perpetual endowment—of the great and beneficent historical personality of the Hindus—the calm, unbroken continuity of the natural, subjective evolution of their strongly idiosyncratic, traditionary civilisation. The first thing to do is to take the whole of your higher education more into your own hands. In our English system of education far too much of time and energy is spent on English literature and far too little on Hindu i.e. Sanskrit and the literature of the literary *Prakits*, such as Mahratti and Tamil. Of Western literature the most worthy of your study are the poetical and philosophical writings of the Greeks and the Romans; and it is through Greece and Rome that you would approach the literature of England, France, and Germany, not direct.

Science is almost the exclusive creation of modern Europe – the Greeks were on the eve of all our greatest modern discoveries when the cataclysms of the Goths and Vandals swept the whole area of the Roman Empire and placed an everlasting gulf between ancient and modern civilisation in the past. It is to modem Europe therefore that you must directly look for your scientific culture and in the present economic condition of India you cannot have too much pure and applied (technical) scientific instruction in all your schools, primary, secondary and higher. But for your literary and artistic and your philosophical and religious - in a word, your spiritual culture, you already possess your own - the indigenous growth of 4000 years of Aryan supremacy in India; and you must never surrender it, but to the utmost of your ability and power strengthen it and extend its influence.

Of course you cannot help its being modified by the literary, artistic and religious culture of the West,—not if India is to keep an equal place and all worthy of her ancient civilisation, in the international life of the world; but the point is that it must not be forced upon you under alien compulsion through the Government schools and the not less official Indian Universities. The modification must come naturally and spontaneously and gradually, as if *subjectively*, through inevitable commercial and social intercourse—which have ever proved the most powerful influences in stimulating the spiritual advancement of peoples and nations. You can acquire no ingrained, no immanent, and instinctive, no natural and enduring culture save in this voluntary and slow and sure way; and you will never assimilate and receive real nourishment from an alien culture imposed on you under the compulsion of the drill-sergeant's cane. You must go back to Classical Sanskrit and Greek and Latin as essential items in every college curriculum, and leave English Literature for private reading- and my advice to you would be to confine that almost exclusively to our poets and the authorised (not revised) version of the Bible. I know nothing about the genesis of the original Hebrew and Greek - but the English (authorised) Translation is beyond question divinely inspired and a spring of perennial youth and joyfulness and counsel to all who read thereof; and in a word it is the "bed-rock" of the British Empire.

I hope I have not tired you with this long - and you may feel lengthy (which implies *weariness* in its longness) letter; but it is written on the impulse of the pleased and grateful feelings excited in my heart by the excellence of your kind note and to me most fascinating periodical. I wish you all success with it and beg to remain,

Yours most truly,

(Sd.) George Birdwood

To
S. C. Mookerjee, Esq.,
Editor of the *Dawn*, Calcutta.

Appendix III

Satis Chandra Mukherjee's Reply to Sir George Birdwood

As my present letter will amply show my sympathies are entirely on your side in matters which affect the natural, evolutionary, indigenous growth of the great Hindu people. And it is, therefore, that equally with yourself, "I hail with delight every symptom of the spontaneous revival of the indigenous and traditionary, literary and artistic and philosophical and religious life of India - India of the Hindus". I cannot, however, conceal from you what I have always felt that our schools and colleges, *such as they are and have been*, are getting to be a growing hindrance; for it seems to me they have outlived their initial stage of usefulness; and that if they must help on the future evolution of my country they would have to be remodelled on, or informed by, a principle the keynote of which would be a greater help by the people themselves along lines suited to a natural, peaceful, indigenous growth, aided of course, but in a most general way, by the fostering hand of responsible men in authority. As it is, the Indian schools and colleges take their cue from the semi-official universities; semi-official in more senses than one. In the first place, they are controlled by the government officials who naturally and with the best of motives, desire to impress upon them the stamp of a culture with which they are most familiar. But the culture has been, I am afraid, forced at too high a speed; it has not been evolutionary, it is not a growth from within ourselves; and if I must speak out my mind, I must not hesitate to say that if the English were to leave us tomorrow, we should be very much in the same position of helplessness as your ancestors were when, during the declining days of Roman power about the fifth century A.D., the aegis of a great rule stood outside and left the people to work out their own destiny. From this point of view, from this point of view of permanent improvement, of stable, enduring, lasting good, I am of opinion that the English will have to revise their relations and initiate a line of reform such as that which you have indicated in your letter.

In the second place, the Indian universities are getting to be more and more governed by a sensible percentage of my own countrymen who are the products of a system of enforced culture, whose evils I have but indicated in the last preceding paragraph. When the machine has been moving along the right road and everything is in order, it does not require a master-mind to direct its operations; but when it has to be shunted off the line in order that it may pursue an even and less risky course, a more progressive road, it will require all the energies we have, and a comprehensive grasp of facts, a larger foresight than the average Fellow of the universities here possess for a successful issue. And it, therefore, happens as a necessary corollary, that many of our Senators have but little time to spare for their educational duties. As you have rightly remarked, "you will never assimilate and receive real nourishment from any alien culture imposed on you under compulsion of the drill-sergeant's cane". There is, therefore, little of life either in the teachers, or the students, or the University Fellow; the ponderous machine continues to move on no doubt, because of the momentum it has acquired, but at a lesser and lesser speed as the days go by; though in the absence of something better, the motion may continue long enough. And in proportion to the time during which the motion would last, should I be inclined to measure the helplessness of our position. There is life, no doubt, amongst us, but it is the sort of life which cannot, as far as I am in a position to judge, work out its own salvation. The culture has been imposed; and so far as it has penetrated our lives, we are presenting a show of activity; but, unless I am greatly mistaken, the activity is artificial, delusive, and bound sooner or later either to disappear, or to issue forth—not in any great calamity—but in a growing weakening of the whole moral frame of the collective body, who have been the victims of such "enforced"', "alien" culture.

My idea, however, is not to deprecate high English Education as truly mischievous, but to prove that it might be made better to fulfil its functions, if it could be leavened with a higher informing spirit; if its lessons could be learnt in a critical spirit and in the comparative method; if, in short, nothing of English life or civilization be taken on trust, but it be approached in a spirit of truthfulness and fairness and understood and appreciated in constant reference to the civilisation and culture of India's past, which must have been and is still furnishing the motive power for further evolution. It is *with this meaning* that, when I wrote to you last, I spoke of "awakening a purer and higher thought" amongst my Indian countrymen.

Macaulay wrote in 1836 and 1837 (I am not referring to his celebrated Minute of the 2nd February, 1835, which has hitherto decided the fate of Sanskrit Education; but to certain smaller and less known ones given in H. Woodrow's collection): "We aim at raising up an educated class who will hereafter, as we hope, be the means of diffusing amongst their countrymen some portion of the knowledge we have imparted to them. Among them some persons will be found who will have the inclination and ability to exhibit European knowledge in the vernacular dialects. This I believe to be the only way in which we can raise up a good vernacular literature in this country". With Macaulay's views as expressed in his Minute of 1835, February 2, "that a single shelf of a good European library was worth the whole native literature of India and Arabia", it was natural that he should think of developing the vernacular literature of India through the influence of an alien culture. He wished to construct, as it were, a new nation out of a heterogeneous lot of people, united by no cement, who, he thought, had no past worth having, no civilisation whose deep-hid workings might one day effectually stand in the way of the realisation of his hopes. He had found, he imagined, a people freshly created, waiting to be impressed with the stamp of what he conceived to be the "noblest literature in the world". "The languages of Western Europe civilised Russia. I cannot doubt that they will do for the Hindu what they have done for the Tartar". The whole drift of Macaulay's thought was in the direction of a mechanical, if forcible, manipulation of forces; he had, it seems, little conception of the evolutionary development of organisms, whether biological or sociological.

The flaw in Macaulay's reasoning is being seen now-a-days; the actual results of the system of enforced, alien culture, it was not possible to detect, so long as such culture was *protected*, was the passport to official honours and emoluments—so long as English administration in India stood in urgent need of a class of English educated Indians from the Universities.

"But", says Seeley in his Expansion of England, "if India is really to be enlightened, evidently it must be through the medium neither of Sanskrit, nor of the English, but of the Vernaculars, that is, Hindustanee, Hindi, Bengali, &c. Could Macaulay really fancy it possible to teach two hundred and fifty millions of Asiatics, English?" Here, again, there is the same error in detecting the right evolutionary point of view, the point of view as above explained; but yet the recognition of the vernaculars as a medium for enlightening the masses is a step in advance. But the vernaculars are but dialects, i.e., arc all drawn from the Sanskrit as their source of life; and it is because Sanskrit and the Prakrits, are so correlated, that a natural development (as opposed to an artificial manufacture) of the great Hindu people is possible through a cultivation of the vernaculars. Having, it seems to me, missed the evolutionary point of view, Seeley would regard Sanskrit as a mere dead tongue incapable of moulding a nation's life. "Why should there be no choice but between dead languages? Therefore over Sanskrit Macaulay had an early victory." Such were Mr. Seeley's views.

I therefore agree with you in thinking that both Sanskrit and the vernaculars formed out of Sanskrit will have to be cultivated in order to a peaceful evolution of Indian life and thought.

Appendix IV

Schemes of Study Prescribed by the National Council of Education, Bengal, National Council of Education's *Calender* for 1906-08

A. Primary Stage (*extending over three years*)

	Literary	**Scientific and Technical**
First Year	Vernacular	Arithmetic, object lessons and Drawing.
Second Year	Vernacular Reader, Story-telling and Geography	Arithmetic, object lessons and Drawing.
Third Year	Vernacular Reader, Geography and English Alphabetical Primer	Arithmetic, General Laws of Health, Object-lessons and Drawing

B. Secondary Stage—Lower (*extending over five years*)

First Year	Sanskrit or Arabic or Persian, Vernacular Prose and Poetry, English Reader (*chiefly dealing with Indian things*	Arithmetic, object-lessons (comprising things economic, physiological and physical), Workshop Practice and Drawing

	and thoughts), History and Geography (both in *Vernacular*)	
Second Year	Sanskrit or Arabic or Persian, Vernacular Prose and Poetry, English Reader, History (in *Vernacular*) and Geography (in *Vernacular*)	Arithemetic, Science, Workshop Practice and Drawing
Third Year	Sanskrit or Arabic or Persian, Vernacular Prose and Poetry, English, History (in *Vernacular*) and Geography (in *Vernacular*)	Mathematics, Science, Workshop Practice and Drawing
Fourth Year	Sanskrit or Arabic or Persian, Vernacular Prose and Poetry, English, History and Geography (both in *Vernacular*)	Mathematics, Science, Workshop Practice and Drawing
Fifth Year	Sanskrit or Arabic or Persian, Vernacular Prose and Poetry, English, History and Geography (in *Vernacular*)	Mathematice, Physics, Chemistry, Biology, Sanitary Science, Workshop Practice and Drawing

N.B. Up to the Fifth Year of the Secondary Course, all branches of Science were to be learnt with the aid of experiments and without text-books, and no written examinations should be held. Besides, the study of the French, German, Japanese and Pali languages as optional subjects was recommended.

B. Secondary Stage— Upper (*extending over two years*)

I. The Secondary Literary Course

(*extending over two years*)

A. For study only. An Oriental vernacular, English, Logic and elementary Physics and Chemistry.

B. For study and examination -

(1) An Oriental Classic, and

(2) Any one of the following groups: —

(a) History and Economics

(b) Psychology and Ethics

(c) Pali, Hindi and either Marathi or Gujarati or Tamil or Telugu

(d) French and German

Candidates for the Seventh Standard Examination (corresponding to the F.A., or Intermediate Examination of the Indian Universities) and offering the Secondary Literary Course were required to write an essay in English and also an essay in a vernacular on one or more of the subjects prescribed for examination.

C. For Study only. Optional.

One or more of the commercial subjects, viz. Shorthand, Type-writing, Book-keeping, Banking, Insurance, Commercial Geography, Correspondence and Arithmetic.

II. The Secondary Scientific Course

(*extending over two years*)

A. For study only. An Oriental vernacular, English, Logic and elementary Economics.

B. For study and examination—

(1) Physics and Chemistry (with laboratory work) and

(2) Any one of the following groups:-

(a) Mathematics, Drawing and Workshop Practice

(b) Biology and Physiology (with laboratory work)

(c) Geology and Biology (with laboratory work)

(d) Agriculture and Biology (with practical work)

Candidates for the Seventh Standard Examination (corresponding to the F.A. or Intermediate Examination of the Indian Universities) and offering the Secondary Scientific Course were required to write an essay in English and also an essay in a vernacular on one or more of the subjects prescribed for examination.

III. The Secondary Technical Course

(extending over three years)

A. A general course of instruction in -

(i) Physics,

(ii) Chemistry,

(iii) Mathematics,

(iv) Drawing,

and

B. A special course of instruction in—

(i) Machine Drawing,

(ii) Mechanics,

(iii) Steam-engines, Boilers and Prime Movers,

(iv) Hand and Machine Tools,

(v) Pattern-making,

(vi) Brass-moulding,

(vii) Smithy,

(viii) Turning,

(ix) Fitting.

N.B. Apprenticeship Course:- "Students who have not passed any previous examination or passed through any course of studies may be admitted into the Technical Department as outside students for practical instruction in one or more of the arts and industries mentioned above or as many of them as may be provided for by the Council. They shall receive certificates of successful apprenticeship."

C. Collegiate Stage (*extending over four years*)

I. *Literary*

(*i*) Linguistic

A. An Oriental Classical language and literature with an allied vernacular - Sanskrit or Pali, Arabic or Persian and Bengali or Assamese, Uriya, Hindi, Urdu, Marathi, Tamil, Telugu, or Gujarati

B. English Language and Literature

C. Comparative Philology

(*ii*) Historical

Group I. *History*

A. An Introductory Course of Lectures on the importance of historical studies to the Indian students

B. History of the Civilisation of India

C. History of the Civilisation of Europe

D. History of the Civilisation of Greece and Rome

E. History of the Spread of Buddhism

F. History of the Spread of Christianity

G. History of the Spread of Mahomedanism

H. A study of the Period, 1557-1688

I. A study of the period, 1757-1857

J. A study of the histories of Japan, China and America during 1850-1900

K. A study of the following historical characters, their work and their times—

1. Washington

2. Bismarck

3. Victor Emmanuel, Mazzini and Garibaldi

4. Solomon the Magnificent

5. Mutshohito

G. Ferdinand and Isabella

7. Napoleon Bonaparte

8. Peter the Great

9. Frederick the Great

10. Chengiz Khan

11. Abraham Lincoln

12. Kosciusko

Group II. *Economics*

A. History of the Economic Condition of India during

(i) Hindu times,

(ii) Mahomedan times,

(iii) The Company's rule,

(iv) Direct British rule.

B. An Elementary Course of Political Economy, analytical and descriptive, with special reference to India.

C. An advanced course of Political Economy to include discussion of economic writers and systems, methods of investigation of current topics (*opinions not to be taught*), history of Economic theories, etc.

Note: It is desirable that students should have a knowledge of the French language and such knowledge should he insisted on as soon as practicable.

Group III. *Political Science*

A. Introduction to Political Science, Society and State and their mutual relations.

B. Study of the forms and methods of government, legislative and administrative, in India (including the Native States) under Hindu, Mahomedan and British rule.

C. Study of the typical forms of government in

(i) England,

(ii) France,

(iii) Germany,

(iv) Switzerland,

(v) The United States,

(vi) Japan,

(vii) Turkey.

D. History of the theories about (1) the origin, (2) the nature and (3) the ends of the State.

E. Methods and instruments of Government—the Sovereignty of the State and its organs.

F. (a) A general survey of recent political progress.

(b) Tendencies in modern International Relations as affected by Commerce and Labour.

(iii) Philosophical

1. Logic

2. Psychology

3. Ethics

4. Metaphysics

5. History of Philosophy

6. Natural and Comparative Religion

7. Indian Philosophical Systems:—

Group I—Hindu,

or Group II—Muhammadan.

N.B. Candidates were expected to possess a good knowledge of Sanskrit or Arabic; and a knowledge of German was deemed desirable.

II. *Scientific*

1. Pure Mathematics (with Mixed Mathematics as a subsidiary subject)

or

Mixed Mathematics (with Pure Mathematics as a subsidiary subject).

2. Physics as principal subject with Chemistry and Mathematics as subsidiary subjects for study but not for examination.

3. Chemistry as principal subject with Physics and Mathematics as subsidiary subjects for study but not for examination.

III. *Technical*

1. Agriculture including Forestry
2. Manufacture including Mining
3. Commerce and Zemindary Management

N.B. The scheme for Higher or Collegiate Technical Course was not complete at the time of framing the N.C.E' s Schemes of Study in 1906. "It," announced Sir Gooroodass in August, 1906, "would be settled after consultation with experts."

A detailed scheme of studies for the Collegiate Course (Applied), consisting of Mechanical Engineering Course, Applied Chemistry Course and Scientific Pharmacy Course, was adopted by the N.C.E. for the National College session from August, 1908 and was published in almost all the dailies of Calcutta as well as in the August, 1908 issue of the *Dawn Magazine*. It is also to be found in the N.C.E's *Calendar* for 1906-08.

IV

1. Medicine
2. Engineering
3. Pedagogics
4. Law

Manufacturing Courses of Study in the Bengal National College

I

College Mechanical Engineering Course (*Four Years*)

A. Mechanical Engineering:—

(a) Manufacturing and repairing of machines and tools &c. with drawing and designing—as principal subject.

(b) Manufacturing and repairing of Scientific apparatus in Physics including Electrical appliances, with drawing and designing—as subsidiary subject.

B. or *Vice versa.*

N.B. Only those students who have passed the 7th Standard Examination in the Secondary Scientific Course 2 (a) of the Scheme of Studies prescribed by the National Council of Education will be eligible for admission to the College Mechanical Engineering Course and those who have not gone through the Secondary Technical Course shall have to complete that course in the first two years of their College Course.

The Secondary Scientific Course 2 *(a)* aforesaid, includes Mathematics, Drawing, Workshop Practice, Physics and Chemistry (both with laboratory work). The Secondary Technical Course includes a special course of instruction in Machine Drawing, Mechanics, Steam-Engines, Boilers and Prime Movers, Hand and Machine tools, Pattern-making, Brass-moulding, Smithy, Turning and Fitting.

Those who take up 2 *(b)* as their principal subject shall be required to go through such higher portions of Mathematics and theoretical and practical Physics as may be necessary.

II

College Applied Chemistry Course

{Four Years)

First Stage

(a) Full Course of Chemistry inorganic and organic (theoretical and experimental) including analysis, qualitative and quantitative.

(b) Manufacturing processes including the manufacture of substances of industrial importance—oxygen, chlorine, bleaching powder, hydrochloric, nitric and sulphuric acids, phosphorus, soda, soda products, pearl-ash, alkalis, plaster of Paris, quicklime, pencils, inks, matches, alloys and solders.

(c) Mechanical Engineering so far as it is necessary for chemical works.

Second Stage

(a) General principles of Agricultural, Commercial and Manufacturing Chemistry with demonstration.

(b) Select methods of Analysis.

1. Qualitative and quantitative analysis of soils and manures.

2. Qualitative and quantitative analysis of food articles, natural waters and ordinary animal products.

3. Qualitative and quantitative analysis of minerals, (especially coal and iron), fuel, gas, oil, fats.

4. Qualitative and quantitative analysis of textile fabrics, sizing materials, bleaching stuffs, dye-stuffs.

(c) Manufacturing Processes: —

(1) Bleaching and dyeing (2) soap and candle (3) manure (4) lac, indigo, ink, (5) paints, polishes, varnishes (6) Electroplating.

N.B. Only those students who have passed the 7th Standard Examination in either Secondary Scientific 2 (a) or 2 (b) of the Schemes of Studies prescribed by the National Council of Education, Bengal will be eligible for admission to the College Applied Chemistry Course. The Secondary Scientific Course 2(b) aforesaid includes Biology and Physiology (with laboratory work).

III

College Scientific Pharmaceutical Course

(Four Years)

(1) Medicine: No general Scheme of medical study has been framed but the study of the following preliminary subjects is prescribed for Proficiency Examination in Scientific Pharmacy and as a preparation for the study of Medicine:

(a) Chemistry .

Primary Stage:

(i) General—(inorganic and organic)—theoretical and experimental, analysis both qualitative and quantitative.

Secondary Stage:

(i) Physiological—optional except for those who intend to study medicine.

(ii) Pharmaceutical

(b) Botany

(i) General

(ii) Pharmaceutical

(c) Materia Medica (Indian and European)

Optional except for those who intend to study medicine	*(d)*	Zoology (including Proto-zoology)
	(e)	Anatomy (comparative and human with dissection
	(f)	Physiology

N.B. Only those students who have passed the 7th Standard Examination in Secondary Scientific 2 (b) of the Scheme of Studies prescribed by the National Council of Education, Bengal, are eligible to the College Scientific Pharmaceutical Course.

Appendix V

Recommendations of the National Education Committee (Report of the Proceedings of the National Education Committee, 23rd Februrary, 1923-6th March, 1923, at Kashi Vidyapeetha)

I

The Purpose of Education

1. The purpose of Education (it should be borne in mind) is to teach the Educable how the Spiritual and the Material Happiness of Mankind may be attained.

II

The Qualifications of the Educator

2. Persons with the missionary spirit, embodying, in some noticeable degree, in their life, self-denial and benevolence as well as special knowledge (*tapas* or *zohd* and *vidya* or *ilm*) should be teachers. Teachers of children in schools should ordinarily be persons inspired by parental feeling, who can take care of others' children in the parental spirit. Heads of institutions, especially, whether the institutions be large or small, should be senior persons, who, besides their special knowledge may have knowledge of the essentials of general psychology and physiology, and especially of the adolescent.

The relations of teachers with each other and with students should be those of members of a joint family (*Guru-kula*).

The status of teachers with each other and other office-bearers in an Educational Institution should not depend upon their incomes.

III

The Educable

All persons desirous of receiving education regularly, and willing to abide by the rules of the institutions concerned, should be eligible, without reference to their caste or creed, for receiving such education, in the National Educational Institutions, as is suitable for their capabilities and requirements, and for which there may be facilities in the institutions.

For other classes of persons, not able to attend the institutions regularly, provision may be made for popular lectures (*katha, vyakhyana, imla*) as far as possible.

The education of persons suffering from mental, moral, or physical defect, may be dealt with by special institutions.

IV

The Nature, Scope and Subject-Matter of Education

Education consists in educating, developing, and training to good uses, the powers of the head, heart, and limbs, *i.e.,* the intellectual, moral, and physical faculties of the Educable, so that they may become able to take care of themselves and their families and dependents, and to serve society, spiritually and materially.

The following branches (all organically connected with one another) are included within the scope of Education:

I. Cultural:

a. *Religious and Moral Education.*

b. *Intellectual and Aesthetic Education.*

c. *Physical Education.*

II. Technical, Vocational or Practical Education

IV-I *(a)*

Religious and Moral Education

(i) Nature of the Instructions; and Text-Books

a. Graduated text-books should be prepared, for the use of teachers, for each religion-Hindu, Muslim, Christian, Sikh, Jain, Parsi, and Buddhist.

b. A Text-Book of Comparative Religion and Morals should be prepared, on a systematic plan, for the use of teachers of Religion, and also for the use of students in the college stage, which should deal as fully as possible with the points common to all religions, while stating and comparing the specific features of each.

c. The special text-books of each religion should state the main ideas and practices of that religion prominently, then explain the principal details broadly, and, finally, mention the differences of ideas and customs that have arisen, within the pale of that religion, in respect of these details.

d. In the actual teaching of any religion, while the important tenets and practices of that religion are taught, attention should be specially drawn to the elements common to other religions also.

(***Note:-*** Thus, when teaching the existence of the Supreme Being, the corresponding names in the various religions, Param-atma, Allah, Jehovah, God, etc., should be mentioned. When teaching the practice of prayer, it should be explained that the essential idea is the same behind the different words 'Sandhya-vandana,' 'Namaj,' 'Prayer,' etc.).

(ii) *To Whom should Religious Instruction be given*

a. Religious instruction (dharma-shiksha, mazhabi-talim) should be given in the principal religions to the students belonging to them respectively, Hindu, Muslim, Christian, Sikh, Jain, Parsi, Buddhist; but in the school stage if the parent of a child expressly wishes that the child should not receive any religious instruction, the child should be exempted.

(*Note*:- In any given institution, provision would ordinarily be made for the teaching of that religion to which the majority of the pupils belong. But if the financial conditions permit, or special funds are provided by donors, provision should be made for the teaching of other religions also, to which minorities among the pupils may belong).

b. In the college stage, students who may have conscientious objections need not be compelled to receive religious instruction. Educational institutions should rely on the excellence of their religious teaching to make their students not only willing but eager to receive it. And, especially, religious instruction should be given in the spirit and manner which will promote proper understanding of and peace with other religions.

(iii) Moral Instruction, especially through extra- college and extra-school activities

Students should, as part of their moral education, be encouraged and trained to take part in activities relating to national reconstruction, under the guidance of teachers, and consistently with the regular prosecution of their intellectual and practical studies, besides the instruction in good habits and good manners which should be given in class, from time to time, on appropriate occasions as they arise.

(iv) Moral Instruction in regard to Sex

The broad idea of purity in matters of sex, of complete sex-cleanliness, as necessary part for the healthy growth of body and mind, during the student-stage, should be put into the atmosphere of educational institutions, generally, and without ostentation, so that it may be assimilated by the pupils from their earliest years, gently and quietly.

For specific advice to pupils, a Committee should be appointed to prepare a pamphlet for the use of parents and teachers in conveying the needed instruction to their children and pupils.

IV-*I (b)*

Intellectual and Aesthetic Education

The subject matter of Intellectual and Aesthetic Education may be divided into:

A. Material Science (Apara-vidya, Ulum-i-Dunya).

B. Spiritual Science (Para-vidya, Brahma-vidya, Adhyatma-vidya, Paramartha-shastra, Ulum-i-Din).

A. Material Science, the Science of Matter, the Science of the Finite, includes, as its three main sub-divisions, the following:

I . The Sciences (Shastra, Ulum) and Arts (Prayoga, Funun) which make possible *the proper Organisation* (vyuhana, sangrahana, or tanzim) and *Preservation* (rakshana or hifazat) of Society: (Dharma-shastra, Ulum-i-tanzim-i-jamaat).

(a). *Organisation*

(i) Languages and Linguistic Sciences, (ii) Law and Jurisprudence (Vyavahara-Dharma, Mamilat-i-Fiqah). (iii) Sociology (Purana, Samaj-shastra, Ijtima-iat), History (Itihasa, Tarikh), Politics and Civics (Raja-Dharma, Danda-niti, Siasiyat, Madani-yat).

(b). *Preservation*

(i) Medicine (Ayur-veda, Tibb), General Hygiene and Sanitation (Shaucha-vidhi, Arogya-shastra, Safai, Hifz-i-sihat). (It) Military Science (Shustravidya, Ilm-i-jung).

II. The Sciences and Arts which make possible *the lawful Enrichment of Society* (Artha-shastra, Ulum-i- Daulat).

(a) The Chemical (Rasayana-shastra, Kimia), Physical (Bhautika-shastra, Ilm-i-tabai), and Biological Sciences (Jiva-shastra, Ilm-i-hayat).

(b) Mathematics (Ganita, Ilm-i-riyazi) (c) Economics, Agriculture, Rearing of Domestic Animals, Commerce, Engineering in all its branches, and all Applied Science generally (Varta-shastra, Ulum-i-iqtisad), i.e., Science applied to the production of Wealth which makes possible the securing of Necessaries as well as refined Comforts, and also the securing of rich Public Possessions of common use, for the families that make up Society.

III. The Sciences and Arts which make possible *the refined Worldly Happiness of Society*; the Science of Domestic and Social Life, and all subsidiary Arts that refine and ennoble the individual, the family, and the race (Kama-Shastra, Kala-Shastra, Ilm-i-Khanadari, Ilm-i-Majlis, Funun-i-Latifa), viz., the Science of Eugenics, and Sex-Physiology and Hygiene; and all the Fine Arts, Poetry, Drama, General Literature, Music, Painting, Sculpture, Architecture, Horticulture, etc.

B. (IV). Spiritual Science, the Science of the Infinite Spirit, which Science explains the nature, meaning, and purpose of life and the universe; unifies, co-ordinates, and supplies first principles and foundations to, all the Sciences of the Finite; and makes possible the *realization of the deepest Spiritual Happiness.*

It includes, (a) Metaphysics or Philosophy (Darshana, Moksha-shastra, Falsafa, Ilm-i-Ilahiyat); (b) Psychology (Adhyatma-vidya, Chitta-shastra, Nafasiyat); (c) Logic or the Science of Reasoning (Tarka shastra, Pramana-shastra, Mantiq; (a) Ethics (Achara-shastra, Niti, Akhlaqiyat); (b) Comparative Religion (Dharma-Tattva-Samiksha, Ilm-ul-Adyan)

Some Details Re Intellectual and Aesthetic Education

1. The School course may be divided into two periods, (i) a Primary or Elementary course, *adya or ibtidai*, of five or six years, and (II) a Secondary or Preparatory, *madhya* or *sanavi*.

Primary Stage

2. In the primary stage stress should be laid on, and methods should be followed which will help, the developing and strengthening of the child's faculties rather than the storing; of much information in his mind. In the earlier years of this stage, books should be used only to a minimum extent. In the later years, voluntary reading of good, healthy, and interesting literature by the pupils should be

encouraged. Special care should be taken to impart education more through observation, conversation, and story-telling, than through books.

3. In the course of the story-telling or his history-telling and conversation, and by means of patriotic songs and recitations, information should be conveyed to the pupil on the following subjects: Manners and Morals (*Shishtackara, sadachara, adab-ikhlaq*); National History; Geography of India and general Outlines of World Geography; Biographies of great men and women; Incidents from Epics; Contemporary events and matters of General Information; the simpler and more familiar Natural Phenomena; Hygiene and Sanitation.

(*Note*: To help in this work, a graduated series of special readers should he prepared which will - each one - convey information on all these subjects in an interesting, and, as far as possible, connected form, as e.g., by narratives of travels, episodes, and dialogues, embodied in a biographical history. Into the history may also be interwoven selections of good poetry, drama, fairy tales, and such other pieces of fine literature as may be suited to the capacities of the pupils, and be fit for memorisation).

4. Pupils should be encouraged to acquire, under the guidance of teachers, general information about natural phenomena, by means of direct observation principally.

5. The following should also be taught; Reading and Writing, Elementary Arithmetic, (including rule of three, simple interest, measurement of areas, mental arithmetic), and simple Account-keeping.

6. Hindustani should be taught as a compulsory Lingua Indica (with either the Nagari Script, or the Urdu Script, or both Scripts when the mother-tongue of the pupil is Hindustani, according to local convenience) in the later stage of Primary Education, or, where this is not possible, for any special reasons, there at some stage of Secondary Education. The particular stage and the extent of

knowledge of the language to be expected from the pupils should be decided by the institutions according to provincial conditions.

Secondary Stage

7. The Secondary stage may be divided into two parts, the first of three years, the second of two.

In the first, the following subjects should be studied:

The Mother-tongue (Language and Literature).

(*Note*: Special readers should he prepared which will include information about the elementary essentials of Civics, Politics, Sociology, Psychology, Physiology, and Ethics).

Hindustani (*i. e*., intelligent reading of books in the language, if not already done in the Primary stage).

Mathematics (amount to be decided by the Institutions).

General History of India, including the Indian Constitution, and General Geography.

Also any two of the following:

(a) Samskrit or Arabic or any other classical language.

(b) A modern European language.

(c) Elementary Science.

(*Note*: Besides the above, instruction in Religion and in some Technical handicraft would be given, of course, as recommended elsewhere under the appropriate heads).

8. In the last two years of the Secondary stage, one of four possible courses may be chosen. The study of the Mother-tongue (Language and Literature) should, however, be compulsory, and common to all the four courses.

9. The four possible courses are,

(a) An Arts Course;

(b) A Science Course;

(c) A Commerce Course;

(d) A Fine Arts Course.

10. Under (a) the Arts Course, the following subjects should be studied:

Compulsory: (i) A Classical language or (ii) a modern European language;

and,

any three out of the following :

i) A modern Indian or Asiatic language other than the mother-tongue.

ii) History with special reference to the struggles of peoples for their rights; and Indian Administration.

iii) Geography.

iv) Civics (*i.e.*, Politics and Economics).

(v) Mathematics.

(vi) Further Mathematics.

(vii) Logic

(viii) Psychology.

ix) A modern European language, not already taken under the head *Compulsory*.

x) A classical language, not already taken under the head *Compulsory*.

(*Note*: Specially circumstanced Institutions may, instead of having a classical or modern European language as compulsory, allow students to choose any *four*- instead of any *three*- subjects out of the optionals).

11. Under (b) the Science Course, the following subjects should be studied:

Compulsory: (i) One modern European language; *and* (ii) Mathematics;

and

any one of the following groups:

Group (i)-(a) Further Mathematics, (b) Chemistry, (c) Physics.

Group (ii)-(a) Biology (*i.e.*, Botany and Zoology), (b) Chemistry.

Group (iii((a) Chemistry, (b) Physiology.

12. Under (c) the Commerce Course, the following subjects should be studied:

Compulsory: (i) One modern European language, (ii) Accountancy, (iii) Commercial Geography with special reference to Indian industries, (iv) Business management,

and

one of the following:

(i) Commercial Law.

(ii) Industrial History

(iii) Elements of Banking.

13. Under (d) the Fine Arts Course, the following subjects should be studied:

Compulsory: (i) one modern European language, (ii) one modern Indian language other than the mother-tongue, (iii) History and Geography of India with special reference to the development of the Fine Arts, (iv) One classical language,

and

one of the following :—

(i) Painting (including Drawing).

(ii) Music.

(iii) Sculpture (including Drawing).

(iv) Architecture (including drawing).

(*Note* i: It is the aim of National Education that a student should be able to complete the whole course of Education without having knowledge of any European language. But as literature in several branches of knowledge, especially the scientific branches, is not yet to be found in the Indian tongues, it has been found necessary to make a modern European language compulsory in those subjects during the transitional period. This provision will not affect the mother tongue as the medium of instruction).

(*Note* ii: In the school stage, not more than three subjects should be taught, under *Intellectual and Aesthetic Instruction*, on one and the same day).

College Stage

14. The College stage should ordinarily cover three years, and be devoted to specialisation in some one subject. Students should take up one sub-head of the subject (when there are sub-heads) as principal and two others as subsidiary, in consultation with their teachers.

Possible subjects:

i) Language and Literature in all their branches, viz. Grammar, Philology, Rhetoric, Belles Letters etc.,

The sub-heads Under this would be a) A Modern Indian Language and its Literature; b) Another Modern Asiatic Language and its Literature; c) a Modern European Language and its Literature; d) a Classical Language and its Literature.

(ii) Philosophy in all its branches, *viz*. Psychology, Experimental Psychology, Logic, Ethics, Metaphysics, Comparative Religion, History of Philosophy, etc.

The sub-heads here would be the various schools of Eastern and Western Philosophy, *e.g.* Nyaya, Vaisheshika, Sankhya, Yoga, Mimansa, Vedanta, Jaina, Bauddha, etc. Darshanas, Arabian Philosophy, Greek Philosophy, Modern European Philosophy, etc.

But a grounding in Eastern Philosophy, Indian or Arabian, should be necessary in every combination under Philosophy.

(iii) The Social Sciences, in all their branches, i.e. Sociology, History (General as well as that of some special period and country), Civics and Politics and Economics.

(*Note* : A student taking any of these four as principal subject will be expected to take up two of the other three as subsidiary).

(iv) Mathematics in all its brandies, pure and applied, including Astronomy.

(v) A Physical Science, *viz*., Chemistry (Pure and Applied); Physics (Pure and Applied); Botany; Zoology; Physiology; Anthropology; or Geology.

(vi) Cultures, Aryan (*i.e*., Bharatiya or Indian) and Islamic.

(vii) Law in all its branches, *viz.*, Jurisprudence, Substantive Law, Procedural Law, Civil Law, Criminal Law, Comparative Iurisprudence, International Law, etc.

The sub-heads here would be (a) Hindu Law, (b) Muslim Law (c) Roman Law, (d) A modern European Legal System.

(Note : Either Hindu or Muslim law should be taken up compulsorily, under this head, either as principal or as subsidiary).

(viii) A Fine Art in all its branches, theory, practice, history, comparison between different schools, etc., (a) Music, (b) Painting, (c) Sculpture, (d) or Architecture.

IV-*I* (*c*).

Physcial Education

Physical Education may be sub-divided .into three parts, as below:-

(i) Exercises For the sake of health, strength, and shapeliness,

(a) Without apparatus,

1. Breathing exercises.

2. Running, leaping, tree-climbing, *kabaddi*, *dand*, *baithak*, *banh*, *kalai*, *panja*, somersaults, and many other sorts of pushes and pulls (of Indian and Japanese varieties), etc.

3. Simple drills and swadeshi team games.

(b) With apparatus,

1. *Mudgar* (or Indian clubs), dumbbells, etc.

2. Gymnastics, with ropes, bars, etc.

3. Drills with flags, lanterns, weapons, etc., and team-games with apparatus, such as cricket, hockey, football, tennis, chaugan, polo, etc.

(ii) Exercises for the sake of acquiring physical accomplishments,

1. Swimming; 2. Boxing; 3. Wrestling and Mal-khambha; 4. Fencing with sticks, swords, daggers, etc.; 5. Shooting with bows and arrows or guns, spear-throwing, etc. 6. Riding; 7. Driving; 8. Rowing; 9. Cycling; 10. Motor- driving., 11. Etc.; 12. Scout-work.

(iii) Exercises for professional gymnastics and acrobatics

Physical exercises of the first kind, for the sake of health and strength and suppling the limbs and giving shape to the body, without apparatus, should be compulsory on all students; also some boxing and fencing with sticks. Breathing exercises, especially, and drills, should be very carefully planned and encouraged. Over-exertion, and sudden changes of temperature, from heat to cold, or cold to heat, - the two great dangers connected with exercise must be very carefully avoided.

Other exercises, with apparatus, and for physical accomplishments, especially swimming, should be encouraged as conveniently possible. Swadeshi games should be encouraged by preference, and expensive ones of all kinds discouraged. Swadeshi and inexpensive team-games and Scout-work should be encouraged especially to develop habits of concerted as well as self-reliant, independent and helpful action.

Tournaments between educational institutions may be arranged as convenient.

Exercises of the third kind need not be considered here.

IV-*II*

Technical Education

(i) Primary Stage

Technical, vocational, industrial or practical Education should be given side by side with Religious and Intellectual instruction during the elementary stage, in a general manner; and, after the elementary stage, *on paid apprentice lines*. Every student should be required during the years of general studies, corresponding to the school-period to learn some handicraft, which would enable him to become self-dependent, and for which local conditions may afford facilities.

Higher and more specialised technical instruction should be given in special institutions, corresponding to colleges.

Manual Training

During the elementary or primary stage, *i.e.* up to the eleventh or twelfth year of age of the student, manual training should be given as preparation for technical instruction proper, in such simple works as the following:

1. Ginning, carding with small bows, sliver making, spinning, bobbin-reeling, tape-making.
2. Clay-modelling, as preparation for pottery and ceramic work.
3. Cane and bamboo work.
4. Envelope-making, pad- making, file-making, book-binding.
5. Ink-making.
6. Simple tin-works.
7. Elementary carpentry.

8. Rope-making and coir-work.

9 Ordinary sewing.

10. Drawing.

11. Gardening and elementary agriculture.

12. Etc.

Generally, about three hours should be given in the forenoon for the other kinds of instruction (religion and moral, intellectual and aesthetic, *i.e.* preferably musical and physical exercises and drill, etc.) and about two hours in the afternoon should be devoted to practical and technical instruction, during this elementary or primary stage.

(ii) The Secondary Stage.

During the secondary stage, *i.e.*, up to the sixteenth or seventeenth year of age of the student, the technical instruction should comprise higher stages of all the items mentioned before and any others for which local conditions may be favourable, such as the making of matches, soap, paper (in the indigenous way), oils, boot-polishes, leather-goods, and electro-plating, mirror-silvering, etc.

Relation of Students to Workshops

Such technical instruction should be arranged for by (a) attaching and (b) *apprenticing* students, respectively, in the Elementary and the Secondary stages, to workshops belonging either to the Educational Institution itself, or to private concerns in the neighbourhood.

Special and Ordinary Secondary Schools

Provision may also be made for secondary schools (or courses) which would give practical and technical instruction of a fuller and more advanced kind than the ordinary secondary schools (or courses) with intellectual education as subsidiary.

In the ordinary schools (or courses), generally about four hours should be given to the intellectual instruction, and two to the technical.

In the specialised schools (or courses), the proportion should be reversed; and the mother-tongue and mathematics should be compulsory, on the intellectual side.

(*Note*: Students leaving from such special schools would ordinarily take up their vocation at once, and would not be able to join the higher technical colleges directly.)[1]

(*iii*) *Higher Technical Education.*

In the period of specialised studies (or the college period), intellectual studies and practical or technical courses would, ordinarily, not be combined, but be alternatives. But if some students taking up one alternative, wish to add to it some knowledge of the other also, facilities may be provided for them to do so, if possible. And, if the local conditions of any educational institution specially require it, it may combine the two kinds of studies.

The technical branches of study may be as below:

1. Medicine in all its branches.
2. Engineering (Civil, Mechanical, Electrical, Chemical, Mining, etc.)
3. Metallurgy.
4. Agriculture.
5. Industrial and Applied Chemistry (Dyeing, Bleaching, Tanning) etc;.
6. Weaving (of cotton-cloths, silk-cloths, woolen cloths, silver-and-gold-cloths, etc)
7. Pottery and Ceramics.
8. Glass-making.
9. Enamelling.

10. Paper-Manufacture.

11. Etc.

(*Note*:- National Colleges situated in or near capital towns may endeavour to specialise in one or other of the above or similar works.)[2]

V

The Time

(*a*) *Early Years of life*

Education (in the specific sense, as distinguished from that which ought to be received from very birth, through the home-life) should ordinarily begin between the fifth and eighth year and end between the twenty-first and twenty-fifth year of age.

(*b*) *Hours of the day*

The mornings and the afternoons are the best times of the day, for studies, generally, in India, the hours varying with the weather.

(*c*) *Holidays*

Holidays should be according to weather, to religious observances and festivals, and to the need for rest and change from routine (ordinarily once a week). Such holidays should, when possible, be utilized for excursions and nature study.

For the general studies or school stage of education, holidays should be short and frequent; for the higher stage, of specialized or college studies, there may be fewer short holidays and one or more long holidays in the year, according to special circumstances. Holidays should not ordinarily exceed one hundred and twenty days in the year.

(*d*) *School period*

Ten or eleven years may be spent on what may be called the courses of general studies, or school courses (*Patha-shala*, *Madrassa*) which would include some common and optional subjects.

(e) *Period of Specialization*

The subsequent years may be given to specialized (or college) studies (*Vidyalaya, Kullia*, or *Dar-ul-ulum*) *i.e.* specialization in culture or technical subjects, it being understood that one subject is principally s tudied for a period for at least three years.

An alternative course of lesser specialization may be provided for, in which the student may study not more than four subjects on an equal level during the period of three years.

Provision may be made for higher research work after the completion of the above courses.

VI

The Place

In the earlier years of education, children should ordinarily reside with their parents; in the later, youths may live in the buildings of the colleges, if possible, and if convenient to all concerned.

Schools for children in the earlier years should be placed as near the children's homes as possible. For the studies of the later years, institutions should ordinarily be located on the out-skirts of habitations, neither too far from, nor too near to, crowded quarters.

VII

The Manner

(i) The Medium

The medium of instruction should ordinarily, be the mother tongue of the province in which the educational institution is located. Where Hindustani is not the mother-tongue, it should be taught as a compulsory second language, for the purposes of a *Lingua Indica.*

(ii) Tests or Estimations of acquirements; Affirmations: Mutual Recognition.

Pramana-patra or *Sanads* should be given to students by the Universities (Vidya-pitha or Jamia), on the basis of estimations (as contra-distinguished from the current system of examinations). The estimations should be principally made by the teachers themselves of the students. The estimations should relate to the students' progress, from day to day, in proficiency in the subject concerned (whether science, art, or handicraft), to their diligence, and to their character and conduct. Special tests may also be made by the teachers themselves, from time to time, as they may think fit, or whenever the student leaves. The University should issue the affirmations on the basis of the recommendations made by the Institution concerned, the Institution being affiliated to, or recognized by, the University.

In any particular case in which the University authoritics find any special reason to disagree with the recommendations, they may withhold the affirmation until satisfied.

Teachers in national institutions and private candidates desirous of receiving affirmations from a University, should produce the recommendation of an affiliated or recognized Institution; and the Institutions should grant a recommendation after specially testing the worthiness of the candidates in such ways as it thinks fit.

A University may grant an affirmation for the compositions of any work of merit in an Indian language or any invention or discovery of note which may be promotive of any art or handicraft.

Affirmations of National Universities should be recognised by each other, for purpose of admission of students; and facilities should be provided (in the way of special coaching in the provincial mother-tongue) for students coming from other provinces; and, in making estimation of the acquirements of such students, minor imperfections in his use of provincial language, such as do not throw the meaning into doubt, should not be counted against him.

VIII

General Administration

(a) Governing Bodies

It is desirable that National Educational institutions should be autonomus, and should be made self-supporting as early as possible. On the managing or governing body of each, there should be an adequate representation of lay opinion, and especially of the donors, in order that the ordinary householder's requirements and views may be kept before the mind of the specialist educationists engaged in carrying on the daily outline of the institution.

The administration of each institution, whether School or College, should be in the hands of a governing body which should work for a minimum of at least five years. A Vidya-Pitha or Jamia should have for its governing body a Senate, (Niyamaka or Niriksha Sabha, etc.) as the executive body of the Senate a Syndicate (Prabandha Samiti or Parishat, etc.) And the Senate should have on it representatives of various affiliated bodies.

(b) Affiliation

It is desirable the National Schools and Colleges should be affiliated to Central Vidya-Pithas or Jamias.

(c) Economy

Expense on buildings should be minimised. For economy here, hostels should be built with at least a sufficient number of rooms of large size, which should hold classes during class- hours, and be used as living rooms by the resident students during the rest of the day.

Library and laboratory buildings should be substantial. The living and other rooms should be of a simple but neat character. Open air teaching should be encouraged, especially in villages.

Furniture should be of a simple character, of Indian make and style as far as possible. Students may bring their own *asans* (mats) to the class; but care should be taken that they do not have to bend down during study hours.[3]

(d) Library

Every institution should try to possess a good library of well-chosen books.

(e) Interchange of Teachers

National Institutions should arrange to interchange teachers, for short periods, from time to time. The fact that long vacations are observed in different months and seasons in different parts of the country, for climatic reasons, should help in such interchange.

(f) Building up Teachers

The growth of the class of Teachers of the right kind, possessing the intellectual and ethical qualifications needed for work in National Educational Institutions, may be helped forward in the following ways:-

1.By training.

2.By special honour from the public.

3.By schemes of allowances which will ensure freedom from financial worry.

As regards the first, every Vidya-Pitha or Jamia (National University) should have a department of Teaching, for training teachers. There should be two courses, one to begin after completion of general studies (school), and the other after the completion of specialised studies (college); each course to last not less than one year,

(*Note*: In view of what has been said before, under II- "THE QUALIFICATIONS OF THE EDUCATOR", it is obvious that Teachers should ordinarily be somewhat mature persons, with families of their own; but, during the transition period, unmarried young men also be entrusted with teaching work).

As regards the second means: Since National Educational Institutions require teachers who may be inspired, not by mercenary motives, but by the self-denying and philanthropic missionary spirit, for which the only recompense that the public can give is honour and gratitude, all teachers in such institutions should be given the honorific designation of Bhai, Pandit, or Maulavi.

As regards the third means: Schemes of *vritti* or *wazifa,* (scholarship or fellowship, honoraria) should be framed by all National Educational Institutions, with due regard to local and special conditions, such as will ensure their workers against financial worry.

(*g*) *Relation between Home and School*

Teachers should keep in touch with parents, as far as possible, and should encourage visits by them to the schools and colleges, request them for suggestions, invite them to holiday functions and do all that is possible to induce parents and the general public to take active interest in the welfare of the institutions and their members, as being 'their own'.

(*h*) *Text-Books*

(*i*)Text-Book Committee.

For the early preparation of much needed text-books a Text-Book Committee should be appointed.

[It should consist of one representative nominated by each National Vidya-Pitha or by a corresponding institution in a linguistic province which has no Vidya-Pitha as yet.]

The functions of the Committee should be,

1. To collect information about all the good and useful books extant and available in all the main living languages of India.

2. To prepare classified and descriptive lists of these under two heads:

(a) Those suitable for direct use as text-books, in the original and in translations, (i) in colleges, (ii) in schools.

(b) Those good for general reading as sources of information, and of material for the preparation of new text-books suitable for class-use.

3. To send such lists to all Vidya-Pithas, with any special recommendations they may wish to make.

4. To collect and circulate information as to the special facilities which the several Vidya-Pithas may possess, in the shape of specialists, of libraries, of laboratories, of local conditions, etc., for the preparation of text-books on any subject or subjects.

5. To compile and publish lists of foreign books (Japanese, English, French, German, etc.) which may be specially suitable for reproduction-with all needed correction of the foreign writers' national or racial bias-in living Indian languages, as text-books, on various subjects.

6. To enter into communication with authors and publishers of repute, in the various provinces who are writing and publishing in the living languages of India, and to secure their help in the preparation and publication of text-books.

(ii) Teachers and Text-Books

The teachers of the Vidya-Pithas should be requested and encouraged and given facilities to write out text-books on their several subjects, on the basis of their lecture-notes, after having taught the subject for some time in the linguistic mediums of their respective provinces.

(iii) Technical Words

For technical words, the current words, whenever available, of an Indian language, preferably Hindustani, should be adopted. In other cases, where conveniently possible, equivalents may be coined out of either Sanskrit or Arabic bases, but should be given such a shape or will not accentuate their Sanskrit or Arabic origin, but will tend to make them generally acceptable, in all provinces, in scientific use and teaching. Current signs and symbols may be adopted intact.

(i) Employment of Alumni

Appeal should be made to the Indian public generally to give preference to the alumni of the National Educational Institutions in engaging employees, when all other needed qualifications are equal.

Notes and References

* All sciences and arts whatsoever, eastern and western, ancient and modern, may be arranged tinder these four main heads, the value of this particular classification consisting in its *purposiveness*.

In the eastern tradition and ancient Indian culture, Education is subservient to the Ends of Human Life. These are dual (a) predominantly Material Happiness in the first half of life, the Path of Pursuit, and (b) predominantly Spiritual Happiness in the second half of life, the Path of Renunciation. Refined Material Happiness befitting the human being, is possible only by means of Wealth ; and the accumulation, preservation, and equitable distribution of that is possible only by means of Law, i.e., by means of definition and enforcement of rights and duties. Hence, the First End of Life is sub-divided into three, viz., Dharma, Artha, Kama, Virtue, (whence) Profit, (whence) Pleasure. The second, and higher, End of Life is Salvation.

To subserve these four Ends, the Knowledge, with which Education has to deal, is organised into four departments also, as above; and Education is throughout made culturo-vocational in one. Technical instruction may be said to be subsidiary to Artha-shastra, and Religious and Moral Instruction to Moksha-shastra.

It may be repeated here that such a *purposive* classification of sciences does not imply separation of their subject-matters in Nature. Nature is organic: Unity; because the God of Nature is One; and that Universal Consciousness holds together all the infinite parts of Nature in a perpetual Unity. Man's limited mind proceeds by analysis. Nature is always a limitless Synthesis. All classifications are only a matter of practical convenience, for the special purposes that may be in view.

Educational institutions may well endeavour that all their *alumni* should learn at least the essential elements, in broad outlines, of all the four great departments of knowledge, in due course.

[1] Shri Purushottam Das Tandon made a suggestion, as below, which it was unanimously agreed, should be put into a note : " There might be two classes of institutions, (1) Those providing education to students who have private means to pay for their education entirely ; (2) Those meant for students who have to earn their upkeep entirely or partly (during their educational career. With regard to the latter, technical education, including agriculture and fruit-culture, may be divided into two branches: (a) that meant to provide a livelihood for a student while he is a student, (b) that meant to be adopted as the profession in life of the student. Every student must go in for the first, since the underlying principle of education in the particular institution in question is, *ex hypothesi*, that the student should support himself without any, or with Very little, aid from his parents, during his student life."

[2] Thus: (1) There are National Medical Colleges, Madrassas or Pathashalas, teaching the European, Ayurvedic, Yunani, or other systems of Medicine, in Bombay, Calcutta, Delhi, Lucknow, Benares, Dacca, Pilibhit, etc.; (2) Calcutta has a National Engineering College whose alumni are said to be in great demand. The National Arts College of Bombay is doing something in the way of (5). The Vrindavana Prem-Maha-Vidyalaya is teaching (2), (4), and (7) near Poona, Bahjoi in Aligarh, Umballa, Naini, Jubbulpore, etc., have glassworks which might be utilised, by arrangement with the Managers, for the technical education of students of National schools. And so on. The idea throughout, in all stages of technical instruction, is that educational institutions and local industries should utilise and act and react on and help and improve each other. Class-room instruction should improve the intelligence; workshop practice should improve the finger-skill; the two together, combined in the same individual, should improve the industry. The poverty of India forbids any more expensive and ambitious and at the same time wide-spread system of technical training—not to say anything about the principles underlying the great controversy of "Factories *vs*. Handicrafts" and "Mechanico-Industrial Civilisation *vs*. Agricultural-Pastoral Civilisation."

[3] Two suggestions, which, it seems, are being practiced in the some places, may be noted. (1) Students to bring their own *asanas* to sit on, and the institution supplies strong *chaukis* (benches) of wood, about six feet long, by one and a half broad, which can be used as desks in class by three students at a time comfortably. Two of these put together, side by side, make a bedstead or chauki, six feet by three, for one resident student, for use in the night. (2) Low walls of mud are used as desks; but, of course, they cannot be moved about, and are difficult to keep in shape and with a smooth and level surface.

Bibliography

[A] Primary Sources

Abott, A., and Wood, S.H., *Report on Vocational Education in India*, Delhi, 1937.

General Report on Public Instruction in Lower Provinces of the Bengal Presidency for 1843-44, Calcutta, 1844.

Ghose, Benoy, (ed.), *Selections from English Periodicals of the 19th Century*, Calcutta, 1981.

National Archives of India, proceedings of Home Department.

i. Proceedings of Education branch.

ii. Proceedings of Political branch.

iii. Proceedings of Public branch.

Quinquennial Reviews of the Progress of Education in India.

Reid, H.S., *Reports on Indigenous Education and Vernacular Schools in Agra, Aligarh, Barreli, Etwah, Farrukhabad, Manipuri, Mathura, Shajahanpur, 1850-51 to 1853-54*, Agra, 1852-54.

Report of the Indian Education Commission, 1882.

Report of the Indian University Commission, 1904.

Reports of Census of India. (1872-1941)

Reports of the Proceedings of the National Education Committee, 23rd February, 1923, to 6th March, 1923

Reports on Basic Education:

i. *Report of the First Conference of Basic National Education*, Poona, 1939.

ii. *Report of the Second Basic Education Conference*, Delhi, 1941.

iii. *Third Annual Report, Hindustani Talimi Sangh*, Wardha, 1941.

iv. *Sixth Annual Report, Hindustani Talimi Sangh*, Wardha, 1944.

v. *Eighth Annual Report, Hindustani Talimi Sangh*, Wardha, 1946.

Selected Works of Mahatma Gandhi, Ahemdabad, 1968.

Selections from educational records :

i. Sharp. H., (ed.), *Selections from Educational Records, Part I (1781-1839)*, Calcutta, 1920.

ii. Richey, J.A., (ed.), *Selections from Educational Records, Part II (1840-1859)*, Calcutta, 1922.

iii. Kirpal, Prem, (ed.), *Selections from Educational Records of Government of India, Vol. I, Educational Reports (1859-71)*, New Delhi, 1960.

iv. Naik, J.P., (ed.,) *Selections from Educational Records of Government of India, Vol.II, Development of University Education (1860-87)*, New Delhi, 1963.

v. Bhargava, K.D.(ed.,) *Selections from Educational Records of Government of India, Vol. IV, Technical Education in India (1886-1907)*, New Delhi, 1968.

Thornton, R., *A Memoir on the Statistics of Indigenous Education within the North-Western Provinces of the Bengal Presidency*, Calcutta, 1850.

[B] Secondary Records

Journals

Dawn (Calcutta)

Indian Historical Quarterly (Calcutta)

Indian Review (Madras)

Manthan (Delhi)

Modern Review (Calcutta)

Proceedings of the Indian History Congress

Studies in History (Delhi)

Unpublished Theses/dissertations

Aptc, Malati G., *The Growth of National Education in India with Special Reference to Maharashtra*, University of Bombay, 1953.

Griffin, Hazel M., *Thomas Babington Macaulay and the Anglicist Orientilist- Controversy in Indian Education, 1833-37*, University of Pennsylvania, 1972.

Kendel, Paul M., *Evangelical Impact on India in the Early 19th Century*, California State University, 1999.

Kundu, Mahima Ranjan, *The Educational Theory and Practices of Mahatma Gandhi and its Impact on Education in India*, Graduate School of University of Oregon, 1967.

Schaefer, Herbert George, *Basic National Education in India, From 1937 to 1957*, Ohio State University, 1969.

Vishwanathan, Gauri, *The Ideology of Literary Education in British India, 1813-1880*, ColumbiaUniversity, 1985.

[C] Other Published Secondary Sources

Ahmad, M.M.Z., *An Examination of the Wardha Scheme of Education and the Suggestion of an Alternative Scheme of Primary Education*, Junagarh, 1938.

Ahmad, M.M.Z., *Present Day Problems of Indian Education*, Bombay, 1935.

Ali, B. Sheikh, *Zakir Husain – Life and Times*, New Delhi, 1991.

Ali, Muhammad Mohar, *The Bengali Reaction to Christian Missionary Activities*, 1833-1857, Chittagong, 1965.

Anand, Mulk Raj, *The King-Emperor's English*, Bombay, 1948.

Andrews, C.F., *The Renaissance in India*, Calcutta, 1912.

Apte,P.S.,(ed.), *Maharastranteel Rashtriya ShikshanachaItihas* (Marathi), Poona, 1958.

Aryanayakam, E. W., *Story of Twelve Years*, Wardha, 1949.

Aurobindo, Sri, *A System of National Education*, Madras, 1924.

Aurobindo, Sri, *Brain of India*, Pondicherry, 1955.

Avinashilingam, T.S., *Gandhiji's Experiments in Education*, Delhi, 1960.

Bagal, J.C., *History of the Indian Association*, 1876-1957, Calcutta, 1953.

Bagal, J.C., *Pramatha Nath Bose*, Calcutta, 1955.

Balhachett. K., *Social Policy and Social Change in Western India, 1817-1830*, London, 1957.

Bannerjee, Surendra Nath, *A Nation in Making*, Calcutta, 1925.

Bannerjee, Gooroo Dass, *A Few Thoughts on Education*, Calcutta, 1904.

Bannerjee, Gooroo Dass, *The Education Problem in India*, Calcutta, 1914.

Bannerjee, Pramath Nath, *Hundred Years of the University of Calcutta*, Calcutta, 1957.

Basu, A.N., *University Education in India-Past and Present*, Calcutta, 1944.

Basu, A.N., ed., *Reports on the State of Education in Bengal*, 1835, by William Adam, Calcutta, 1941.

Basu, A.N., *Indian Education in Parliamentary Papers*, Part I, (1832), Bombay, 1952.

Basu, A.N., *Education in Modern India, A Brief Review*, Calcutta, 1945.

Basu, Aparna, *Essays in the History of Indian Education*, New Delhi,1982

Basu, Aparna, *The Growth of Education and Political Developments in 1898-1920*, Delhi, 1974.

Basu, Aparna, *Women's Education in India, 1813-1866*, Bombay, 1973.

Basu, B.D., *Education in India Under the East India Company*, Calcutta,1940.

Basu, Swapna, *Bhudev Mukhopadhyaya and the Indian Tradiation*, Calcutta, 2000.

Bhattacharya, Bhabani, *Socio-Political Currents in Bengal: A Nineteenth Century Perspective*, Ghaziabad, 1980.

Bhattacharya, Sabyasachi, Joseph Bara, and Chinna Rao Yagati, *Educating the Nation: Documents on the Discourse of National Education in India, 1880-1920*, New Delhi, 2003.

Bhattacharya, Sabyasachi, ed., *The Contested Terrain: Perspectives on Education in India*, New Delhi, 1998.

Bayly, C.A., *Empire and Information: Intelligence Gathering and Social Communication in India, 1780-1870*, Cambridge, 1990.

Besant, Annie, *Higher Education in India-Past and Present*, Madras, 1932.

Besant, Annie, *How India Wrought for Freedom*, Adyar, 1915.

Bevan, E., *Indian Nationalism*, London, 1913.

Bhargava, M.L., *History of Education in Uttar Pradesh.*, Lucknow, 1958.

Boman Behram, B.K., *Educational Controversies in India : The Cultural Conquest of India under British Imperialism*, Bombay, 1943.

Burstion, W.H.,(ed.), *James Mill on Education*, Cambridge, 1969.

Carnoy, Martin, *Education as Cultural Imperialism*, New York and London, 1974.

Chakravarty, Vasudha, *Sister Nivedita*, New Delhi, 1965.

Chandavarkar, Ganesh, L., *Maharishi Karve*, Bombay, 1985.

Chandra, Bipan, et.al., India's Struggle for Independence, 1885-1947, New Delhi, 1989.

Chandra, Bipan, *Modern India*, New Delhi, 1971.

Chandra, Bipan, *Nationalism and Colonialism in Modern India*, New Delhi, 1979.

Chandra, Bipan, *Rise and Growth of Economic Nationalism in India*, New Delhi, 1966.

Chandra, Bipan; Tripathi, Amles; and De, Barun, *Freedom Struggle*, New Delhi, 1972.

Chandra, Sudhir and Bhalla, A., (eds.), *Indian Responses to Colonialism in the Nineteenth Century*, New Delhi, 1993.

Chatterjee, Bhola Chandra, *Indo-British Cultural Confrontation*, Calcutta, 1979.

Chatterjee, Santimoy, (ed.), *Studies in the History of Science*, Calcutta, 1992.

Chattopadhyaya, Gautam, *Awakening in Bengal in the Early 19th century*, Calcutta, 1965.

Chaudhary, K.K., *Maharashtra and Indian Freedom Struggle*, Bombay, 1985.

Chopra, P.N., Puri, B.N., and Das, M.N., *A Social, Cultural and Economic History of India, Vol III: Modern India*, Madras, 1974.

Clive, John, *Thomas Babington Macaulay: The Shaping of the Historian*, London, 1973.

Cohn, B.S., *Colonialism and its Forms of Knowledge*, Delhi, 1997.

Collet, S.D., *The Life and Letters of Raja Ram Mohan Ray*, London, Calcutta, 1962.

Concept of National Education in India, Calcutta, 1967.

Dalton, Dennis Gilmore, *Indian Idea of Freedom : Political Thought of Swami Vivekananda, Aurobindo Ghose, Mahatma Gandhi and Rabindra Nath Tagore*, Gurgaon, 1982.

Dar, S.L., and Somaskandam, S., (eds.), *History of the Banaras Hindu University*, Banaras, 1966.

Das Saal Ka Kaam, Wardha,1947.

Datta, K.K., and Narain, V.A., eds., *A Comprehensive History of India*, New Delhi, 1985.

Datta, K.K., *Renaissance, Nationalism and Social Changes in Modern India*, Calcutta, 1965

Datta, T.K., *What English Education has Made of Us*, Lahore, 1942.

Dayanand Saraswati, Swami , *English Translation of Satyartha Prakash*, Tr. by Durga Prasad, Lahore, 1908.

Desai, A.R., *Social Background of Indian Nationalism*, Bombay, 1959.

Devi, Raj Kumari and Rameshwari, Pruthi Romila, *Sister Nivedita: Social Revolutionary*, Jaipur,2003.

Dewey, J., *Democracy and Education : An Introduction to the Philosophy of Education*, New York, 1948.

Dharampal, *The Beautiful Tree: The Indigenous Indian Education in the 18th Century,* Delhi, 1983.

Di Bona, Joseph, *One Teacher One School, The Adam's Reports on Indigenous Education in 19th Century India*, New Delhi, 1983.

Dikshit, S.S., *Nationalism and Indian Education* , Jullundur,1966.

Dutt, Sukumar, *Problem of Indian Nationalism*, Calcutta, 1926.

Embree, A.T., *Charles Grant and British Rule in India*, London, 1962.

Fleming, D.J., *Schools with a Message for India*, Madras, 1948.

Fraser, Lovat, A., *India under Curzon and After*, London, 1911.

Gadgil, D.R., *The Industrial Evolution of India in Recent Times*, Bombay, 1944.

Gandhi, M.K., *Hind Swaraj*, Ahmedabad, 1983.

Gandhi, M.K., *Towards a New Education*, Ahmedabad, 1953.

Gandhi, M.K., *True Education*, Ahmedabad, 1962.

Gandhi, M.K.,*The Problem of Education*, Ahmedabad, 1962.

Gandhi, M.K., *Basic Education*, Ahmedabad, 1951.

Gandhi, B.N., *Indian Economic Thought: 19th Century Perspectives*, New Delhi, 1977.

Gandhi , M.K., *New Education*, Ahmedabad, 1953.

Ghosh, Aurobindo, Sri, *The Renaissance in India*, Calcutta, 1946.

Ghosh, Suresh Chandra, *Birth of a New India*, Delhi, 2001.

Ghosh, Suresh Chandra, *Indian Nationalism, A Case Study for the First University Reform by the British Raj*, Ghaziabad, 1985.

Gupta, Atul Chandra, (ed.), *Studies in the Bengal Renaissance*, Calcutta, 1958.

Gupta, R. K., (ed.), *Readings in Basic Education*, Delhi, 1968.

Gurukul Kangri Viswa Vidyalaya, Diamond Jubilee, Hardwar, 1960.

Halappa, G.S., *History of Freedom Movement in Karnataka*, Bangalore, 1964.

Hampton, H.V., *Biographical Studies in Modern Indian Education*, London, 1947.

Hardayal, *Our Educational Problem*, Madras, 1922.

Hartog, Sir Philip, *Some Aspects of Indian Education: Past and Present*, London, 1939.

Hasan, Mushirul, (ed.), *Knowledge, Power and Politics: Educational Institutions in India*, New Delhi, 1995.

Heimsath, C.H., *Indian Nationalism and Hindu Social Reform*, Princeton, 1964.

Howell, Arthur, *Education in British Indian, Prior to 1854 and in 1870-71*, Calcutta,1872.

James, H.R., *Problems of Higher Education in India*, London, 1916.

James, H.R., *Education and Statesmanship in India*, 1797-1910, London, 1917.

James. Kenneth, W., *The New Cambridge History of India, III.1*, Cambridge, 1989.

Jha, Hetukar, *Colonial Context of Higher Education for India*, New Delhi,1985.

Jordens, J.T.F., *Dayanand Saraswati, His Life and Ideas*, New Delhi. 1978.

Joshi, V.C., (ed.), *Ram Mohan Ray and the Process of Modernisation in India*, Delhi, 1975.

Kabir, Humayun, *Education in New India*, Bristol, 1956.

Karve, D.K., *Looking Back*, Poona, 1936.

Kashi Vidyapith: Hearak Jayanti Abhinandam Granth, Varanasi, 1983.

Kaushik, P.D., *The Congress Ideology and Programmes*, 1920-1947, Bombay, 1964.

Keer, Dhananjay, *Lokmanya Tilak : Father of Our Freedom Struggle*, Bombay, 1959.

Kelkar, N.C., *Life and Times of Bal Gangadhar Tilak*, New Delhi,1987.

Kopf, David, *British Orientalism and the Bengal Renaissance, 1773-1835*, California, 1969.

Kopf, David, *The BrahmoSamaj and the Shaping of the Modern Indian Mind*, Princeton, 1979.

Kriplani, J.B., *The Latest Fad*, Bombay, 1946.

Kumar, Deepak, (ed.), *Science and Empire (1700-1947)*, Delhi, 1991.

Kumar, Deepak and Roy Macleod, eds., *Technology and the Raj: Western Technology and Technical Transfers to India 1700-1947*, Delhi, 1995.

Kumar, Krishna, *Political Agenda of Education*, Delhi, 1991.

Kumar, Krishna, and Oesterheld, Joachim, eds., *Education and Social Change in South Asia*, New Delhi, 2007.

Kumar, Ravinder, *Western India in Nineteenth Country*, London, 1968.

Laird, M.A., *Missionaries and Education in Bengal, 1793-1837*, Oxford, 1972.

Lal, Sundar, *Bharat Main Angreji Raj*, Delhi, 1982.

Law, N.N., *Promotion of Learning in India by Early European Settlers up to about 1800 A.D.*, London, 1915.

Leitner, G.W., *History of Indigenous Education in the Punjab since Annexation and in 1882*, Patiala, 1973.

Limaye, P.M., *History of Deccan Education Society*, Poona,1935.

McCully, B.T., *English Education and the Origins of Indian Nationalism*, Columbia, 1940.

Majumdar, R.C., *Glimpses of Bengal in the 19th Century*, Calcutta, 1960.

Majumdar, B.B., *History of Indian Social and Political Ideas from Ram Mohan Roy to Dayananda*, Calcutta, 1967.

Majumdar, Bhagwan Prasad, *First Fruits of English Education, 1817-1857*, Calcutta, 1973.

Majumdar, R.C. (ed.), *The History and Culture of The Indian People, Vol X: British Paramountcy and Indian Renaissance*, Bombay, 1974.

Majumdar, R.C., *History of Freedom Movement, in India*, 3 Vols., Calcutta, 1962-63.

Malik, Haffez, (ed.), *Sir Syyed Ahmad Khan's Educational Philosophy: A Documentary Record,* Islamabad, 1989.

Malik, S.G., ed., *Indian Movement: Some Aspects of Dissent, Protest and Reform*, Delhi, 1970.

Mani, R.S., *Educational Ideas of Eminent Indians*, Delhi, 1965.

Mcdonald, Ellen E., and Start, C.M., *English Education: Nationalist Politics and Elite Groups in Maharashtra, 1885-1915,* Berkeley, 1969.

Mckee, William J., *New Schools for Young India*, Chapal Hill, 1930.

Mehrotra, S.R., *The Emergence of the Indian National Congress*, Delhi, 1971.

Misra, B.B., *The Administration History of India, 1834-1947*, New Delhi, 1971.

Misra, B.B., *The Indian Middle Classes*, Delhi, 1961.

Mohammad, Shan, (ed.), *Writings and Speeches of Syed Ahmad Khan*, Bombay, 1972.

Mukharjee, Haridas, *Satis Mukherjee: A Father of the Bengali Revolution*, Calcutta, 1948.

Mukherjee, Haridas, and UmaMukharjee, *The Origins of the National Education Movement*, 1905-1910, Calcutta, 1957.

Mukharjee, Hismanshu Bhusan, *Education for Fullness,* Bombay, 1962.

Mukharjee, Radhakumud, *Fundamental Unity of India*, London, 1913.

Mukharji, S.N., *Education in India: Today and Tomorrow*, Baroda, 1960.

Mukherjee, S.N., *History of Education in India*, Baroda, 1957.

Murdoch, John, *Education in India*, Madras, 1881.

Murdoch, John, *Letter to the Right Hon'ble Baron K.T. Napier, on Government and University Education etc. in India*, Madras, 1872.

Musaraf, Hossain, *Swami Vivekananda's Philosophy of Education*, Calcutta,1980.

Naik, J.P. and Nurullah, S., *History of Education in India during the British Period*, Bombay, 1955.

Naik, J.P., *A Review of Modern Education in India (1813-1942)*, Poona, 1943.

Nair, V. Sankavan, *How Students Wrought for Freedom*, New Delhi, 1993.

Narain, V.A., *Social History of India: The Nineteenth Century*, Meerut, 1972.

Natarajan, S., *A Century of Social Reform in India*, Bombay, 1954.

Natesan, G.A., (ed.), *Speeches and Writings of Annie Besant*, Madras, 1921.

National Council of Education, Bengal : A History and Homage, Calcutta, 1956.

Nayar, D.P., *Towards a National System of Education*, New Delhi, 1989.

Nehru, Jawaharlal, *An Autobiography*, London, 1936.

Nivedita, Sister, *Hints on National Education in India*, Calcutta, 1967.

O'Mally, L.S.S., *India and the West*, London, 1941.

Oak, V.V., *English Education Policy in India*, Madras, 1925.

Pal, Bipin Chandra, *Nationality and Empire*, Calcutta, 1916.

Pal, Bipin Chandra, *Swadeshi and Swaraj (The Rise of New Patriotism)*, Calcutta,1954.

Panday, Dhanpati, *The Arya Samaj and Indian Nationalism, 1875-1930*, Delhi, 1972.

Pandey, B.N. (ed.), *A Centenary History of the Indian National Congress, 1885-1985*, New Delhi, 1985.

Pandit, K.G., *The Deccan Education Society, 1885-1960*, Poona, 1960.

Pandit, M.P., *Builders of Modern India: Sri Aurobindo*, New Delhi, 1983.

Panikkar, K.M., *Essays on Educational Reconstruction in India*, Madras, 1920.

Pannikkar, K.N., and Thaper, Romila, (eds.), *The Intellectual History of Colonial India*, Delhi, 1986.

Paranjpe, M.R., *A Source Book of Modern Indian Education (1797-1902)*, London,1938.

Parulekar, R.V., *Literacy in India in Pre-British Days*, Poona, 1940.

Parulekar, RV., *Survey of Indigenous Education in the Province of Bombay, 1820-1830*, Bombay, 1951.

Poddar, Aravind, *Renaissance in Bengal : Quests and Confrontations, 1800-1860*, Simla, 1970.

Pradhan, G.P., *LokmanyaTilak*, New Delhi, 1994.

Purkait, B.R., *New Education in India*, Ambala, 1987.

Purohit, B.R., *Hindu Revivalism and Indian Nationalism*, Bombay, 1965.

R.V. Parulekar, *A Source–Book of History of Education in Bombay Province, Part I, Survey of Indigenous Education*, 1820-1830, Bombay, 1945.

Raj, Lajpat, *History of Arya Samaj*, Bombay, 1967.

Raj, Lajpat, *The Arya Samaj*, Calcutta, 1915.

Raj, Lajpat, *The Problem of National Education in India*, New Delhi, 1966.

Raleigh,T., (ed.), *Lord Curzon in India (Speeches)*, London, 1906.

Ranade, M.G., *Essays on Indian Economics: A Collection of Essays and Speeches*, Bombay, 1898.

Ranade, M.G., *The Miscellaneous Writings of Mr. Justice M.G Ranade*, Delhi, 1992.

Ray, Chaudhury, H.C. Majumdar, R.C. and Dutta, K.K., *An Advanced History of India*, London, 1946.

Ray, P.C., *Autobiography*, Calcutta, 1958.

Life and Experience of a Bengali Chemist, 2 vols. Calcutta, 1996.

Renold, Leah, *A Hindu Education: Early Years of the Banaras Hindu University*, Oxford, 2005.

Review of Education in India, 1947-1961, Delhi, 1962.

Roy, Ram Mohan, *The English Works of Raja Ram Mohan Ray*, (ed.), Calcutta, 1885.

Rudolph, S.H., and Rudolph L., eds., *Education and Politics in India*, Delhi, 1972.

Sankhadher, B.M., ed., *Encyclopedia of Education System in India*, New Delhi, 1999.

Sarkar, Benoy Kumar, *Education for Industrialization*, Calcutta, 1946.

Sarkar, Sumit, *Bibliographical Survey of Social Reformation in 18th and 19th Century*, New Delhi, 1975.

Sarkar, Sumit, *Modern India : 1885-1947*, New Delhi, 1983.

Sarkar, Sumit, *Swadeshi Movement in Bengal, 1903-1908*, New Delhi, 1973.

Sarkar, Susobhan, *On the Bengal Renaissance*, Calcutta, 1979.

Seeley, Sir John, *The Expansion of England*, London, 1897.

Seal, Anil, *Emergence of India Nationalism*, Cambridge, 1968.

Sen, Ashok, *Ishwarchandra Vidyasagar and his Elusive Milestones*, Calcutta, 1977.

Seth, Sanjay, *Subject Lessons: The Western Education of Colonial India*, Oxford, 2008.

Sharma, Braj Bihari Lal, (ed.), *Raja Mahendra Pratap Janma Shatabdi Smarika*, Vrindavan, 1986.

Sharma, Shri Ram (ed.), *Our Education Mission*, Lahore, 1925.

Shrimali, K.L., *The Wardha Scheme*, Udaipur, 1946.

Singh, Poornima, *Indian Cultural Nationalism*, New Delhi, 2004.

Singh, Yogendra, *Modernization of Indian Tradition*, Jaipur, 1986.

Singh. R.P., *Education in an Imperial Colony*, Delhi, 1979.

Sinha, D.P., *The Educational Policy of East India Company in Bengal up to 1854*, Calcutta, 1964.

Sitaramaya, P., *History of Indian National Congress*, Bombay, 1969.

Smith, George, *The Life of Alexander Duff*, London, 1879.

Smith, George, *The Life of John Wilson*, London, 1878.

Spears, Percieval, *Oxford History of India*, New Delhi, 1974.

Sri Aurobindo and the Mother on Education, Pondicherry, 1960.

Stokes, E., *The English Utilitarian and India*, Oxford, 1959.

Subbarao, C. S., *Basic Education in Practice*, Secunderabad, 1958.

Subbarao, C. S., *Basic Education in Principles*, Secunderabad, 1960.

Sunthanker, B.R., *Maharashtra : 1858-1920*, Bombay, 1993.

Suraj Bhan, *Dayanand, His Life and Work*, Jullundhar, 1954.

Swami Vivekananda on India and her Problems, Calcutta, 1963.

Ram Swarup, *On Hinduism: Reviews and Reflections*, New Delhi, 2000.

Tandon, Prakash, *The Punjabi Century, 1857-1947*. New York, 1961.

Tarachand, *History of the Freedom Movement in India*, 4 Vols., Delhi, 1961-72.

Thapar, Romila and Bhattacharya, Sabyasachi, (eds.), *Situating Indian History*, Delhi, 1986.

The Besant Spirit, Adyar, 1939.

The Indian Year Book of Education, New Delhi, 1964.

Tilak, B.G., *Samagra Lokmanya Tilak, Vol. VII*, Poona, 1975.

Tonkhi, S,M., *Aligarh and Jamia: Fight for National System of Education*, New Delhi, 1983.

Trevelyan, C.E., *On the Education of the People of India*, London, 1838.

Tripathi, Amles, *The Extremist Challenge*, Calcutta, 1967.

Tucker, Richard P., *Ranade and the Roots of Indian Nationalism*, Bombay, 1972.

University of Bombay, (1857-1957): Centenary Souvenir, Bombay, 1957.

Varkey, C.J., *Wardha Scheme of Education an Exposition and Examination*, Humphrey Milford, 1940.

Vidyalankar, Satyaketu, and Vidyalankar, Haridutt, *Arya Samaj Ka Itihas*, New Delhi, 1984.

Vidyalankar, Satyaketu, *Arya Samaj Ka Itihas*, Vol. III, Delhi, 1983.

Vikuntham, Y., *Education and Social Change in South India, 1880-1920*, Madras, 1982.

Vishwanathan, G., *Masks of Conquest*, Delhi, 1991.

Vivekananda, Swami, *Complete Works*, Calcutta, 1970.

Vyas, K.C., *Development of National Education in India*, Bombay, 1954.

Walport, S., *Tilak and Gokhle*, California, 1962.

Wellock, Wilfred, *Nai Talim and Social Order*, Wardha, 1950.

Zacharia, H.C.E., *Renascent India: From Ram Mohan Ray to Mohandas Gandhi*, London, 1933.

Zastoupil, Lynn and Moir, Martin, Eds., *The Great Indian Education Debate*, Surrey, 1999.